O9-BRY-442

THE SOUND OF LAUGHTER

BY BENNETT CERF:

The Sound of Laughter
A Treasury of Atrocious Puns
Laugh Day
Riddle-De-Dee
Out on a Limerick
The Laugh's on Me
Reading for Pleasure
The Life of the Party
An Encyclopedia of Modern American Humor
Good for a Laugh
Laughter, Incorporated
Shake Well Before Using
Anything for a Laugh
Laughing Stock
Try and Stop Me

Edited by Leonora Hornblow
and Bennett Cerf:

The Take Along Treasury

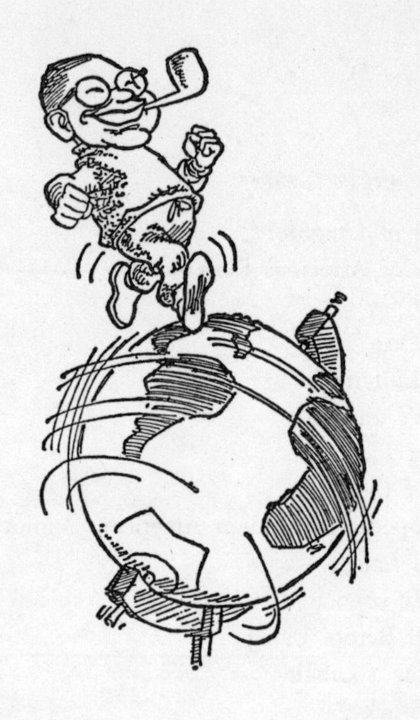

THE SOUND OF

WITH ILLUSTRATIONS BY *Michael K. Frith*

BENNETT CERF'S

LAUGHTER

DOUBLEDAY & COMPANY, INC.
Garden City, New York

Library of Congress Catalog Card Number 72-125527

Printed in the United States of America

CONTENTS

FOREWORD

Heaven knows there's been no lack of sound in the U.S.A. these past five troubled years, but the one I've been straining hardest to hear has proven the most elusive—the sound of laughter. It's been all but drowned out by the angry caterwauling of racists, hawks, doves, panthers, weathermen, drug addicts, campus wreckers, and extreme rightists and leftists of every description. Smaller grow the ranks of those of us who still prefer to stress the brighter side of life!

Five years ago, when I published *Laugh Day,* my last book of stories, I noted, "We're not laughing enough these days—and any country that has lost the inclination to laugh—particularly at itself—is in serious trouble." That was in 1965. Now, in 1970, we scarcely are laughing at all—and just look at the mess we're creating for ourselves!

Instead of the two years it's taken me in the past to collect enough good stories for a full-sized book, this compilation's taken five—and at that it hasn't been easy. Laughter is so hard to come by these days that it had to be taped mechanically for Christmas last season and sold by the bag!

The occasionally more serious stories and bits of history and folklore scattered through *The Sound of Laughter* are all designed to stress the cheerier side of life. Along with them, of course, you'll find the heartwarming quotations, riddles, limericks, quickies, ingenious signs, and above all, the "atrocious" puns to which I long have been addicted. They are indexed by categories so that a hard-pressed banquet M.C., party host, disc jockey, or columnist can find a tidbit appropriate for almost any conceivable emergency.

The Sound of Laughter, in brief, is aimed straight at your jocular vein, and I can only hope that detractors may be limited to a Booing 747!

BENNETT CERF

Barbados and New York
Spring and Summer 1970

(The greater part of the material in this volume appeared originally over a five-year span in my syndicated King Features column "Try and Stop Me.")

THE CREDIBILITY GAP

1. *Ingenuity*

In need of some cash to finance a leisurely trip around the world, a man went to a bank where he had done business for years and applied for a reasonable loan. He was told that because of the money crunch, there wasn't a dime available to him. Another bank, where he was a total stranger, loaned him the money with a minimum of fuss.

So our hero bought a ten-pound fish, had it wrapped, and put it in his safe-deposit box in bank number one as he cheerfully left town for six months.

∴

"It's easy enough to make money," asserts Joan Rivers, "if only you know how." For example, she points to an immigrant who landed here penniless and though he learned only three words of English is worth a fortune today. The three words were, "Stick 'em up!"

∴

Fortunate was the Wilmington lady who lost her handbag in a shopping center recently: an honest lad found it and returned it to her. "Funny," commented the lady. "When I misplaced the bag there was a ten-dollar bill in it. Now I find ten one-dollar bills."

"That's right, lady," agreed the honest lad. "The last time I found a lady's purse, she didn't have any change for a reward."

∴

That great inventor, Thomas Edison, had also a keen appreciation of U.S. currency. Every time he showed his constant stream of visitors the new inventions and gadgets that filled his summer estate, someone was sure to ask, "Why do you still have that anachronism here: that turnstile we all have to force our way through on the way to the garden?" And Mr. Edison would invariably reply happily, "My friend, every single soul who pushes his way through that turnstile pumps seven gallons of water into the tank on my roof."

∴

Pert Barbara Felton admits she was slightly discombobulated at her home the other morning. She was taking a bath when the doorbell rang. Grabbing a small towel, she made for the door and asked, "Who's there?" "Blind man," was the reply. Barbara opened the door to discover a fine figure of a lad who inquired appreciatively, "Where do I put these blinds?"

∴

Playwright Sam Behrman, intent upon acquiring a new rug for his study, encountered one Armenian merchant who gave him a ten-minute lecture on the superior qualities of all the floor coverings in his emporium. Seeking to stem the flow of eloquence, Behrman exclaimed reverently, "Mr. Kabvotzian, you certainly know the rug business." Mr. Kabvotzian replied, "Mister, I know the business so well that rugs are afraid of me!"

∴

For his birthday, a Philadelphia merchant received from his wife a group photograph of her entire family (eighteen persons in all), in a sterling silver frame. What to do with this marvelous gift? The ingenious merchant solved the problem. He took the photograph to his office and gave it to his receptionist. "Study this picture well," he instructed her, "and if anybody in it ever comes to this office, say I've gone to Tokyo on business."

∴

Eligible for membership:

—The girl who took a whistle with her one evening. She had a date with a basketball star.

—The finance company head who advertised, "For the man who has everything—but hasn't paid for it."

—The psychiatrist who had an electric vibrator installed in his couch and picked up a fortune in loose change.

—The bachelor who reminded each new girl, "I may be a thing of beauty—but I'm also a boy forever."

∴

A story from Nob Hill stars a gentleman and a very lovely companion who stepped into a telephone booth and set up a portable tape recorder which began playing typical office sounds: phones ringing, typewriters banging away, and a babble of business talk. Once the tape was playing to the gentleman's satisfaction, he winked at his girl, dialed a number, and announced sorrowfully, "I can't get home for dinner, darling. That confounded boss of mine has got me tied down again at the office."

When he hung up, he tucked the recorder under his arm, and he and his girl disappeared contentedly into the gloaming.

∴

In the good old days when trolley cars clanged their way through street after street of the Borough of Brooklyn, related John Straley, an inspector climbed aboard one open car to check on the integrity and competence of brand-new Conductor Dinty O'Toole. First, he counted the passengers, then he noted the number of fares O'Toole had rung up. "Ah ha, lad," he roared. "Caught you in the act. There are two more passengers on board this car right now than the fares you've registered." Dinty carefully made a count himself, then addressed the passengers: "Bejabbers, the inspector is right! Two of yez will have to get off!"

∴

Myron Cohen tells about the lady who was asked, "Sadie, if you found a million dollars in the street, what would you do with it?" "That depends," answered Sadie. "If I found it belonged to somebody very poor, I'd give it back."

∴

There's a perky little lady who lives alone at Fire Island—and loves it. When the beach in front of her house gets too crowded for her own comfort, she simply circulates quietly among the sun worshipers and bathers, shades her eyes, and exclaims, "Goodness, isn't that a fin out there?" In no time flat, she has the beach to herself.

∴

A nervous millionaire was interviewing an applicant for the post of chauffeur. "My last man," grumbled the millionaire, "took too many unnecessary chances. I want somebody who'll always play it absolutely safe." "I'm your man, sir," said the applicant cheerfully. "Can I have my first month's pay in advance?"

∴

A suspicious lady accosted a drugstore clerk to demand, "Is it true that that new hair restorer you're pushing is guaranteed to work in twenty-four hours?" "Positively, ma'am," nodded the clerk, "and we can prove it. See that fat female over at the soda fountain? Yesterday afternoon she pulled the cork out of one of our bottles with her teeth, and when she woke up this morning she had a mustache!"

∴

Attention has been called to a very smart Madison Avenue secretary whose boss sends her out without fail every working day about noon to a deluxe delicatessen down the block to order him a club sandwich and a container of milk. The secretary has learned to make the club sandwich at home, bring a container of milk to the office with her, and clears a dollar and fifteen cents every day on the transaction.

∴

Winning a battle with a computer system is getting to be more fun than sneaking into the subway through an exit gate used to be when we were kids. Let's give a great big hand to latest winner Jerome T. Parker. Mr. Parker, for reasons unknown to him, received a bill from an oil company for several consecutive months for $0.00. He laughingly showed the bills to friends and waited for the bills to stop coming. When he got one marked "Final Notice," however, plus a threat to turn the account over to a notoriously tough collection agency, he wrote out a check for no dollars and no cents, signed his name thereto, and mailed it to the oil company with a note saying, "This pays my account in full."

Darned if he didn't get a form letter in return thanking him for his patronage.

∴

Woody Allen knows a man who has built up a fine business as a caterer to wedding parties, and is particularly proud of innovations he has introduced thereto. One of his boasts is, "I am the only caterer ever to make a miniature groom out of potato salad."

∴

If the garbage workers in your community ever go out on strike you might like to know how a wise New Yorker disposed of his refuse for the nine days the sanitation workers were off the job last summer. Each day he wrapped his garbage in gift paper. Then he put it in a shopping bag. When he parked his car, he left the bag on the front seat with the window open. When he got back to the car the garbage always had been collected.

∴

"Who," a precocious office boy dared to ask his boss, "were those two ladies I just ushered out of your office?" "One was my wife," joshed the indulgent boss, "and the other was Sophia Loren." "Which one was Loren?" asked the lad with a perfectly straight face.

The boss whipped a dollar bill out of his wallet and handed it to the office boy. "It's a loan," he explained. "When you succeed me as president, I want you to remember that I once loaned you money."

2. *Advertising*

A stout-hearted fellow, tired of doing undercover work for the espionage department of a country we won't identify, applied for a post with a Madison Avenue advertising agency. The job application blank included the question, "What qualifications do you have?" Whimsically, the applicant wrote, "Spying, arson, burglary, kidnapping, etc." Furthermore, he got the job.

A year or so later, combing the files, he came across his personnel folder. On his job application form, a top executive had written, "This fellow obviously is one of us. Grab him!"

.:.

Young Horace answered the front doorbell and discovered on the steps an eager salesman of a brand-new detergent with a brand-new secret ingredient. "Come quickly, Mom," he called inside. "It's a live commercial!"

∴

A canny Illinois merchant claims that this ad pulled four times as many inquiries as any he had previously tried: "LADIES! Earn a lot of money in your spare time. Rent one of my electric rug-shampooers for only 2 dollars a day. Then tell your husband you spent 30 dollars to have the rug cleaned."

∴

A poignant story going the rounds concerns the trials and tribulations of the adman entrusted with a very big cigarette account. His operatives ferreted out a Tennessee mountaineer who had been smoking incessantly for ninety years. A photographer and copywriter were dispatched immediately to contact this oldster—just in time for his hundredth birthday party.

"Ever been to New York?" they asked. "Nope," he answered. Nor had he ever been up in a plane, it developed. "Tell you what we're going to do, pop," proposed the copywriter. "Friday morning we're going to put you on a jet, fly you to Manhattan, install you in the biggest suite at the Waldorf, and then Monday morning we're going to interview you on a coast-to-coast TV program. What do you think of that?"

"Sounds jim-dandy," enthused the old boy, reaching for a cigarette. "But the morning TV show is out. You'll have to do it much later in the day." "Why?" he was asked. "You see, boys," he explained, "I don't stop coughing till noon."

∴

The owner of a prosperous department store in a medium-sized midwestern town was a firm believer in the power of advertising—and every one of his ads for years on end featured the line, "The owner of this store is a decorated veteran of World War Two." A new agency, anxious to get the account, assured the owner he could cut his ad appropriation by 10 per cent and no loss of business by simply eliminating this slogan, but was met with an adamant, "Nothing doing. I'm convinced it increases sales." "Hmphh," snorted the agency man. "I'll bet you weren't even in World War Two." "I certainly was," the owner answered angrily. "What branch of service?" persisted the agency man. "The Luftwaffe," replied the owner.

∴

Noteworthy classified ads:

1. In a Los Angeles daily: "Wanted: man to work on nuclear fissionable isotope molecular reactive counters and three-phase cyclotronic photosynthesizers. No experience necessary."

2. In the Southern Illinois University student newspaper: "Sweet little old lady wishes to correspond with S.I.U. undergraduate. Prefers six-foot male with brown eyes answering to initials J.D.B. (Signed) His Mother."

3. From a Miami Beach throwaway: "Having trouble with your husband coming home late—or not at all? Let us make a confidential investigation for you. Special discount if your husband is over 75 years of age."

∴

When Burma Shave's top brass decided to abandon their famous roadside signs, they persuaded Frank Rowsome, Jr., to collect a passel of them in a beguiling little volume called *Verse by the Side of the Road*. Here are a few of the Burma classics included:

"His face was smooth and cool as ice, and Oh, Louise, he smelled so nice."

"He had the ring; he had the flat—but she felt his face, and that was that."

"The bearded lady tried a jar: she's now a famous movie star."

"No lady likes to dance or dine, accompanied by a porcupine."

"The whale put Jonah down the hatch, but coughed him up because he scratched."

∴

Herb Shriner said he spent his boyhood in an Indiana hamlet so tiny that it was located between the first and second line on a Burma Shave ad. "I had to travel to the next town," insisted Herb, "to discover how the poem came out."

∴

Told that she would surely give birth to twins, a proud mother-to-be demanded a glass of Schaefer's beer. "Why must it be that particular brew?" she was asked. "Don't you remember?" she answered impatiently. "Schaefer's is the one beer to have when you're having more than one."

∴

There's a rising young advertising executive in New York whose somewhat outlandish taste in suits, shirts, and haberdashery is a source of acute embarrassment to his ultra-conservative mother in Detroit. To complete her confusion, he grew a Fu Manchu mustache last year. "I'm ashamed to let my old mah jong and canasta friends look at you these days," she protested bitterly. "If you have any love left at all for your mother, you'll at least shave off that hideous mustache. If Joe Namath could do it, you can!"

The young man's next visit to Detroit was occasioned by his mother's birthday, and to surprise and please her, he shaved off the Fu Manchu mustache on the morning of his trip. He spent three happy days home with his family, but to his consternation, his mother not only failed to thank him for his noble sacrifice when she met him at the airport, but never brought the subject up once during his entire visit.

As he bade her good-by, he finally blurted out, "Mom, I shaved off my beautiful mustache just to delight you—and you never thanked me once for doing so. Didn't you even notice that it was gone?"

His mother embraced him warmly. "Of course I noticed, you silly boy," she told him, "but just before you arrived, I promised your father that no matter how long you stayed, I'd never mention that mustache once!"

3. *Fables*

A very ugly girl was sitting alone at the beach, when the waves washed a bottle to her feet. She opened it—and out blew a huge genie in a billow of smoke. "I've been a prisoner in this bottle for five thousand years," cried the genie, "and now you've freed me! As a reward, I will fulfill any wish you make." Ecstatic, the ugly girl announced, "I want a figure like Sophia Loren, a face like Elizabeth Taylor, and legs like Ginger Rogers." The genie looked her over carefully, then sighed, "Baby, just put me back in the bottle!"

∴

A jaguar persuaded a cat to teach him how to pounce. After a few successful experiments, with bugs and insects, the jaguar, his appetite whetted, decided to try out his new technique on the cat itself. The cat, however, jumped out of danger like a flash, and the jaguar landed in a heap.

"That isn't fair," whined the jaguar. "You didn't teach me that trick."

"A smart teacher," the cat reminded him, "never teaches a pupil ALL his tricks."

∴

Once, writes Roger Price, a businessman was fishing in a lake when he hauled in a fish of a type he never had seen before. It had golden scales and silver fins which gleamed and flashed as it thrashed about on the bottom of his boat. Suddenly the fish startled the businessman by speaking! "Kind sir," implored the fish, "throw me back in the lake and I'll grant you three wishes."

The businessman considered carefully and then said, "Make it five and we've got a deal." "I can only grant three," gasped the fish. "Four and a half," proposed the businessman. "Three," said the fish, barely audible. "Okay, okay," said the businessman. "We'll compromise on four wishes. How about it?"

But this time the fish made no reply at all. It lay dead on the bottom of the boat.

∴

An impoverished but stout-hearted mother, unable to afford a blanket to shelter her son from the extreme cold and the snow which sifted in through the cracks of her hut, covered him with boards and driftwood. One night the boy wrapped his arms around her and exclaimed contentedly, "Mom, what do poor people do on cold nights like this, who have no boards or driftwood to put over their children?"

∴

A wise old king once had a heavy stone placed right in the middle of a busy thoroughfare. Passers-by stepped gingerly over it, or kicked it angrily—but not one of them made the slightest effort to remove it. Finally one goodhearted fellow came along and single-handed managed to roll it to a ditch paralleling the road, thus clearing the way for all who followed him.

Under the stone he discovered a purse filled with gold, which the king had placed there.

∴

This is a story worth reflection that is told by Rev. Purnell Bailey. In pre-Communist China, a farmer lost his axe, and immediately suspected his neighbor's young son. Thereafter he watched the lad very carefully. Every time he passed by he looked guiltier, and more anxious to escape attention. Then one day the farmer found his axe, tossed absent-mindedly in an old bin in his barn. The next time the neighbor's boy came by, there was no air of guilt whatever about him. He walked upright, and was humming a gay tune. "What a fine boy that is!" mused the farmer as he shouldered his axe.

∴

There's a 1970 version of the small frog who piped up to a beautiful princess, "If you take me home tonight and put me next to your pillow, I'll be a handsome prince when you awaken tomorrow morning." In THIS version, the princess did—and the next morning his fellow frogs had him committed to the nearest lunatic asylum.

∴

Cliff Mackay has another "beautiful princess" story. In Mackay's version, the princess begins by asking her father what the word "frugal" means. "Frugal," the king tells her means "to save." The princess thereupon decides to have a swim in the castle pool, but gets beyond her depth and hollers for help. Just as she's going down for the third time she spies a handsome prince nearby. "Frugal me! Frugal me!" she screams.

So the prince frugals her and they live happily ever after.

∴

Scott Fitzgerald once told of an attractive young honeymoon couple who boarded a train for Niagara Falls, and indulged in the traditional billing and cooing. Suddenly, however, the baffled bride found herself hurling hateful insults at her husband, with his rejoinders matching hers in bitterness and venom.

And then she discovered a total stranger sitting beside her in the drawing room. "How did you get in here?" she gasped. "Who are you?" The stranger answered softly, "I'm ten years from now."

4. *Liars*

Pat McCormick, searching the highways and byways of California for "the oldest living citizen of the state," claims he found one codger so old his first job was parking covered wagons. Another lady is so advanced in years that birth control pills jump out of their box and laugh at her. And candidate number three, blowing out one hundred candles on his birthday cake, had his dentures melted by the heat.

On the side, Pat McCormick specializes in transplants,

he confides. He put the heart of a mouse in an elephant, for example, and the very next day the elephant ate a cheese factory. But for putting the heart of a dog into a stricken patient, he can't collect payment. The patient keeps burying the bills in his backyard.

∴

"I had a horse once," boasted Farmer Loeb, "that licked an express train on a forty-mile run." "That's nothing," countered Farmer Klopfer (an even bigger liar). "I was driving about twenty miles from my house one day when a heck of a storm came up. I turned my horse's head for home and he raced that storm so perfectly that for the last ten miles I didn't feel one drop, while my dog, just ten yards behind me, had to swim the whole distance!"

∴

Champion Liar Demarest of Iowa won his title hands down with this whopper: He went out to his cornfield one sweltering Saturday to gather some ears. After a spell, however, it got so darn hot that the corn began to pop. The air got so full of popped corn that it looked like a blizzard was raging. When Demarest's mule saw this, he lay down in his tracks and froze to death.

∴

Vance Randolph, of the Ozark country, tells of a pioneer who cut a great big hickory tree on a steep hillside. It rolled to the bottom of a hollow, then halfway up the opposite side. Then it came rolling back toward the chopper, and kept on bouncing back and forth, until the woodcutter got bored and went home. Six months later he came back, and the tree was still rolling, but it was just about petered out. It was so worn down, in fact, that the pioneer picked it up, stuck one end of it in the fire, then lit his pipe with it.

∴

Trainer John Sullivan insisted he once had a two-year-old stallion who continually ran off the track to follow any automobile that drove by. "We figured that he imagined he was an automobile himself—so we found the way to cure him," concluded Sullivan. "We poked him through a car wash a couple of times."

∴

An applicant for a job in a computer laboratory listed among his qualifications: "I graduated first in my class at MIT. I turned down a vice-presidency at IBM. Money means nothing to me, so I don't care what salary I get. And I'm prepared to work sixty-five hours a week." "Lordy," gasped the superintendent. "Haven't you ANY weaknesses?" "Just one," admitted the applicant after some reflection. "I'm a TERRIBLE liar!"

THE ANIMALS ALL ARE HERE

Dogs, Cats, Wildlife, Horses, Birds, and Suchlike

Mr. A. A. Thomson has an Irish setter named Brigid, of whom he is inordinately fond. In fact, he is convinced her powers in following a scent border on the miraculous. For instance, he writes, she once spotted a disreputable-looking character lolling on a bench in Hyde Park, and, quivering all over, darted across and perched in front of him in the setting position.

Thomson said, "Good morning, sir. This is my dog Brigid, who has a remarkable nose. You haven't by any chance some game in your coat pocket?" "I certainly have not," cried the character angrily, "and if you don't remove this beastly hound immediately, I'll call a policeman as sure as my name is Algernon Partridge."

∴

A Miss Culberston took a shine to a puppy cavorting in a pet shop window and entered the shop to inquire about the pup's pedigree. "The mother," the proprietor told her earnestly, "is a purebred Scottie. As for the father—well, the father comes from a very good neighborhood."

∴

A great big overfriendly sheep dog who was firmly convinced that he was a lap dog was consigned to a kennel, where it was hoped he might learn to stop jumping up on every arrival. At the kennel he fell into conversation with a perky little poodle. "What's your name?" inquired the poodle. "I'm not really sure," confessed the sheep dog, "but I THINK it's Downboy."

∴

Five-year-old Rosie was overheard talking to her brand-new puppy. "You mustn't chew me," she was saying. "Bones are for chewing, silly. People are for lapping."

∴

What type of human does a dog hate most? Remind yourself of all the jokes you've heard in this category. Mailmen win handily, though a good score has been rung up by butlers, gardeners, irascible homeowners, milkmen, and policemen. Bearing these statistics in mind, an ingenious Rochester pet food expert has introduced a line of "People Crackers," the biscuits being shaped like the proven hates of the pooches. The biscuits modeled on mailmen, predictably, seem to have the biggest canine appeal. At twenty-nine cents a box, they're selling like—well, like hot biscuits.

A Culver City mail carrier complained to his boss that a dog had bitten him on the leg that morning. "Did you put anything on it?" asked his boss. "No," replied the mail carrier. "He liked it just as it was."

Then there was a tramp who hollered for help when a watchful bulldog clamped his jaws on his posterior. "Call off your dog," pleaded the tramp to the farmer who appeared to investigate the cause of the commotion. "I can't," answered the farmer—not too unhappily. "His name is Sick'm."

A carpet layer had just put the finishing touches to a big wall-to-wall job. It had taken him all day. Now, as he stepped back to admire his handiwork, he was horrified to notice a small lump right in the middle of the room. In a flash he realized what had happened. His pack of cigarettes was in none of his pockets. Not one to panic, he made sure nobody was watching, then picked up his hammer and pounded on the lump until the carpet was level. Pleased with himself, he went into the kitchen for his tool kit—and there on the table was his pack of cigarettes.

Just then a little boy's voice was heard upstairs: "Mommy, where's the cat?"

∴

When ex-schoolteacher Sam Levenson was a boy, he had a cat named Hamlin, who specialized in getting in Mama Levenson's way. When, in the darkness, Mrs. L. would step on Hamlin's paws, and the cat howled, she would say in self-defense, "Who tells it to walk around barefoot?"

∴

Mama and Papa Levenson desired above all else that their children be "cultured," but they couldn't quite cope with the textbooks the kids brought home from public school. "I read here," complained Papa one day, "that the cow says, 'Moo, moo,' the pig says, 'Oink,' the dog says, 'Woof, woof.' What's the matter with these animals? Can't they speak ENGLISH?"

∴

Clancy and his wife were equally fond of their mangy, mean-tempered cat. "Pat," demanded Mrs. Clancy as her husband climbed into bed one night, "did yez put out the cat?" "Oi did," maintained Pat. "Oi don't belave yez," countered Mrs. C. "Right-o," conceded Pat. "If yez think Oi'm a liar, get up and put her out yerself."

∴

Adlai Stevenson, who knew how to tell a good story, broke up a Long Island rally one night by recalling the prudish, tight-lipped old maid who wouldn't even allow her pet cat out of the house after dark. Headed for New York on one of her infrequent outings, she paused to remind the maid about locking up that cat each evening.

This time in New York, however, the old maid encountered a handsome old rogue who swept her off her feet. After four nights of blissful romancing she wired her maid, "Having the time of my life. LET THE CAT OUT!"

∴

Young Reginald was ordered to bring in the cats one evening, and there followed a crescendo of meowing and spitting. "What are you doing to those poor cats?" demanded Reginald's mother. "Nothing at all," protested Reginald. "I'm being especially careful. I'm carrying them by their stems."

∴

A suburbanite lady on the Main Line outside Philadelphia was distressed to notice that her beloved young cat was getting suspiciously fat. "She simply CAN'T be having kittens," she explained to the vet she had summoned. "The only time she ever leaves this house is when I have her on a leash."

Just then another cat padded arrogantly across the drawing room floor. "Aha," chuckled the vet. "That looks definitely like a tomcat to me."

"Oh, you don't understand," said the suburbanite impatiently. "He's only her BROTHER!"

∴

A Tacoma husband inserted a classified ad in a local newspaper offering a one-hundred-dollar reward for the return—with no questions asked—of his wife's pet cat. "That's a mighty big reward for a cat," observed the clerk accepting the ad. "Not for this one," said the husband cheerfully. "I drowned it."

∴

When Mr. Bauman had to go to London on business, he persuaded his brother to take care of his Siamese cat while he was away. Mr. Bauman dearly loved that Siamese cat, but the brother definitely did not. The very moment Bauman set foot back at Kennedy Airport, therefore, he phoned his brother to check on his cat's health. The brother announced curtly, "Your cat died"—and hung up.

For days Mr. Bauman was inconsolable. Finally, however, he phoned his brother again to point out, "It was needlessly cruel and sadistic of you to tell me that bluntly that my poor, poor cat had passed away." "What did you expect me to do?" demanded the brother. "You could have broken the bad news gradually," grumbled Bauman. "First, you could have said the cat was playing on the roof. Later you could have called to say he fell off. The next morning you could have reported he had broken his leg. Then, when I came to get him, you could have told me he had passed away during the night. Well—you didn't have it in you to be that civilized. Now tell me—how's Mama?"

The brother pondered momentarily, then announced, "She's playing on the roof."

∴

A couple of intrepid African hunters were having a few snifters in their tent late one afternoon, when the more restless one suddenly announced, "I think I'll go out into the bush and shoot me a lion." "Nonsense," snapped the other. "It's too dark out there now." "You underestimate my talents," jeered the first. "I'll bet you fifty bucks I can kill a lion within the next thirty minutes." Scarcely had the bet been accepted when the proposer was out of the tent, trusty rifle under his arm.

Thirty-five minutes later a huge lion poked his head into

the tent. "Are you the guy," he inquired politely enough, "who made a bet with that poor sap out there?" "That's me," was the ungrammatical reply. "Good," nodded the lion, licking his chops. "You'll never be able to collect, but I thought it might amuse you to know that he owes you fifty dollars."

∴

An Englishman, about to embark upon his first tiger hunt, received this bit of last-minute advice from an experienced big-game hunter: "Conceal yourself carefully on a moonless night. When the tiger approaches, his eyes will be shining in the dark. Aim between them. He'll fall dead from your first shot."

On his return, the Englishman had to report that he had bagged nary a tiger. Furthermore, he was considerably scratched up and one arm seemed to be missing. "Somebody has wised up those blasted tigers," he complained. "They now travel in pairs—and each one closes an eye!"

∴

Relates Jean-Pierre Hallet in his fascinating book *Animal Kitabu:* At a hostel in the Congo's Albert National Park, the hippos sometimes plod a full mile from their haunts along the Rwindi River, just to hover outside the restaurant and watch the tourists dining, chatting, and playing cards. During the day the same tourists trek down to the river to watch the same hippos.

∴

Back from their African safari, the Robinsons' prize exhibit was the head of a huge lion, killed, it turned out, by *Mrs.* Robinson. "What did she hit it with?" wondered an admiring neighbor. "That great new rifle you gave her?" "Not at all," answered the husband. "With the 1964 station wagon I hired."

∴

A waiter from the Stage Delicatessen took his son to the Bronx Zoo, where the boy was struck by the offhand way an attendant tossed a slab of raw meat into the cage of a pacing tiger. "Papa," asked the boy, "why didn't that man serve the meat nicely like you do?" The waiter whispered to his son, "Confidentially, Sammy, tigers are rotten tippers."

∴

An attendant at the London Zoo was intrigued by two Beatle-haired youths strumming guitars earnestly outside the lions' cage. "My brother's the cool one," announced one of the boys modestly. "You put him in that empty cage over there and let one lion at a time into it and you'll see how even the wild beasts fall for his music."

So the zoo attendant led the brother into the empty cage, then shoved the first lion in with him. Almost at once the lion seemed to smile and began dancing daintily to the music. A second lion was produced and proceeded to execute a cross between the twist and a gavotte.

Then a third lion entered the cage. In less time than it takes to tell he had pounced upon the poor guitarist and eaten him up. The zoo attendant patted the surviving brother sympathetically on the back. "I was afraid that would happen," he said sadly, "when I let that deaf lion in there."

∴

An elephant was frolicking happily in a swimming pool one day, when a mouse came along and implored him to come out of the water. The elephant ignored the mouse for a while, but it became so insistent that the elephant finally lumbered out of the pool to demand, "What on earth do you want?"

The mouse squeaked, "I just wanted to see if you were wearing my bathing suit."

∴

A certain amount of confusion occurred at the zoo in Central Park in New York recently when the directors decided to part with some excessive livestock—a couple of husky bears, for example, plus four elk, and some African wild sheep. Guards were equipped with tranquilizer guns, just in case one beastie got out of hand and panicked spectators.

The excitement came when the tranquilizer gun of one guard was accidentally discharged, pinging an innocent bystander squarely in the midsection. Then, while he was being bundled off for repairs, another tranquilizer bullet felled a 500-pound male bear—who promptly fell asleep on his feet, then fell over on his back in the pool. Keepers had to drain the pool and hoist out the unconscious bear with ropes.

By now a good time had been had by all—and the crowd went back to feeding the seals and monkeys.

∴

There's an animal trainer who's been haunting the agents' headquarters with a great big brown bear who, he claims, is in a class by himself as a clown, juggler, bicycle rider, skater, and heaven knows what else. One agent stopped the boastful owner cold by inquiring, "If this bear of yours is so smart, how come he got caught?"

∴

Riding alligators? There's really nothing to it—if you believe what blond, twenty-eight-year-old Barbara Parra told Larry Merchant between innings at a Yankee ball game recently.

"You can't try it with the big 'gators," began Barbara, reasonably enough, but then continued. "The four-footers, however, can give you a right good ride. You get in front of one and hold down his jaws; they're real weak. Honest! Then you slip on his back, making sure you don't let him whip you with his tail. You guide him by holding on to the sides of his eyes and pressing them. That's all there is to it."

Tennis, anyone?

∴

Animals of distinction:

1. The elephant in Ringling's Circus who got his trunk caught in his mouth—and swallowed himself.

2. The ardent mole who sighed, "Do I *love* her? I worship the ground she tunnels under!"

3. The baby mouse who saw a bat swoosh out of the window and excitedly squeaked, "Look quick, Mom! An *angel*!"

4. The most unusual eagle in Idaho. He had a sailor tattooed on his chest.

5. The bashful debutante centipede who crossed her legs hurriedly and cried, "No! A hundred times, no!"

6. The housefly, escorting her daughter across the head of a completely bald man, who observed, "How quickly times change! When I was your age, my dear, this was just a footpath."

7. The little pig who in due course became a ham, which

was then sliced up into enticing sandwiches by a beautiful young hostess. "He died a gentleman," proclaimed the pig's mourners. "His last act was to give his seat to a lady."

8. The very intelligent but sensitive cow who became increasingly distressed by all the billboards she saw extolling the virtues of homogenized milk, vitamin-charged milk, pasteurized milk, and the like. "All of them," she mooed sadly, "make me feel so INADEQUATE!"

∴

Distinguished Judge Albright, a recognized authority in cattle circles, was selecting the winners in a Fort Worth show when the committee in charge, bent on enlivening the proceedings somewhat, asked if he would judge a group of heifers not on the program. "Certainly," nodded the obliging judge, whereupon a bevy of beauteous girls in scant bikinis pranced into the ring.

Judge Albright never batted an eyelash. He simply boomed over the loudspeaker system, "Folks, I'm not accustomed to judging heifers with their blankets on. If the owners will now remove the blankets, I'll proceed with the judging."

∴

An elephant who had been a steady customer at a neighborhood bar for months suddenly dropped out of sight, then just as suddenly lumbered back to the eight bar stools he was wont to occupy. "Where you been, Big Boy?" demanded the bartender. The elephant answered, "I've been on the circus wagon."

∴

A youngster spotted a deer and asked the keeper, "What kind of an animal is that?" "What," teased the keeper, "does your mother call your father every night?" The youngster, startled, cried, "Don't tell me that's a skunk!"

∴

The hero of this story is Steve Ingram, a student at Pensacola Junior College in Florida. Steve's exhibit of white mice copped a blue ribbon at a Florida Regional Science Fair and Steve took his white mice home—flushed with triumph. Disaster fell on the Ingram homestead that very night, however. The white mice ate Steve's blue ribbon.

∴

A Lexington Avenue cavalier encountered a young lady bustling along with a small pig cradled in her arms. The cavalier inquired, "Where did you get that pig?" The pig answered, "I won her in a raffle."

∴

A very worried farmer called up his vet and reported, "That danged old mare of mine is really sick this time. She can only stand on her feet for about fifteen minutes at a time. Is there anything I can do with her?" "Yes," said the vet. "The next time she's standing up—sell her!"

∴

A nag who started life pulling an ice wagon worked his way up in the world to the day he came in first in the Kentucky Derby. Obviously, this was one horse with a whinny way.

∴

Kathleen Szast's *Petishism* is not only a fascinating study of the lengths to which some people will go to pamper their pets—be they dogs, cats, monkeys, or even alligators and skunks—but is replete with choice tidbits like the following:

1. The Earl of Cranbrook feeds his favorite bats on a choice mixture of egg yolk, cream cheese, and banana.
2. The number of new animal hospitals in the U.S. is going up nine times faster than new human hospitals.
3. The owner of a Great Dane dressed him up in top hat and tails so the dog wouldn't feel out of place at a fashionable wedding.
4. An Italian housewife was granted a divorce because her pet-loving spouse shared his bed with thirty cats and six dogs—and made her sleep in another room.
5. Two ladies in Louisville once inherited a $115,000 estate from a pampered goat named Sugar.
6. A New Yorker listed his dog's own personal phone number in the directory in case any of his friends felt the urge to call him.

⁂

"It's wonderful the power I got over dumb animals," boasted Mr. Schwartz to his wife. "You'll notice dogs, cats, horses, no matter how mean, they all come up and lick my hand."

"Maybe," sniffed Mrs. Schwartz, "if you'd eat with a knife and fork once in a while, they wouldn't be so friendly."

∴

John Fuller tells about an understanding mother who watched with growing concern while her young son indulged in lengthy and involved conversations with a stuffed toy frog. Finally she decided that this fantasy was getting a bit out of hand. She told him, "I know how much you love that frog, Freddie, but you should realize that his talk is only PRETEND talk. He doesn't really talk to you."

The boy looked shocked, and ran out of the room with his frog. He came back empty-handed and told his mother, "You've got to be more careful, Ma, while my frog is with us. He THINKS he can talk!"

∴

"Papa," asked a city lad on vacation with his parents, "what makes cocks crow so loudly every morning?" "I suspect," answered his father wearily, "they merely are making the most of their opportunity before the hens wake up."

∴

A barn full of chickens came upon a pile of torn-up racing forms in the backyard of a gentleman farmer one evening and ate them all. The next morning they were laying odds.

∴

The inimitable Robert Benchley may have written the very last word on the subject of roosters when he pointed out, "The rooster is an entirely different sort of bird from the hen. He has a red crest on the top of his head—put there by Nature so that the hen can see the rooster coming in a crowd and can hop into a taxi or make a previous engagement if she wants to. One of the happiest and most successful roosters I ever saw was one who had had his red crest chewed off in a fight with a dog. He also wore sneakers."

∴

Once upon a time there was a parrot who could say only three little words: "Who is it?" One day when the parrot was alone in the house there was a loud knock on the door. "Who is it?" screeched the parrot. "It's the plumber," the visitor responded. "Who is it?" repeated the parrot. "It's the plumber, I tell you," was the reply. "You called me to tell me your cellar was flooded." Again the parrot called, "Who is it?" By this time the plumber became so angry that he fainted. A neighbor rushed over to see the cause of the commotion, and, gazing at the unfamiliar face of the prostrate plumber, asked, "Who is it?" The parrot answered, "It's the plumber."

∴

A lady who had bought a parrot returned him a fortnight later, demanding her money back. "This bird," she told the pet shop proprietor, "is a nuisance around the house. He's bad-tempered and fidgety." "Allow me to make one suggestion," said the proprietor. "Try putting a mirror in his cage. Parrots are vain, and love to preen themselves."

A week later the proprietor met the lady on the street and inquired, "Well, has your parrot's behavior changed?" "It has," answered the lady grimly. "He's hired a press agent."

∴

If you're under the impression that a baby quail cannot be turned into a household pet, you should read *That Quail, Robert,* by Margaret Stanger. Robert wandered into the Stanger household uninvited one day and promptly took over.

The Stangers didn't even dare to change her name when "she" started to lay eggs. She even became housebroken (well, almost housebroken) in due course, and only kicked up a rumpus when she felt she wasn't getting enough attention. On one such occasion she deliberately paddled through the mint jelly and showered a half-dozen guests with broccoli and butter sauce. The Stangers never ruffled her feathers again!

Robert died—of old age—at three and a half. She was mourned by the whole town where she had lived. The book about her is a joy.

⁖

A bold ornithologist crossed a turkey with an ostrich, intent upon developing bigger drumsticks. The experiment, however, was a dismal failure. All he came up with was a scrawny bird who insisted on hiding his head in the mashed potatoes.

⁖

Farmer Jones, of Clinton, New Jersey, made history at the State Fair one day when he bought a prize rooster for the highest price ever paid in the history of the poultry trade. When he got it home, however, he found he simply could not control the rooster's romantic tendencies. Not only the hens, but the ducks, geese, and swans, not to mention a few stray nanny goats and sows, fled before the rooster's tireless onslaughts.

Farmer Jones finally collared his gay bird and grumbled, "I didn't pay a record price for you to waste your energies on every form of animal life in New Jersey. You are henceforth to confine your activities exclusively to the hens. Keep on the way you're going, and you'll die of exhaustion."

The rooster made light of his owner's fears, but sure enough, Farmer Jones found him a few mornings later flat on his back, his eyes glazed, his legs straight up in the air, with a couple of buzzards ominously circling closer and closer above him. "What did I tell you, you durn fool?" roared the farmer. "I knew the life you were leading would get you sooner or later!" But then, to his amazement, the supposedly expired rooster opened one eye and whispered hoarsely, "Pipe down, will you? When you're trying to romance a buzzard, you've got to play it their way!"

THE MOVING FINGER WRITES

1. *History*

Advice to readers of *The Sound of Laughter:* skip this section if you're anything like the deep thinker who announced, "History bores me. The way I feel about it, let bygones be bygones!"

∴

Recent discoveries:

1. What Achilles said after he was wounded in the heel: "My feet are killing me."

2. What happened when Hannibal crossed the Alps with an elephant: he got a mountain that remembered everything.

3. What happened when Julius Caesar, houseguesting at a villa on the Italian seashore, disapproved of the manner in

which the butler was preparing the dinner entrée: "Here," ordered Julius, "give me that bowl and ladle and let ME mix that salad." It's been called Caesar's salad ever since.

4. What happened when Pope Sixtus summoned artist Michelangelo and asked him what he'd charge to paint the walls and ceilings of the Vatican's Sistine Chapel: "That all depends," answered the cautious Michelangelo, "on whether you want one coat or two."

∴

The historian Henry Edward Fox tells us that when the news of Napoleon's death reached England, the king's minister, Sir E. Nagle, rushed to be the first to give the welcome tidings to his monarch. "Sir," he exclaimed joyously, "your bitterest enemy is dead." "Is she, by God," nodded the tender husband.

∴

John Gunther, in his book *Twelve Cities*, recalls the day the blunt Marshal Blücher, the Prussian strategist who helped beat Napoleon at Waterloo, was shown London from the dome of St. Paul's Cathedral. "What do you think of our fair city?" asked his guide. Blücher smacked his lips and answered, "What plunder!"

∴

One of the first of the great international statesmen to be irked by what he termed "the outrageous way I am misquoted by irresponsible rumor-mongering journalists" was Otto von Bismarck, iron-willed Chancellor of Germany from 1871 to 1890. London's top foreign correspondent at the time was W. H. Russell of the *Times*, and he reminded Bismarck one day, "You'll have to admit that I am one newspaper man who has respected your confidence. You have conversed with me on all sorts of subjects and never once have I repeated a word you said." Bismarck cried angrily, "The more fool you! Do you suppose I'd ever say a word to a man in your profession that I didn't *want to see in print?*"

∴

In a fascinating book called *Monsoon Seas,* author Alan Villiers demolishes the legend built up about the notorious "Pirate King," Captain Kidd. Far from being really big-team stuff, Captain Kidd, insists Villiers, made off with only one rich prize in his whole evil career—the barque *Queda Merchant,* bound West across the Indian Ocean, loaded with treasure from the Far East. Even this accomplishment availed him little, for his undisciplined crew of cutthroats promptly fell to quarreling over the spoils.

Kidd eventually turned up in New York, virtually penniless, was immediately arrested and hustled back to England. There he was hanged on May 23, 1701, so flabby and fat that the rope broke twice under his weight, necessitating his being strung up three times.

Poof, there goes another illusion! Apparently fortune hunters who still form occasional expeditions to unearth the fearsome Captain Kidd's "lost treasures" would have a better chance of copping a jackpot on a carnival slot machine!

∴

A prize example of tact and diplomacy was presented by Albert, King of the Belgians, one day on the eve of the outbreak of World War One. He was entertaining a powerful chieftain from the Belgian Congo at the palace, and after dinner, at a signal, the royal orchestra filed into the hall, and began tuning their instruments.

"Tell me the kind of music you like best—and my orchestra will be happy to oblige," proposed King Albert. "That's it," enthused the chieftain. "They're playing it now." The King nodded graciously—and for the remainder of the evening the assembled guests listened while the orchestra tuned up.

∴

Professor Russell Miles, of the University of Illinois, would like to convince you that when Adolf Hitler was obviously about to become the absolute dictator of Nazi Germany, a cautious carriage maker in Düsseldorf concluded, "I might as well continue to make shay while the Hun shines."

∴

The surest way to understand the character and motives of an adversary, insists Mayor John Eusthy, assistant dean of the USAF Academy, is to read a book he has written. Take the case of *Mein Kampf,* written by Hitler at a time when his political power index was close to zero—and regarded for too long as the fantastic dream of a frenzied visionary—so vast in scope and so incredibly ambitious as to be totally ridiculous. Yet, for every word in *Mein Kampf,* 125 lives were destined to be lost, for every page, 4700 lives, for every chapter, more than 1,200,000 lives! The fantastic dream of a frenzied visionary poisoned the world from 1933 to 1945!

∴

In 1941, a master sergeant at Fort Dix steadfastly resisted pressure to change his name, which happened to be Hitler. "That's my name," he insisted, "and it's going to stay my name. Let the other guy CHANGE HIS!"

∴

Turning the spotlight back to our own shores, Nat Benchley has been doing a little research on the deal by which the Dutch bought the whole of Manhattan along about 1626 for the sum (still considered exorbitant by curmudgeons) of twenty-four dollars—in trinkets and firewater.

The Indians who sold the island did just fine for themselves —because they didn't own it. Peter Minuit's agents made their offer to a passel of Canarsies, in from Long Island to gander the 1626 equivalent of Radio City Music Hall, whereas the real owners were the Weckquaesgeek Indians, centered around what is now Washington Heights and the Bronx, and blissfully unaware until too late that their property was being sold right out from under them.

It turns out that the Canarsies were strictly small-time con men at that. The real sharpies were the Raritan Indians. They sold Staten Island to the Dutch SIX consecutive times!

∴

I'm sure you learned in grade school that the name of Robert Fulton's famous steamboat was the *Clermont*. Wrong, says Charles Rice. Fulton christened his ship *The North River Steam Boat*. Clermont was just its port of registry. An early historian got the facts mixed up, and the error has been perpetuated ever since.

∴

Early in his military career, Ulysses S. Grant complained about the inadequacy of the officer who shared his command in a certain operation. Grant's senior general demurred, "You underrate the man," he snapped. "Remember, he's been through ten campaigns." Grant replied, "So has that mule over there, General—but he's still a jackass, isn't he?"

∴

In his early days as a country lawyer, Abraham Lincoln rather fancied himself as a horse trader and readily agreed to an unusual swap with a rival bargainer—the most important judge in that part of Illinois, in fact. Lincoln was not to see the judge's horse beforehand, and the judge was not to see Lincoln's.

Came the morning of the trade, and a big crowd turned up to see who would prove the shrewdest hornswoggler. The judge hove into view first, dragging behind him the oldest, sorriest-looking nag that ever managed to stand on four feet. The crowd was still chuckling when Lincoln came along, carrying a carpenter's wooden sawhorse.

For a long minute, Mr. Lincoln stared at the judge's horse without speaking. Then his face lit up with that wonderful smile of his, and he exclaimed, "Judge, this is the first time I ever got the worst of it in a horse trade!"

∴

General Sam Houston, when served his first helping of vanilla ice cream, is reputed to have expostulated, "Madam, it is not my intention to slander your hospitality, but this here pudding is froze."

∴

An alleged horse thief took the stand to defend himself in the kind of western outpost so familiar to TV fans. "Prisoner," growled the justice of the peace, fondling his shooting irons, "there's one thing I want to tell you before you get sworn in on that Bible. There's a Divine Justice up there who's bigger than you and me. There's an Eternal Providence looking down on these here proceedings—and He ain't gonna be took in by no lying hoss thief!"

∴

A character in another western frontier town, whom nobody liked or trusted, was accused of stealing a horse, and promptly strung up by an enthusiastic posse. His carcass was still dangling when the real culprit rode up on the stolen mustang and shamefacedly admitted his guilt.

This left to the sheriff the pretty problem of explaining to the hanged man's widow. He proved equal to the occasion. "Ma'am," he stated cheerfully, "we just hung your husband, but then discovered he was convicted by mistake. 'Twas another varmint entirely. So it looks like the joke's on us."

∴

Joe Babcock, a grizzled guide in the Grand Canyon area, gives this capsule history of the Wild, Wild West: "First them pioneers tamed the West. Then them confounded women tamed the pioneers. And now, by God, they got a symphony orchestry in Deadwood Gulch."

∴

Nobody who had the guts to ride out sudden panics or depressions has ever lost money on New York real estate. Sam Himmell offers a few isolated examples that spectacularly prove the point. That corner of Broad and Wall streets, where the prestigious house of J. P. Morgan now stands, changed hands in 1789 (and that's less than 250 years ago!) for the then handsome price of $1125. . . . In 1818, Robert Lenox bought the land now bounded by Seventy-first Street, Seventy-fourth Street, Fifth Avenue, and Park Avenue for the round sum $500—and thought it necessary to explain to his family in writing, "My motive for this move is a firm persuasion that this empty land may well be, at some distant day, the site of a village." . . . In 1829, John Jacob Astor, who could have taught all the real estate giants of today put together a thing or two, conned a shnook named Medclef Eden into selling him a farm on what is now Forty-second Street to Forty-sixth Street on Times Square for exactly $25,000. You couldn't get that property today for forty million!

∴

Ever think how tough it would be for you—let alone your teenage daughter—to get along without a telephone in your home? Yet it was as late as 1877 that the very first telephone company in New York City was organized. A Roosevelt—Hilborne H. Roosevelt—was president, and the first subscriber was a well-heeled Brooklynite named James R. Haight. His line stretched five miles from his home to his steel mill in South Brooklyn.

∴

And while Brooklyn is on our mind, the famous Brooklyn Bridge was opened in 1883. For some years it was a toll bridge, charging "one cent for pedestrians, five cents for cows, and ten cents for horse-drawn vehicles." Today cows can cross it for nothing!

∴

On the subject of prophecies, cast your eye over this one, made by the eminent diarist George Templeton Strong in 1865: "By the year 1900, Brooklyn undoubtedly will be the city, and Manhattan will be the suburb. Brooklyn has room to spread; Manhattan has not. The New Yorker uptown on Thirty-fifth Street already finds it a tedious and annoying job to commute to his business downtown and home again. Can you imagine him fighting his way all the way up to the pig farms on One Hundredth Street forty years hence?"

∴

In a beguiling new book, *The Polite Americans,* Gerald Carson reminds us that "a Virginia aristocrat in 1853 would never be 'so gauche as to throw up to a Yankee the misfortune of his birthplace.'" And forty years later, in the same milieu, a lady reproached her servant for kicking an inquiring reporter downstairs. "After all," she pointed out. "The person was only trying to earn an honest living in a most disagreeable way."

∴

Here are a few other memorable bits of Americana unearthed by Mr. Carson: 1. The first Harvard man to have his ears cut off was one Joshua Parker—for forging a deed. 2. The

American president who sported by far the longest set of whiskers was Rutherford B. Hayes. 3. A visitor at a Fifth Avenue mansion, anxious to impress his hostess at dinner, actually remarked, "In Eastern Uganda, one hears it is no longer compulsory to take part in the rain-making dances."

∴

There was a wild night in a saloon in the frontier town of Mingusville, South Dakota, way back in 1880. A Bad Lands drunk had just shot up the premises and sent the bartender to cover behind the counter when he spied a bespectacled tenderfoot minding his own business at a rear table. The drunk announced boldly, "Four Eyes will now set up drinks for the house."

Four Eyes turned slowly, and after two shots from the drunk went wild, knocked him senseless with a single punch to the solar plexus.

After that Tenderfoot Theodore Roosevelt was affectionately known in those parts as "Old Four Eyes."

∴

Tidbits from an Overseas Press Club book presentation, *Heroes of Our Times:* A nosey brat once evaded flunkies and made his way into Winston Churchill's study and asked, "Are you the greatest man in the world?" "I certainly am," snapped Sir Winston. "Now buzz off!" . . . A not too reverent member of Mahatma Gandhi's retinue was overheard to sigh, "If only Gandhi realized how much it costs us to keep him in poverty!" . . . Eleanor Roosevelt, noting that her dress seemed to be coming apart at a state function, despaired, "There seems sometimes to be a hopeless discrepancy between me and my clothes!"

Incidentally, the prestigious Overseas membership answers the unfortunate question of FDR's Chief of Staff Admiral

Leahy, "Who the Hell is Harry Truman?" by placing him tenth among its twelve selected *Heroes of Our Times.*

∴

In his best-selling biography *Huey Long,* the eminent historian T. Harry Williams tells about the first time the ebullient Huey campaigned in rural, predominantly Catholic southern Louisiana. A veteran local boss advised him at the outset of the tour, "Remember one thing, Huey. South Louisiana's a lot different from your northern part of the state. We've got a lot of Catholic voters down here." "I know," nodded Long.

And so at every whistle stop on the tour Huey would declaim for openers, "When I was a boy, I'd get up at six A.M. every Sunday, hitch our old horse up to the buggy, and take my Catholic grandparents to Mass. I'd bring them home, and at ten A.M. I'd hitch the old horse up again, and take my *Baptist* grandparents to church."

The audiences responded heartily, and the boss finally told Huey admiringly, "You've been holding out on us. We didn't know you had any Catholic grandparents."

"Don't be a damn fool," replied Huey. "We didn't even have a horse!"

∴

Molly Berkeley, a very proper Bostonian indeed, now turned eighty, has written her memoirs, called *Winking at the Brim,* and a very engaging chronicle it is, replete with intimate bits about such important buddies as the Cabots, the Lowells, Henry Adams, Justice Oliver Wendell Holmes—and Franklin D. Roosevelt. Near the end you'll come across this prophetic vignette: "My husband built me a swimming pool with the understanding that no one would be permitted to enter the drawing room in a bathing suit. To my dismay, in marched one day young John F. Kennedy (his father at the time was our Ambassador to Britain), just out of the pool, his bathing suit dripping. He threw off his top, plumped himself down beside my husband—and got away with it. I thought to myself, if you can get away with that, you can get away with anything!"

∴

President Harry Truman liked to reminisce every now and then during a lull in the White House about his brief experience in the haberdashery business. He recalled one pesky customer who couldn't seem to find the shirts he was looking for. "Here's our most expensive line," Mr. T. said finally. "They wear like iron. They just laugh at the laundry." "Yes, I know," grumbled the customer, unimpressed. "I bought a half-dozen just like these. They came back with their sides split."

∴

When John O'Brien served a brief term as mayor of New York in the 1930's, he carried on a running feud with City Hall reporters, who kidded him continuously and unmercifully. One day a columnist asked him for an advance copy of a speech he was scheduled to deliver that evening. O'Brien, thinking he was turning over a carbon copy of the speech, handed the columnist a sheaf of blank paper by mistake. "Why, Mr. Mayor," chided the columnist, "This is the same speech you made last Tuesday."

The mayor had him barred from City Hall for a month.

∴

To give you a graphic example of how radically things have changed in forty years, when Herbert Hoover was inaugurated as President in 1928, he waited some days to summon his Secretary of War, then asked him, "Do you know of anything

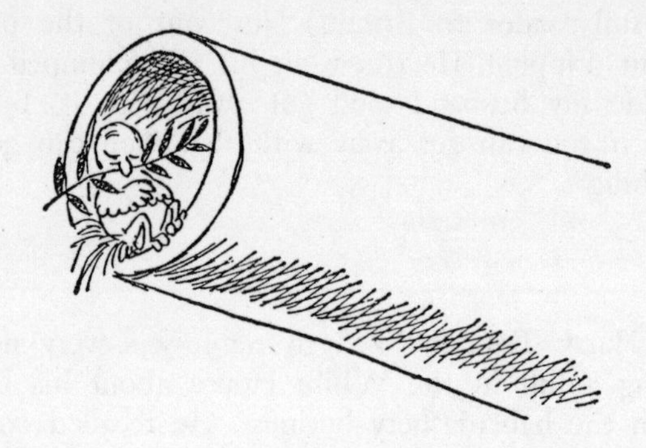

particular going on in your sphere about which I should be concerned?" "Not a thing in the world, Mr. President," was the response. Hoover never had occasion to huddle with the War Secretary one other time for the balance of his administration!

∴

Can you guess what well-known personage mesmerized an audience with this rabble-rousing speech?

"The streets of our country are in turmoil. The universities are filled with students rebelling and rioting. Communists are seeking to destroy our country. We are in danger from within and without. What we need now is restoration of law and order. Elect us and I promise you that bringing back law and order to our streets, our courts, and our schools will be our first obligation."

These words, which may have a slightly familiar ring, were a bit of campaign oratory by Adolf Hitler in Hamburg, Germany, in 1932.

2. *Politics*

A habitually cautious Congressman had several too many at a luncheon party one day, and that afternoon rose to make a few remarks. So carried away was he by his own eloquence that before he wound up he had declared himself on eight key problems that were up for grabs in the House at the time.

When he sat down, several colleagues rushed over to congratulate him, one going so far as to say, "Brother, you sure told it to 'em today! You made it crystal clear which way you stood on every controversial question plaguing this body."

The Congressman turned deathly pale. "Good God!" he groaned. "I DID?"

∴

Some elections back, Republican headquarters in Washington received this query over the phone: "Can you please give us the name of the Democratic candidate for governor in Vermont?" The clerk was temporarily stumped, then chirped brightly, "Why don't you call the Democratic National Committee? Surely they'll be able to give you the information."

There was a pause, then a sad voice replied meekly, "This *is* the Democratic National Committee!"

∴

"Gentlemen," begged the Republican chairman of a bipartisan congressional committee, "permit me to tax your memories for a moment." "Golly," whispered a Democrat member to a crony, "why haven't we thought of that?"

∴

A live action political campaign story comes from Ohio, where, to wind up his last pre-election speech with a flourish, a Congressman pulled his overcoat off the seat, waved it grandly to the crowd, cried, "Next stop, Washington!"—and plunged headfirst into the organ pit.

∴

A recent governor of North Carolina was greeting an endless line of constituents after a long, long oration on a hot, hot day. The inevitable pest showed up who wouldn't let go of the governor's hand, and roared, "I just bet you can't tell me my name." "Of course, I can," lied the governor, trying to pry his hand loose. "Why, you and me, we've been workin' for the same things now together for years and years." "Sure, sure," cackled the constituent, not to be put off, "but just you tell me my name now."

After one more unsuccessful attempt, the governor called over an aide and instructed him in a loud stage whisper, "For God's sake, find out this twerp's name and tell him what it is. He's forgotten it and he's trying to find it out from me!"

∴

Rhode Island's Theodore Francis Green, who died not long ago at the ripe old age of ninety-eight, was still active in the U. S. Senate only six years before—a genial, jaunty, humor-loving, conscientious politician who believed in giving his constituents a square deal. Senator Green was still playing tennis at eighty-eight, and flirting with pretty girls at ninety-four. He loved parties. At one Washington cocktail soiree, his hostess caught him leafing hurriedly through his pocket date book. "Ah, Senator," she chided. "Trying to find out where you're due next, eh?" "Not at all," replied Senator Green. "I'm trying to find out where the hell I am now."

∴

When it came to the gentle art of hedging, Massachusetts Senator Henry Cabot Lodge, Sr., bowed to nobody. Asked his opinion one day on a certain controversial bill, the good Senator replied without hesitation. "Well, some say this and some say that, but what I have to say on the subject is that there's no knowing and no telling, and mark my words, son, I'm right."

∴

In the heat of a spirited election campaign, a visitor to the Williamson home declaimed, "I will never vote for a mud-slinging candidate." The Williamsons' four-year-old daughter seemingly was paying no attention whatever to the remarks of the grownups, but the following afternoon her mother caught her and a playmate in the backyard slinging handfuls of mud at each other. "What on earth are you two scalawags doing there?" demanded Mrs. Williamson. Her daughter explained, "We're playing candidate."

∴

Translation of congressional oratory by Charles McDowell, Jr.:

GREAT AMERICAN: An American.
GREAT SOVEREIGN STATE: A state.
DISTINGUISHED SENATOR: A Senator.
SCHOLARLY ADDRESS: A long speech.
FACT-FINDING TRIP: A junket the user of the phrase went along on.
JUNKET: A fact-finding trip the user of the phrase did NOT go along on.

∴

Senator Fred Harris likes to tell about the close-mouthed politician who shot his girl friend and was convicted of murder in the first degree. Just before he was hanged, he was asked, "Have you anything you wish to say?" His answer was, "Not at this time."

∴

A half-dozen top-ranking Congressmen had a secret meeting at an exclusive Washington club to decide strategy for beating a bill they all detested. As they got down to brass tacks, they noticed that the waiter took a station near the door. Furthermore, he flatly refused to leave. "If you don't vamoose immediately," thundered one red-faced Congressman, "I will report your insubordination to the manager of this club." "It was the manager who ordered me to STAY here," replied the unperturbed waiter. "He's holding me responsible for the silverware."

∴

A local Chamber of Commerce had a notoriously long-winded and boring Senator wished upon it for its annual banquet. Maybe the chairman was weighing his words very carefully when he instructed the official photographer, "Don't take his picture while he's speaking. Shoot him before he begins!"

∴

Subtle reporting by a new man sent to cover a debate between two old windbags in the Texas House of Representatives: "Rep. Blank and Rep. Blunk engaged in intellectual combat this morning. Both were unarmed."

∴

Fattest President by far that we've ever had in the U.S.A. was the good-natured William Howard Taft. Visiting friends one summer day in Long Branch, New Jersey, he was disporting himself languidly in the surf when his host's two young sons asked if they could have a swim before lunch. "You'll have to wait till later," their father told them gravely. "The President is using the ocean."

∴

"The most impartial man I ever met," Bugs Baer liked to emphasize, "was Charles Evans Hughes. In fact, he was so impartial that he even parted his beard down the middle."

∴

Do you think politicians' set speeches today leave something to be desired? Have a look at what Senator William McAdoo once said about the perorations of President Warren Harding: "His speeches leave the impression of an army of pompous phrases moving over the landscape in search of an idea. Sometimes these meandering words actually capture a straggling thought and bear it triumphantly a prisoner in their midst until it dies of servitude and overwork."

∴

Unexpectedly clobbered in an election he was expected to win by a landslide, a defeated politico alibied, "I was going great until one night I made the mistake of saying 'Let's look at the record'—and dammit, they did!"

∴

Cal Coolidge, never a man to waste words, hit one whistle stop while campaigning for election where the total population was about three hundred. He sized up his audience at a glance and retreated precipitately to his private compartment. "This crowd," he explained tersely, "is too big for an anecdote and too small for an oration."

∴

Shortly after his election as President, "Silent" Cal was asked the secret of his success in politics. Drawled the President, "It was very simple. I just listened my way along!"

∴

One of my favorite Coolidge stories concerns the evening he was seated next to Alice Longworth at a Washington dinner party. Mrs. Longworth was a famous and brilliant conversationalist and was determined she'd succeed in drawing the taciturn President out of his shell. After several vain assaults, however, she finally exploded, "These formal dinners obviously bore you to death, Mr. President. Why do you attend so many of them?" President Coolidge swallowed a generous slab of beef and remarked, "Well, a man has to eat somewhere."

∴

To a distinguished jurist who was being urged to run for a high state office, but demurred because he felt he would be compelled to make some questionable and distressing compromises, the always realistic President Franklin D. Roosevelt summed up his whole concept of politics in one short sentence: "First get elected, Judge; then get honest!"

∴

FDR, when told that Wendell Willkie had his eye on the presidential chair: "Yes, but look what I've got on it."

∴

The late and admirable Norman Thomas, perennial Socialist candidate for President, was hailed with delight at a banquet in the forties by Alf Landon, who boomed to his wife, "Come over and meet Norman Thomas—the fellow I beat so badly in 1936!"

∴

While Dwight Eisenhower was President, his popular first lady Mamie saw an item she liked in a big Washington department store and ordered it sent to the White House. "What's that address again?" asked the saleslady, obviously unaware of her customer's identity. "Sixteen hundred Pennsylvania Avenue," said Mamie Eisenhower, smiling. The saleslady asked, "What apartment?"

∴

James Michener, author of *Hawaii* and *The Source*, declined a dinner invitation at the White House during the Eisenhower administration, but his explanatory letter to the President made full amends. "Dear Mr. President," wrote Michener. "I received your invitation three days after I had agreed to speak a few words at a dinner honoring the wonderful high school teacher who taught me how to write. I know you will not miss me at your dinner, but she might at hers."

Commented the understanding Ike: "In his lifetime a man

lives under 15 or 16 Presidents, but a really fine teacher comes into his life but rarely."

∴

Ohio Rep. J. William Stanton understandably treasures a letter he received from the Chamber of Commerce in Painesville, Ohio, dated 1949, when he offered to bring a new Congressman as the featured speaker of a fund-raising dinner. The letter reads, "We feel that this year we really need a big name speaker who'll be a drawing card so we're hoping to bag the head football coach at John Carroll University. Thanks anyhow for suggesting Rep. John F. Kennedy."

∴

On the desk of the late President Kennedy in the White House stood a small plaque bearing this inscription: "Oh God, thy sea is so great and my boat is so small."

∴

Arthur Daley retains this pleasant memory of the late Senator Bobby Kennedy: Shortly after his brother, President Jack, had appointed him Attorney General, Bobby took his wife, Ethel, to a movie one evening in downtown Washington. They drove around block after block, vainly searching for a parking space, and finally he dispatched her to buy tickets while he made one more try for a free space. When he returned, he obviously was pleased. "Where did you find a space?" asked Mrs. Kennedy. "At Jack's place," he explained triumphantly. "Jack's place" was the White House.

∴

In Ted Kennedy's heartbreaking eulogy of his martyred brother Bobby, the best-remembered lines were, "Some men see things as they are and say, 'why?' He dreamed things that never were and said, 'Why not?'"

The quotation comes from one of George Bernard Shaw's plays, *John Bull's Other Island.*

∴

One of Lyndon Baines Johnson's favorite windups to speeches he made at countless banquets was, "I think it essential that the U.S.A. remain a two-party country. I'm a fellow who likes small parties, too—and the Republican Party can't be too small to suit me."

∴

LBJ's devotion to his superb wife, Ladybird, was one of the first things obvious to anybody fortunate enough to be invited to the White House during his incumbency. He was wont to observe, "Only two things are necessary to keep one's wife happy. First is to let her think she's having her own way. Second is to let her have it."

∴

A few days before Lyndon Johnson evacuated the White House, he put in an unexpected appearance at a congressional reception in the House Office Building. After greeting the Senators and Representatives warmly, he explained, "I've learned that it never hurts a private citizen to have an in with a few fellows in public life."

∴

President Nixon tells about a supervisor at the Income Tax Bureau who phoned a certain Baptist minister to say, "We're checking the tax return of a member of your church, Deacon X., and notice that he lists a donation to your building fund of three hundred dollars. Is that correct?" The minister answered without hesitation, "I haven't got my records available, but I'll promise you one thing: if he hasn't, he WILL!"

∴

Three cracker-barrel cronies spent a pleasant hour giving their definitions of the word "FAME."

"Fame," opined the first one, "is being invited to the White House to dine alone with President Nixon."

"No," corrected the second. "Fame is dining alone with Nixon and when a ring on the Hot Line from Moscow interrupts the conversation, Nixon answers impatiently, 'I can't talk to you now. I'm entertaining a very important visitor.'"

"You're both wrong," declared the third. "Fame is when the Hot Line rings, Nixon answers, then hands you the receiver and says, 'It's for you!'"

∴

Caution was the watchword of Richard Nixon at the beginning of his comeback trail that ended in the White House. He was so careful, according to a San Diego scribe, that when he stopped to look at the male Siamese twins at a circus side show, he hazarded, "Brothers, I presume?"

∴

They say that on Vice-President Agnew's recent stopover in Viet Nam, a GI accosted him and demanded, "Say, aren't you Spiro Agnew?" "Sure I am," grinned the V.P. The GI exclaimed, "Man, that's what I call a draft board!"

∴

At a star-spangled banquet at the Waldorf, Bob Hope, in rare form, and irreverent as always, declared that New York's

Cardinal Cooke's unfavorite song of the year was, "Wedding Bells Are Breaking Up That Old Gang of Mine" and that Vice-President Agnew, after a lightning tour of Far East bastions, went about for three days remarking how quiet everything was before he realized he was back home in the U.S.A.

The V.P. and the Cardinal joined in the burst of laughter.

∴

Political expediency once dictated the appointment of an admittedly inferior man as Assistant Secretary of State. The President then occupying the White House was challenged by an idealistic adviser. "This fellow," spluttered the adviser, "is not only thoroughly incompetent: he is a liar, a vulgarian, and a snob beyond belief." "Good," nodded the President. "Then we won't have to break him in."

∴

Dick Roraback vows that he rode in the club car of a Washington-bound train and spotted Congressman Emanuel Celler taking a nap, while Chicago scribe Irv Kupcinet was writing a column on the seat to his left and baseball great Leo "The Lip" Durocher perused a sports magazine on the seat to his right. "Ho, ho," cackled Roraback. "There's Manny, asleep twixt Kupp and the Lip."

∴

When Senator Muskie was campaigning through Maine some years ago, an opponent named Bill Trafton gave him a very tough fight. At Bangor one evening, Muskie asked a grizzled native, "Do you think I have a better chance than Trafton?" "I don't know too much about that," admitted the native, "but if bumper stickers mean anything, you'd better look out for this fellow Ausable Chasm!"

∴

With politicking very much the order of the day, pundits are recalling some of the extraordinary statements made on TV or the radio in previous campaigns. A few examples: 1. "Vote for me and I'll roll up my hands and go to work." 2. "What I'm telling you about my distinguished opponent is more truth than poultry." 3. "The great Senator of this sovereign state who introduced me this evening has said such

flattering things about me that I feel like the fifth wheel on a horse." 4. "Our rally tomorrow night will be a great show. Don't miss it if you can."

∴

After departing completely from his planned speech at a big public rally, a big-wig Washington politico apologized to his audience, "There I go again—an unreconstructed text deviate!"

∴

A too jovial bear of a man was running for mayor and strode through a hall greeting everybody as a long-lost friend. One individual he clapped on the back with a hearty, "Surely, I've seen that face before." "Very likely," agreed the voter. "I've been a guard at the county jail for the past thirty years!"

∴

The wittiest public official of our day undoubtedly is New York's Mayor John Lindsay, a self-styled ham to his finger-tips. One morning a secretary at City Hall called him at home to tell him, "You'd better get down here on the double." Quipped his honor, "Why? What's playing there this week?"

∴

Mayor Lindsay defines the abbreviated miniskirt as a functional thing: "It enables young ladies to run faster—and because of it they may have to."

∴

Roger Devlin, of Tulsa, detects a distinct trend toward political conservatism among today's collegiate set, and cites as an example a lad who has been a frequent guest in his home—a second son to all intents and purposes. "For a long time," recalls Devlin, "he was far left politically and economically. Really far out. But recently he expressed such opposite views that I was startled. 'How come?' I asked him, 'that you've so drastically changed your tune? Why no longer a super-liberal?' 'I found out,' explained the student calmly, 'that they're counting on ME to pay YOUR old age pension.'"

∴

A Congressman from the deepest South was aiming both barrels at sex education in the schools recently. "I don't want my twelve-year-old son to hear such filth," he ruminated, "and what's more, I've felt just that way since the day the stork brought him!"

"PRESENT ARMS!"

The Military

Under active fire in Viet Nam for the first time, two U.S. draftees (in this war they're called "grunts") huddled under a bush on a hillside, listening apprehensively while bombs exploded on all sides of them. "Buck up," counseled the braver of the two. "Remember, not one of those bombs is going to hit you unless its got your name stenciled on it." "I guess you're right," conceded the other with a weak smile.

Just then a Viet Cong soldier popped up behind them to tap the frightened American on the shoulder and inquire politely, "Pardon me, sir, but exactly how do you spell your last name?"

∴

At a neighborhood bar, in the wee hours of the morning, a chronic stutterer announced, "If they r-r-really w-w-wanted to, they c-c-could end this d-d-damn w-w-war in V-V-Viet Nam in about t-t-two w-w-weeks!"

"Humph," snorted his companion. "That's easy for *you* to say!"

∴

A cocky Texan was a member of a small Marine detachment that was ambushed by a Viet Cong force ten times as large. A bullet caught him in the thigh, but when the enemy withdrew, he charged after them, hurling invectives, and bleeding profusely. "Come back," shouted his captain. "You're wounded, you idiot." "I know," yelled back the Texan, "but I think I know who did it!"

∴

Stationed for a long spell in a remote village in South Korea, a bored captain wrote home to his wife telling her of the shortage of good books and music—and his trouble in warding off all the attractive babes who sought to help him wile away the lonely hours. "Maybe if I had a harmonica, it would help," he suggested.

So his wife sent him a harmonica. When he finally got back home, she met him at the airport, embraced him, then commanded, "Okay, my faithful hero: let's hear you play that harmonica!"

∴

"Just read the letters on that chart," ordered a draft board doctor. "I don't see any chart," answered the draftee happily.

"You're absolutely right," snapped the doctor. "There isn't any chart. You're 1-A!"

∴

A distinguished, elderly Senator, visiting a hospital in Viet Nam, was escorted by a new navy nurse, eager, beautiful, and proud of her just acquired ensign's bars. As the two of them passed through a wardroom full of tough, wounded marines, a chorus of joyous wolf calls resounded through the corridor. "Goodness," exclaimed the flustered nurse. "Do you suppose those boys are whistling at ME?" The Senator chuckled and answered, "I hope so, missy. I certainly hope so!"

∴

One of the many top comedians and singers who have risked their lives to entertain our troops in Viet Nam was describing some of his experiences at one of his old Broadway haunts. "More than once," he recounted, "we'd give a performance and then run like heck for our lives." "Hmmph," sniffed one veteran but not too successful vaudevillian. "That's the story of my whole professional career!"

∴

Speaking about all the polls being taken to ascertain the degree of public approval of our Viet Nam policy, don't overlook the one reported from an Indian reservation in New Mexico. Twenty-one per cent of the people questioned there thought we should get out of Viet Nam. Ninety-nine per cent thought we should get out of New Mexico.

∴

After six lonely weeks of jungle training, an army unit returned to its home base—just down the road from a WAC detachment.

The wise CO of the army unit suggested to the head of the WAC that she keep her girls restricted after duty hours. "If you don't," he warned, "I predict trouble." "Not with my girls," scoffed the WAC leader. "My girls," she explained, tapping her temple, "have it up here."

"Ma'am," exploded the army CO, "I don't care where your girls have it. My men will find it. Restrict them!"

∴

A Congressman, shaken by what he had seen in a ten-day tour of Viet Nam, sought some relaxation in Japan before returning to Washington. In Tokyo, he ran into a high-flying newspaper man from his hometown, and was immediately steered to the most expensive restaurant in the entire Far East. As the meal came to a close, the newsman summoned the waiter, and struggling over every syllable, spoke to him in Japanese.

The Congressman remarked kiddingly, "Is that all the Japanese you've learned here in over two years?"

"It's enough," the newsman assured him. "I told him to give you the check."

∴

A draftee was assigned as chauffeur to a colonel who had a keen eye for a pretty girl. One afternoon the colonel spotted a real beauty ankling along Park Avenue in the opposite direction and ordered the chauffeur, "Turn the car around on the double and pull up alongside that young lady."

The driver promptly stalled his motor in carrying out the directive, and by the time he got it going again, the beauty had disappeared in the crowd. "Soldier," snapped the irritated colonel, "you'd be a total loss in an emergency."

"I think you're wrong, sir," hazarded the soldier. "That was MY girl."

∴

An army barber was just finishing cutting a draftee's hair. "Like to keep these sideburns of yours?" he asked solicitously. The draftee, a hipster, answered fervently, "I sure would." "Okay," chirped the barber. "CATCH!"

∴

A general, determined to keep morale high among his troops, stopped to question new recruits during an inspection. "How does the food strike you?" he asked one likely-looking lad. "It's horrible," was the frank reply. Taken aback, the general said, "That distresses me. What, for instance, did you have for breakfast this morning?"

The recruit answered, "Orange juice, scrambled eggs and a rasher of bacon, toasted English muffins, and two cups of coffee." "But that's a wonderful breakfast," exclaimed the general. "It should be," nodded the recruit. "It cost me four bucks at the PX."

.˙.

In Charlotte, N.C., there's an eatery whose proprietor, an honored veteran of three wars, likes to wear his medals as he personally serves favored customers. The other day several of the medals fell into a jurist's chicken soup. The jurist now boasts, "I've got the only stomach in town with the air medal and four oak leaf clusters."

.˙.

A callow draftee was out on the rifle range for the first time and delivered a truly atrocious performance. When his card was brought in, in fact, it was so bad that he mopped his brow and groaned, "I think I'll shoot myself." His captain heard him, and suggested unfeelingly, "Better take two bullets."

.˙.

On an inspection tour to Viet Nam, a top army officer resented the presence of a very shy, puny civilian on his committee. He had been instructed particularly to give this civilian all the advance briefing he possibly could, so, trying unsuccessfully to hide his distaste, he handed the civilian a book outlining the whole history and culture of Viet Nam, and suggested, "Begin reading this now, and with a lot of luck, you just may digest it in six months." "That's possible," said the little man calmly. "It only took me two months to write it."

.˙.

Mrs. Gumberg had plenty of advice to give her son Monroe before he set sail for Viet Nam. "Get plenty of rest and nonfattening food in that Army," she counseled, "and try to get a nap every afternoon. And if you're shooting Commies, don't stay out too late." "Mama," interrupted Monroe, trying to humor her, "what do you think I should do if a Commie happens to kill me?" "Don't be foolish, Monroe," reproved Mrs. Gumberg. "What have the Communists got against you?"

∴

At a full-dress inspection at Redstone Arsenal, Alabama, not long ago, Pfc. Jan Curran reports that the commanding officer halted abruptly in front of a freckle-faced recruit and ordered, "Button that pocket, trooper!" The recruit stammered, "Right now, sir?" "Of course, right now," roared the CO.

So the recruit carefully reached out and buttoned the flap on the CO's shirt pocket.

∴

Just before a drafted farm boy made his first parachute jump, his sergeant reminded him, "Count ten and pull the first rip cord. If it snarls, pull the second rip cord for the auxiliary chute. After you land, our truck will pick you up."

The paratrooper took a deep breath, and jumped. He counted to ten, and pulled the first cord. Nothing happened. He pulled the second cord. Again nothing happened. As he careened crazily earthward, he said to himself, "Now I'll bet that darn truck won't be there either!"

∴

It was midnight on New Year's Eve on Times Square, and from a window high in the Alcoa Tower, a happy, happy sailor saluted the arrival of the New Year by emptying a vat of tasty Italian food on the celebrants below.

His bunkmate shouted up at him from below, "I said CONFETTI, you idiot; not SPAGHETTI!"

∴

A barmaid in a German rathskeller near a NATO base was a flirtatious piece and the tall, bronzed Texas GI who invaded the premises was just her cup of tea. The MP on duty had left the bar for a moment, and the barmaid cuddled up to the Texan, murmuring, "Here's your chance, big boy." "You said it," agreed the GI heartily—and drank the MP's beer.

∴

Little Nancy, rummaging around in the attic, came upon her dad's old dog tags from his days in World War Two. Her mother explained to her what they were and let her wear them to school. There she proudly displayed them to her chum. "These belonged to my daddy," she boasted. "He used to wear them when he was a dog!"

∴

One of Notre Dame's immortal "Four Horsemen," "Sleepy Jim" Crowley, liked to tell about the record of his outfit in World War Two. "Our boys destroyed six bridges, blew up two ammunition depots, and demolished a key military installation. Then we were sent overseas."

∴

Near the end of World War Two a newly commissioned army medic, stationed on a South Pacific island, radioed the newest base hospital, "Have a case of beriberi on my hands. What should I do?" Back came a message reading, "Give it to the Marines. They'll drink anything."

∴

A slightly pixilated gent blockaded a full admiral at a cocktail soiree to impart the invaluable information that he, too, had been in the Navy in World War Two. Then he became suddenly aware of all the gold braid adorning the admiral's uniform. He backed off embarrassedly and stammered, "Gad! You're in this thing pretty deep, aren't you?"

∴

Learning that his son, a navy lieutenant, was slated for a leave in Tokyo, a father wrote asking him to send back something he had heard praised in glowing terms: a Japanese back scratcher. The son duly replied, "Dear Dad: I dug up for you the best darn back scratcher in all Japan, but unfortunately, they wouldn't give her an exit visa."

∴

A sailor came running to the officer of the deck and mumbled something about the admiral of the fleet. "I can't understand one word you're saying," protested the officer. "Sing it out, man, sing it out."

The sailor looked mystified, then took a deep breath and sang: "Should old acquaintance be forgot, and never brought to mind, the admiral's fallen overboard, me lads: he's half a mile behind!"

∴

A young sailor lad and his date seemed to be getting along beautifully in a side booth of a Norfolk bar and grille until she suddenly cried authoritatively, "Okay, sailor: all hands on deck!"

∴

A small boy accompanied his parents to watch his big brother arrive home from a hitch in Viet Nam. He was the first to spot the brother, too. "There he is, Pop," he whopped to his father, pointing up to the transport as it eased into the dock. "Where?" queried Pop. "Up there," cried the boy, "with the boat around his neck!"

∴

The most unpopular officer on a carrier had enjoyed shore leave a little too much, and was lurching visibly when he started back up the gangplank. Suddenly, to the infinite delight of the sailors on deck, he pitched over the side. That's when a boatswain hollered, "Well, don't you gobs just stand there! Somebody throw him an anchor!"

∴

The captain of a cruiser made a lamentably faulty maneuver within full sight of his admiral, and waited in dread for his well-deserved dressing down. To his relief, the admiral's prompt message read merely: "To Captain Cruiser. Good. Admiral Flagship." Five minutes later, however, this second communiqué reached him: "To Captain Cruiser. To previous message, please add the word 'God.' Admiral Flagship."

∴

Marine sergeants aren't quite the same since they've learned about psychology. Take the sarge at Quantico, for instance, who was heard bawling out his green rookies: "Take a look at yourselves! Shoes not shined properly, haircuts terrible, ties crooked, and whiskers like you haven't shaved in a week. SUPPOSE SOME COUNTRY SUDDENLY DECLARED WAR ON US!"

∴

Two luscious lasses sadly watched a shipload of marines sail for a destination unknown in Southeast Asia. "I hate to see 'em go," sighed one. "I wonder what they're going to be doing way out there?"

"What will they be doing?" echoed the other incredulously. "How long is it since you've had a date with a marine?"

∴

A gent of middle age, but powerfully built and with a ruddy complexion, was trying to enlist in the Marines, and doing his best to tell everything he could about himself. "I'm a nudist, sergeant," he admitted, "and the father of fourteen children." "Nudist, hell," rasped the irritated sergeant. "You just never had time to dress!"

∴

Word comes from a large naval base in California that a Marine private had the temerity to flag down a jeep doing sixty-five miles an hour—with a doughty navy commander at the wheel.

"Damn it, Private," cried the irate commander. "Do you realize you've stopped the executive officer of this base and that you've made me late for a golf date with a former President of the United States?"

"Sorry, sir," replied the unperturbed private. "I'll write out your traffic violation ticket just as fast as I can!"

∴

Near the end of an oral examination, an army lieutenant, seeking promotion to captain, was asked, "If, while traveling on orders, you observed a young lady to whom you were attracted by the general excellence of a co-ordinated rear action, what would you do?" The unblinking candidate, according to informant H. R. Flanagan, won unanimous approval of the review board by assuring the questioning colonel, "I would first reconnoiter the forward development, sir, to be sure that it matched the rear emplacement that you described."

∴

A sailor, mustered out of service after long service at Pearl Harbor, was nabbed for speeding one evening, and hoping to avoid a ticket, told the cop, who had his summons book in hand, "You'll have trouble with my name, I'm afraid, officer. It's Kamehameha Haleakala Kamakaipo."

"You don't say," nodded the unimpressed cop. "Kamehameha was a king, Haleakala is a mountain, Kamakaipo is a town, and I was an MP in Honolulu for four years. Now, smart guy, what's your name?"

∴

Chet Huntley is responsible for the story of the high-falutin' admiral who was invited for a hunt on a duke's enormous estate. He reported later that he had brought down one animal the likes of which he never had seen before. "All I can tell you," he added, "is that it had great big shoulders, a long nose, and an enormous rear." "Good heavens," gasped an English journalist, "he's shot the Duchess!"

WELL SAID

1. *Quotations*

"Stronger than all the armies in the world is an idea whose time has come."—Victor Hugo

"Today is the first day of the rest of your life."—Harvey Firestone, Jr.

"Memory is given us that we may have roses in December." —Arnold Toynbee

"The worst wheel of the cart makes the most noise."—Benjamin Franklin

"A pig bought on credit is forever grunting."—Spanish proverb

"Don't rob tomorrow's memories by today's penny pinching." —John Mason Brown

"Happiness is a place between too little and too much."—Ching Chow

"The moment of truth occurs when a man learns once and for all whether he is the bullfighter or the bull."—Stimson Bullett

"Any critic can establish a wonderful batting average by just rejecting every new idea."—J. D. Williams

"The measure of a man's character is what he would do if he knew he would never be found out."—Thomas Macaulay

"A man seldom makes the same mistake twice. Generally it's three times or more."—Perry Griswold

"How we do admire the wisdom of those who come to us for advice!"—Ramsey Clark

"Few people blame themselves until they have exhausted all other possibilities."—Paul Porter

"Early to bed and early to rise makes a man healthy, wealthy, and hell-bent to talk about it."—Franklin P. Jones

"A good listener is not only popular everywhere, but after a while he knows something."—Wilson Mizner

"Remember this before you burden other people with your troubles. Half of them aren't the least bit interested, and the rest are delighted that you're getting what they think is coming to you."—Vance Packard

"The only thing necessary for the triumph of evil is for good men to do nothing."—Howard Smith

"There's nothing I'm afraid of like scared people."—Robert Frost

"It's sweet to be remembered, but often cheaper to be forgotten."—Kin Hubbard

"Pipe smokers are almost always model citizens. They're so busy cleaning, filling, and relighting their pipes, they just haven't time to get into trouble."—William Vaughan

"The only reason that some people have a secret sorrow is that the rest of us won't listen to them."—James Forrestal

"Some people who cast their bread upon the waters expect it to return to them toasted and buttered."—Hugh Allen

"One thing I like is long walks—especially when they're made by people who annoy me."—Fred Allen

"Thanks to jogging, more people are collapsing in perfect health than ever before."—Jack Leonard

"Show me a man getting a hypodermic injection from a cheerful nurse, and I'll show you a man taking a friendly needling."—Herb Gochros

"Many of us don't know what poor losers we are until we start dieting."—Tom La Mance

"Don't throw away your empty seed packages. Sometimes they're just the right size for storing your crop."—Thomas La Mance

"My young daughter's favorite food is strawberry jam and chocolate syrup on white: white walls and white sofas."—Joan Rivers

"One reason so many kids are spoiled is that their parents don't think it's quite the thing to spank Grandpa and Grandma."—Groucho Marx

"School days are the happiest days of your life—providing, of course, your youngsters are old enough to go."—Paul Selden

"If you've given up on getting a bottle or jar opened—just forbid your four-year-old to touch it."—Victor Borge

"There's only one thing wrong with the younger generation: a lot of us don't belong to it any more."—Bernard Baruch

"I'm all for the young taking over and thank God I won't be here when they do."—Arthur Treacher

"What this country really needs is some colleges that teach everything the students think they already know."—Jack Knowles

"The biggest difference between men and boys is the cost of their toys."—Dr. Joyce Brothers

"An intelligent girl is one who knows how to refuse a kiss without being deprived of it."—Christopher Plimpton

"Kissing a girl is like opening a bottle of olives. If you can get one the rest comes easy."—Bob Hope

"When women kiss, it always reminds me of prize fighters shaking hands."—H. L. Mencken

"The hardest task of a girl's life is to prove to a man that his intentions are serious."—Suzy Knickerbocker

"A bridge table is the only place I've seen where a wife is usually eager to do her husband's bidding."—Charles Goren

"Why is the husband who constantly complains he can't get a word in edgewise always so hoarse?"—Peggy Weidman

"Many a man owes his success to his first wife—and his second wife to his success."—Jim Backus

"Paying alimony is like having the TV set on after you've fallen asleep."—Henny Youngman

From a speech to a conclave of Hollywood reporters and gossip columnists: "If I had as many love affairs as you fellows have given me credit for, I would now be speaking to you from inside a jar at the Harvard Medical School."—Frank Sinatra

Carved over the fireplace in Katharine Hepburn's childhood home: "Listen to the Song of Life."

Critic Walter Kerr, reviewing one particularly horrendous Broadway opening this spring: "This was the sort of play that gives failures a bad name."

When Nijinsky, possibly the most famous male ballet dancer of all time, was asked how he managed leaps a full two feet higher than any rival could achieve, he explained, "I just jump; then at the top, I pause a moment."

Of the late Howard Lindsay, Brooks Atkinson observed, "Although gentlemen are going out of style, Howard chose to ignore it."

"I'm getting so fat that when I wear a white dress these days, they show movies on me."—Phyllis Diller

"The evening my bride cooked her first dinner for me, I choked on a bone in the chocolate pudding."—Woody Allen

"A woman's driving frequently leaves something to be desired—a tow truck, for instance."—Eddie Bracken

"It takes mighty little to capture a man's imagination, especially when the right girl is wearing it."—Ferris Mack

"Behind every successful man stands an absolutely astounded mother-in-law."—Frank De Buono

"Business? It's quite simple. It's other people's money."—Alexandre Dumas the Younger

"Salesman who cover chair instead of territory always on the bottom."—Long Tack Sam

"People who have an hour or so to waste usually inflict themselves on someone who hasn't."—George Atkinson

"Associate with people of cultivated tastes and some of the culture may rub off on you. Hang around musical folk and you may, with luck, get to know Brahms from Beethoven. But keep company with the very rich and you'll end picking up the check."—Stanley Walker

"I know of no sentence that can induce such immediate and brazen lying as the one that begins 'Have you read . . .'"—Wilson Mizner

"I had a minor disaster on the subway this evening. The paper I was reading got off at Eighty Sixth Street."—Arthur Goodman

"A small town is where you can finish your Sunday paper at breakfast."—Bernie Allen

"If you can keep your head when all about you are losing theirs, maybe you haven't heard the news."—Adam Smith

"Politics is the art of looking for trouble, finding it everywhere, diagnosing it incorrectly, and applying the wrong remedies."—H. L. Mencken

"Only one man in a million understands the international situation. Isn't it odd how you keep running into him?"—William Nichols

"International goings-on are becoming so complicated that now our diplomats are being thrown out of countries we never heard of before!"—Tom Baker

"Politicians are like ships: noisiest when lost in a fog."—Emmet Hughes

"We don't declare war any more: we declare national defense."—Eugene McCarthy

"You won't find one leader in the world today who isn't willing to mediate a just peace—for somebody else."—Art Buchwald

"If a man says to you, 'It isn't the money; it's the principle of the thing,' I'll lay you six to one it's the money."—Kin Hubbard

"St. Petersburg is a quiet little town. Down there they consider a speech by Hubert Humphrey an orgy."—Johnny Carson

"The new TV shows this year prove that people would rather look at anything at all than at each other."—E. F. Houghton

"If the average man saves for the next 20 years at the rate he's been saving for the past six months, he'll be able to retire at the age of sixty owing only a hundred thousand dollars." —Jack E. Leonard

"Are our waters polluted? Well, if you fall into Lake Erie today, you don't drown: you decay."—Jerry Goodis

"Enjoy yourself. These are the good old days you're going to sigh over in 1980."—Gen. Alfred Gruenther

2. *Letters*

A retired California couple received this circular from their young married son in Denver:

"VACATION CONTEST. Free round-trip transportation to beautiful mile-high Denver. Free golf and use of all facilities of new million-dollar country club. Unlimited use of slightly battered station wagon, color TV set, pool table, and set of bongo drums. Maid and laundry service included.

"To enter contest, simply complete the following sentence in 25 words or less, 'We would like to come to Denver and take care of four healthy young children for two weeks while our son and daughter-in-law take a richly earned vacation in the Canadian Rockies because . . ."

∴

According to Juliet Lowell, a western Senator received this letter from a constituent last month: "Dear Senator: I have voted for you three times and I think you're terrific. Please send me $900 at once so I can buy an ice box and repaint my car. P.S. The three times I voted for you were in the election of 1966."

∴

Received by a music teacher: "Thank you for your remarks on our young Bertram's piano-playing ability, but in your next report, will appreciate your not giving us your honest opinion."

∴

Received by a Congressman from a voter in his district: "I beg you not to improve my lot any further. I can't afford it."

∴

Received by the parents of a lad whose group had just completed a tour of Yellowstone Park: "The bears here come right up to your car and beg for candy. At night they eat the garbage. For anybody who eats nothing but candy and garbage, they seem awful healthy."

∴

A collection letter that's producing gratifying results has been devised by an ingenious retailer. It's supposedly a two-page missive, but the first page is missing. The top of the second page (the one that actually is sent) reads, "We're sure you don't want us to do that to you, DO YOU?"

∴

A worried-looking citizen came to the FBI to ask if they couldn't do anything about a series of threatening letters he had been receiving.

"Any idea who might be sending them?" asked the FBI agent.

"I have one little clue," said the helpful citizen. "The envelopes are marked Department of Internal Revenue."

∴

A few of those youngsters' letters home from camp to mythical parents:

1. "Dear Mom: Last night a mad hermit killed all the kids. Your late son, Putney."

2. "I got fined for being late to breakfast this morning. I guess I overwashed. Love, Nancy."

3. "Dear Dad: We took a couple of long hikes this week. Please send my other sneaker. Donald."

4. "Dear Folks: What is an epidemic? Love, Tom."

∴

A canny and sophisticated young sophomore is purported to have mailed this letter to her long-suffering parents:

"Dear Folks: I have two pieces of news for you. First, I'm going to have a baby, and have no idea who the father may be. Second, I'm afraid I've flunked both History and Economics this term. Now hold on a moment, Mom and Dad! The first piece of news is a pure fabrication. DOESN'T THAT MAKE YOU FEEL JUST A LITTLE BIT BETTER ABOUT THE SECOND? Love, Debbie."

∴

An impetuous, oft burned, but irrepressible Argentinean playboy now begins all his passionate love letters, "Idol of my dreams and gentlemen of the jury . . ."

∴

A wealthy steel fabricator spent the better part of two years writing an autobiographical tome, but got only a publisher's carefully worded letter of rejection for his pains. However, his efforts were not a total loss.

He wrote to the publisher, "For two years I've been trying to find a humane way to get rid of my drizzle-puss secretary. Your letter of rejection was so tenderly phrased, so eloquent, so heartbreaking that all I had to do was enclose a copy in her last pay envelope. Not only is she vanished from the scene —she thanked me, with tears in her eyes, for firing her."

∴

Letter received by the editor of a rural weekly: "Sir: My wife and I, unbeknownst to each other, bought subscriptions to your paper, so now two issues are delivered to us every week. One is carefully slipped under our welcome mat, the other is thrown by a boy riding a bicycle and lands somewhere on our front porch, where the pages usually blow apart. Kindly cancel our subscription to the one that blows apart."

∴

A well-loved rabbi, if Bill Adler can be believed, received these queries from youthful members of his congregation:

1. Did you always want to be a rabbi, or did you want to be a third baseman like I do?

2. Is it permissible to wear a miniskirt to Yom Kippur services?

3. Please announce at my bar mitzvah services that I would rather not have money as a gift. P.S. My mother made me write this letter.

∴

The outdoor feature editor of a metropolitan newspaper received this letter from a youthful reader: "Can you tell me a good place to fish within about six miles of the address below? I'm 14 years old and have saved up enough money to buy a rod, reel, and line, but don't know where to go fishing. My dad goes almost every weekend, but he and his friends don't want to be bothered with a kid along, so I have to find a place I can get to alone by bus or on my bike."

The editor sent this letter straight to the boy's father, and this is the reply he got:

"You handed me quite a wallop with your letter and did I ever deserve it! When I think of the opportunity I might have lost, I shudder. Allow me to tell you that I now have a new and wonderful fishing companion, and we've got some great plans for the season ahead. I wonder how many other fathers are passing up similar opportunities?"

GOOD HUMOR MEN

"Humor in the thirties," recalled the late Corey Ford, an expert exponent of same, "may have consisted largely of flying custard pies and snowballs aimed at top hats, but unlike most of what passes for humor today, it was happy and wholesome, and there was no malice concealed in a joke like a rock in the snowball. Fun was our only purpose; humor its own excuse."

∴

Ford was one of the founders of *The New Yorker* magazine and, in fact, provided the name Eustace Tilley for the pompous fop who adorns its anniversary cover each year. "Eustace," explained Ford, "was the name of a maiden aunt and I chose 'Tilley' because it was euphonious." (Rea Irvin is the artist who made Eustace Tilley's a face to remember.)

∴

Typical of Corey Ford's reminiscences are those centered in the famous Players club in Lower Manhattan.

Here it was that an obnoxious member told Oliver Herford that a fellow Player had offered him five hundred dollars to resign. "Don't do it, old man," Herford advised him. "Hold out for a better offer." Here, too, an actor named Ransom, a regular in the poker games, assumed an expression so revealing when he picked up a good hand that Franklin P. Adams ordained, "Anyone who looks at Ransom's face is cheating." And, finally, it was at The Players that Don Marquis, after a month of abstinence, ordered a double martini with the proud declaration, "I've conquered my blank blank will power."

∴

Roger Price, obviously privy to some inside information that has eluded other biblical students, claims that all Noah said to an interviewer after six days aboard the Ark was, "PHEW!" And that Samson tried to ward off Delilah with, "I just CAN'T get it cut. Me and three other guys have formed this hot Singing Group. . . ."

∴

One of the great natural wits of our time was the late and sorely missed Fred Allen. A city boy to his fingertips, Allen, though he shunned the haunts of night owls and "cafe society," loved the hustle and bustle of midtown Manhattan, and found the seashore and mountain resorts far too silent and remote for a man of his temperament.

From Montauk, at the far tip of Long Island, he once wrote a friend, "It's so confoundedly quiet here, I was jolted by the sound of a caterpillar backing into a globule of dew."

∴

From a New England seashore resort he complained, "Things are so tough up here that people who have been living on the cuff are moving further up the sleeve for the summer." From a New Jersey farm: "The mosquitoes in these parts are enormous. One stung a Greyhound bus the other night and it swelled up so badly they couldn't get it through the Lincoln Tunnel."

∴

To bird lover John Kieran, Allen noted, "We have none of your bird activities around our 58th Street apartment, but there is one old slate-colored junco who flies around occasionally. This junco is owned by a real estate operator who builds houses rather hurriedly. When one of the slate-colored shingles blows off the junco flies up and covers the hole in the roof until the real estate operator collects the first payment on the house."

∴

Another of Fred Allen's letters, collected faithfully by Joe McCarthy, includes his famous description of a hotel he abhorred: "The rooms are so small that the mice are hunchbacked." He acquired so many books (he read them, too!) that he wrote, "I am just about three books away from having to use the Empire State Building and the Chrysler Building as bookends."

∴

Allen insisted that two estates he bought for his lovely wife Portland were unique. One was so deep in the North Woods that the previous owner was a bear. The other was so far south that the living room was in the Gulf of Mexico.

.:

From the sayings of Kin Hubbard:

—There's only two ways to handle a woman—and nobody knows either of them.

—When some fellers decide to retire, nobody knows the difference.

—There's two songs that could stand some rewritin': "The Star Spangled Banner" and "Happy Birthday to You"—the first one 'cause nobody kin sing it, the second 'cause everybody kin.

.:

Among the friends of Jack E. Leonard:

—A lady who's such a fussy housekeeper she puts a newspaper under the cuckoo clock.

—An East Side kid whose block is so tough a cop edged

up to him last week and whispered, "Wanta buy a radio patrol car?"

—A neighbor whose eight-year-old dispatched this impassioned request to Santa Claus: "Last Christmas you sent me the baby brother I asked for. This Christmas I'd like you to take him back."

∴

A few nuggets from the Peter Pauper Press's *Best Of Offbeat Humor:*

The day after a spectacular bank robbery, the paying teller phoned a man to tell him, "Your pictures are ready."

When a skyscraper's elevator broke down, one passenger raced down twenty-two floors of spiral stairways so fast that he drilled himself into the basement.

A writer has just completed a new novel about drug addiction. In the last chapter, the hero gets the heroin.

It took one songbird six months to warble "Night and Day." He was an Eskimo.

∴

Jerry Vale avers that the morning Mrs. Rip Van Winkle shook her husband and murmured, "Wake up, you lug! You've been asleep now exactly twenty years," old Rip yawned prodigiously, turned over, and pleaded, "Just five minutes more!" Jerry also states that the Street Cleaning Department in his hometown has come up with a foolproof method for getting rid of snow. They call the method "July."

∴

For the perfect start of an outrageously funny take-off, I give you the opening paragraph of Donald Ogden Stewart's *A Parody Outline of History:*

"On a memorable evening in the year 1904 I witnessed the

opening performance of Maude Adams in 'Peter Pan.' I shall never forget the moment when Peter came to the front of the stage and asked the audience if we believed in fairies. The whole house shouted 'Yes! Yes!'—with the exception of the man sitting directly in front of me. I pounded him on the back and shouted, 'Wake up, man! Hurrah for the fairies! Hurrah!' Finally he uttered a rather feeble 'Hurrah.'

"That was my first meeting with that admirable statesman, Woodrow Wilson."

∴

Peter Lind Hayes recalls a day when the great Frisco, stuttering comedian beloved by the entire theatrical profession, was watching a crew of workmen building New York's Eighth Avenue subway tubes. After some minutes of silent observation, Frisco asked one laborer, "How long before this s-s-subway will be f-f-finished?" "I reckon three years," was the answer. "In t-t-that case," decided Frisco, "I'd b-b-better call a taxicab."

∴

A zealous hotel clerk called Frisco in his room late one night to demand, "Have you got a girl up there with you?" "Yes, I d-d-do," admitted Frisco. "Better s-s-send up another G-G-Gideon Bible!"

∴

Frisco's capsule critique of California was, "The scenery's beautiful, all right, but you can't put c-c-catsup on those mountains."

∴

Johnny Carson has many felicitous definitions of what brings contentment to people in his compact best seller *Happiness Is a Dry Martini.* Among other things, asserts Carson, happiness is "being served with a paternity suit on your seventy-fifth birthday; sitting down to watch slides of your neighbor's vacation—and finding out he spent it at a nudist camp; learning your daughter's boyfriend has had his electric guitar repossessed; and seeing the taxi driver who just ignored you in a blinding rainstorm skid kerplunk into a police car."

.:.

Wayne McDonald has a few ideas of his own on what true happiness consists of: recognizing your new secretary from a center spread in a current girlie magazine; your dentist telling you it won't hurt much and then having him catch his finger in the drill; and discovering the giant plant somebody gave your mother-in-law for her bedside is a meat-eater.

.:.

Dave Garroway nominates as corniest jokes of the year (of course, he hasn't seen *The Sound of Laughter* yet):

1. "Say, Dad, why can't a man have more than one wife?"

"When you grow older, my boy, you will learn that laws are written to protect those incapable of protecting themselves."

2. Clergyman: "Haven't seen you in church lately, Mr. Scott."

Mr. Scott: "That's right. My daughter has started taking harp lessons."

Clergyman: "What's that got to do with it?"

Mr. Scott: "Seems I'm not nearly so keen on going to heaven as I once was."

3. "How's your wife getting along with her new reducing diet?"

"Great. She disappeared completely last week."

∴

One of the most trusting souls in America must be humorist P. G. Wodehouse. When he writes a letter, he disdains walking to a postbox to mail it. He just seals it, affixes a stamp, and throws it out of his third-story window, convinced that some good-natured passer-by will pick it up and mail it for him. He insists, furthermore, that not one of his letters has yet gone astray.

∴

A seldom quoted episode concerning the great Will Rogers took place in 1930, when the Coolidge Dam just had been completed in Arizona. Will Rogers was a unanimous choice for master of the dedication ceremonies. It hadn't rained in those parts for a month of Sundays and as Rogers gazed over the sea of grass and weeds where San Carlos Reservoir was supposed to be filling up, he chuckled, "If that was my lake, I'd mow it!"

∴

REMEMBERED LINES:

In a Ring Lardner story, a young boy asked his father a simple question. Father's response, as reported by Lardner: " 'Shut up,' he explained."

In a Mark Twain tale about his uncle who toiled in a carpet factory: "One day the machinery made a snatch at him. Poor fella. He got wove up."

In Evelyn Waugh's *Decline and Fall:* " 'Meet my daughter,' said the Bishop with some disgust."

The beauteous Juliet embracing a suitor on her balcony, the while admonishing him, "We'll have to figure out some other way of meeting, darling. With daylight-saving time starting Sunday, Romeo will be getting home an hour earlier."

In a convention of witches: "I know I'm an hour late, girls, but Salem was socked in, so I had to land my broom in Pawtucket."

In a supermarket bargain bulletin: "All this talk about soaring prices of meat and vegetables is pure propaganda, circulated by people who EAT."

In Col. Francis Duffy's Corncrib: "It's nice to see folks with lots of get-up-and-go—especially if they're relatives visiting you."

A puzzled wife telling her mother by long distance, "I haven't the faintest idea what he's talking about, Ma, but my husband Robert says I should ask you how things are in Loch Ness."

Bobby Dean, to cop writing out a ticket for jaywalking in Beverly Hills: "Tell me, officer, how fast was I going?"

In a priceless old movie: W. C. Fields to his shrewish wife, Alison Skipwirth: "And what countries have you been ravaging THIS summer, my sweet?"

At a Harvard class reunion: Robert Benchley's "Except for an occasional heart attack, fellows, I feel as young as I ever did."

Bill Forman reports that a Scarsdale lad answered an anatomy quiz at school with "Your legs is what if you haven't got two pretty good ones you'll never get to first base and neither will your sister." Forman also has a friend who gave up cigarettes and started chewing toothpicks. He now has Dutch elm disease.

∴

Steve Allen, sick and tired of being asked if he wears a toupee, assured one nosey housewife, "The hair is absolutely real, ma'am; it's the head that's a fake." Another humorist, Don Herold, made not the slightest effort to camouflage his shiny pate. "There's one thing about baldness," he asserted.

"It's NEAT!" Sam Hoffenstein summed up the situation as follows:

"Babies haven't any hair;
Old men's heads are just as bare.
Between the cradle and the grave
Lies a haircut and a shave."

∴

Mark Twain once was asked by a lady admirer if he believed in luck. "Certainly," he replied. "How else can you explain the success of those you detest?"

∴

Charlie Lederer, accustomed to zany antics by his literary pals, was taken aback, nevertheless, when he received this official announcement in the mail recently: "The National Park Commissioner is pleased to announce that your back yard has been selected for a game preserve. The first shipment of 500 buffalo and 200 yaks will arrive at your home Tuesday at 4:30 A.M."

∴

There is nothing in this world better calculated to put you in excellent humor than an obviously sincere and felicitously phrased compliment from someone you respect.

Here are three I deem worth treasuring:

1. Carl Van Doren, describing the brilliant, deeply loved playwright Moss Hart: "There's something about Moss that makes all the people in a room with him seem a little nicer than they really are."

2. Harry Hopkins, summarizing his friend Robert Sherwood: "Everybody who meets up with Bob leaves him feeling happier and more confident than before he happened along."

3. A college senior, different than the kind getting all the

publicity these days, describing his father: "He doesn't tell me what I should be doing and thinking all the time—but he wants to know what I'm up to and why. He's as interested in my point of view as he is in telling me his. He doesn't need words to make me know he loves me. I think he's wonderful."

∴

And to prove that our leading literary lights are not above punning a bit now and then, it was Clifton Fadiman who reminded us of the gent who was crossing England's river Mersey, and noting its muddy condition, remarked, "The quality of Mersey is not strained." Ogden Nash brought up the case of a hater of spring who refused to bring charge against an intruder who shot him with an autumnatic. And Nunnally Johnson pleads guilty to the story of the amorous male punster who whispered in the ear of a belle of the ball, "How's for coming over to my place for a whiskey and sofa?" To which she, no mean punster herself, whispered back, "Nix on a whiskey and sofa. But you COULD talk me into a gin and platonic."

THE GENERATION GAP

1. *Very Little Girls*

A young mother in Easthampton served her small daughter two fried chicken wings for lunch. "Can't I have something else?" pleaded the daughter. "These are nothing but hinges!"

∴

A harassed mother finally got her three obstreperous children tucked into bed and, with a sigh of relief, changed into a rumpled housecoat and started to shampoo her hair. Just as the suds were beginning to sink in, all hell broke loose in the kids' quarters, and she hurried in to quell the incipient riot. Peace was restored, but as she turned back to the bathroom she heard her three-year-old ask her five-year-old sister fearfully, "Who was that?"

∴

Mr. Pulsifer Henpeck was deeply shaken when his first-born turned out to be a girl. "Why are you taking it so to heart?" he was asked. "Confound it," grumbled Mr. Henpeck, "I was hoping for a boy to help me with the housework!"

∴

A bright eight-year-old girl was being questioned by an inquisitive aunt, "What are you going to give your little brother David for Christmas this year?" "I haven't decided yet," said the girl. "Well," persisted the aunt, "what did you give him last Christmas?"

The little girl answered, "The whooping cough."

∴

"That lump on my twin brother's head," explained a little girl to her teacher, "is where Daddy helped him last night with his arithmetic lesson."

∴

"How come," the hostess of a kid's birthday party asked a little girl in attendance, "that your younger brother is so shy? He hasn't moved from that corner all afternoon."

"He isn't shy at all," answered the little girl. "He's never had on a necktie before—and he thinks he's tied to something."

∴

The budding daughter of a traveling salesman was taught to close her evening prayer, when Papa was on the road, with, "And please watch over my daddy." It sounded just fine to her mother—until one night she heard the little girl add, "And you'd better keep an eye on Mama, too."

∴

Aboard a coast-bound plane that made several intermediate stops, a little girl asked her mother, "What was the name of the city before last that we landed in?" The mother, engrossed in a paperback, grumbled, "How do I know? And why do you suddenly want to know, anyhow?" "Well, for one thing," observed the little girl, "Papa got off there."

∴

Ben Whitehill tells about a little girl who became lost in a New Jersey discount emporium while her mother was hunting for bargains. The manager asked her testily, "Why didn't you hold on to your mother's skirt?" Explained the little girl, "I couldn't REACH it."

∴

The *Catholic Digest* reports that a mother hoisted a young daughter to her lap and said, "You told me a half-hour ago that your earache was better, darling. Why are you still crying?" "I'm waiting for Daddy to come home," explained the little girl. "He's never seen me with an earache."

∴

Note found in a Wisconsin household, penciled by a nine-year-old girl after an argument: "Goodbye, family. You all hate me. I love you anyhow. Bless you! P.S. In case of fire, I'm in the attic."

∴

A proud father, unaware of the sophistication of the youngsters of today, set out to acquaint his small daughter with the value of money. First, he explained the variety of coins, then he lined up a penny, a nickel, a dime, a quarter, and a dollar bill, and asked her which one she'd choose for herself. She eyed him speculatively for a moment, then said, "I'll take the copper one, Daddy—but I think I'll take the little piece of paper along to wrap it in."

∴

Little Claudia, in the first grade, coyly admitted to her parents that she had been kissed in school that day by one Jonathan Buffum. "Is Jonathan in your class?" asked her father, concealing a grin. "No, he's an older man," confided Claudia. "He's in the second grade."

∴

A neighbor of Mary Healy has a darling little seven-year-old daughter whose father likes to question about her days in school. One evening the tot reported proudly, "This morning we started learning math-e-mat-ics. Did you study math-e-mat-ics when YOU went to school, Daddy?" "I certainly did, my dear," he beamed. "How did you like it?" "It was yummy," she told him. "Isn't Page Five GOOD?"

∴

Senator Javits likes to tell about a neighbor's little girl who really believes in the power of prayer. When her brother built a trap to catch sparrows, she prayed hard that he wouldn't catch any. Nor did he.

Some mornings later her mother asked, "What made you so

sure your prayer would be answered?" "Well, for one thing, Mother," replied the devout youngster, "I went back there three days ago and kicked the trap to pieces."

∴

Wistful gents of forty-five and over who long for a blue-eyed, blond, adorable little granddaughter to dandle on their knees, might stop dreaming long enough to listen to Harriet Van Horne's story of the acquisitive little four-year-old who sat on grandpa's lap and played with his gold watch chain. "When I die," cooed loving gramp, "this gold chain will go to you." "It's pretty," nodded the little darling. "When are you going to die?"

∴

In a rather tough neighborhood, a thirteen-year-old girl named Vivian had always shown up the boys in such demanding games as touch football, wrestling, hockey—and playing tricks on the cops. Therefore, when one of the boys complained recently to his mother that they needed a catcher for their baseball team, she asked immediately, "What's the matter with

Vivian? She's never let you down, has she?" "Aw," was his disgusted reply, "Vivian's turning into a girl!"

2. *Very Little Boys*

It is possible that a Mrs. Hugo Flugelheimer, of Cincinnati, has the most gigantic inferiority complex in the world. A few days after her first son was born, she fondled him affectionately and remarked to her spouse, "Just think, Hugo! Some day this son of ours may grow up to be the Vice-president of our country!"

∴

Alan Littman copied this note pinned to the canopy of a baby carriage parked outside a London supermarket: "WARNING: Do not bend over to pet or coo over this child. Although born in wedlock he is a little bastard. [Signed] His Mother."

∴

A five-year-old boy came home from his first day at kindergarten. "How big is your class?" his mother asked him. With considerable disgust, the manly lad replied, "Four other fellows, and about a half a million girls."

∴

Fatigued by a hard day at the office, a father found the racket being made by his two young sons too much for his jangled nerves, and sent them upstairs to their room after a severe scolding.

The next morning he found this note pinned to his bedroom door: "Be good to your children and they will be good to you. Yours truly, God."

∴

A little boy worrying through his very first day at school, raised his hand for permission to go to the washroom, then returned to the class a few moments later to report that he couldn't find it. Dispatched a second time with explicit directions, he still couldn't find it. So this time the teacher asked a slightly older boy to act as guide. Success crowned his efforts. "We finally found it," he told the teacher. "He had his pants on backwards."

∴

A kindly old lady stopped a toddler at Miami Beach and asked, "What's your name?" The toddler answered, "Morris." "Morris what?" persisted the old lady. "What's your last name?" "My last name?" pondered the toddler momentarily, then said brightly, "Oh, I know. Morris Stop That Immediately."

∴

A wily young mother in Enid, Oklahoma, has devised a foolproof method for keeping her two sons out of the cookie jar. She locks the pantry door and hides the key under the cake of soap in the bathroom.

∴

At Disneyland one July afternoon, a mother and her nine-year-old son ran into the boy's teacher at the monorail depot. The mother and the teacher exchanged cordial greetings, but the boy cut her dead. "What a dreadful way to behave," the mother reprimanded him when the teacher was out of earshot. "Why don't you speak to your teacher when you meet her like this?" "What?" protested the boy. "In the SUMMER VACATION?"

∴

A ten-year-old boy protested vigorously when his mother sought to persuade him to let his kid sister accompany him on a fishing expedition. "The last time I let her tag along I didn't catch a single fish," he pointed out. "This time," promised his mother, "she won't say a single word the whole afternoon." "It wasn't the noise, Mom," asserted her son. "She ate all the bait."

∴

Little Sebastian, the nastiest brat in the neighborhood, came home from his very first day in school. "I hope you didn't cry," said his overindulgent mother. "Of course I didn't cry," scoffed Little Sebastian, "but, oh boy, the teacher did!"

∴

"How is that difficult kid of yours doing at that new school you put him in?" asked one commuter of another. "Let me put it this way," was the answer. "I'm still going to the PTA meetings under an assumed name."

∴

When top comic Sam Levenson was a schoolteacher in Brooklyn, he once asked a fifth-grader, "Why did you hit Gregory?" The kid answered, "Because he hit me back first."

∴

Grandma put two apples on the table when Stanley and his little sister came calling. One apple was large and bright red, the other withered and wormy. "Now, my loves," said Grandma,

"I want to see which of you has the better manners." "She does," said Stanley—grabbing the bigger apple.

∴

Old Lady Abernathy hadn't seen her young grandson since his christening and when she heard he was being sent up to her country place to spend his ninth birthday with her, she was so delighted she put five dollars in the collection plate that Sunday at church.

The Sunday after her grandson went back home she put in ten dollars.

∴

Jerome Beatty tells about the principal of an elementary public school in a tough neighborhood who, although used to just about everything by this time, was reasonably startled when his phone rang, and a squeaky, obviously disguised voice announced, "Hello, Mr. Principal, this is my father talking. Elmer won't be able to come to school today."

∴

For weeks, a six-year-old lad kept telling his first-grade teacher about the baby brother or sister that was expected at his house. Then, one day, the mother allowed the boy to feel the movements of the unborn child. The six-year-old was obviously impressed, but made no comment. Furthermore, he stopped telling his teacher about the impending event.

The teacher finally sat the boy on her lap and said, "Tommy, whatever has become of that baby brother or sister you were expecting at home?" Tommy burst into tears and confessed, "I think Mommie ate it!"

∴

At a swinging Easthampton weekend, the ten-year-old son of the house kept getting underfoot and inhibiting his elders. His father finally barked, "Why don't you go down to the beach and play with that surfboard you found yesterday?" "I can't," explained the sterling lad. "I might run into the boy I found it from."

∴

An "A" for imagination goes to the Columbus, Ohio, kid who was caught digging a big hole in his mother's prize garden. "What are you doing there?" cried the horrified mother. The kid answered, "I'm letting some of the dark out of the ground!"

∴

A lad, obviously winded, rushed into a drugstore crying, "Quick! My old man is hanging upside down by his pants leg in a barbed wire fence." "What do you want, boy?" demanded the druggist. "Help—or first-aid supplies?" "Nothing like that," said the boy angrily. "I want another roll of film for my camera!"

∴

Tommy Noonan picked up a nice piece of change mowing lawns for neighbors after school let out. One afternoon his mother noticed he was taking his own good time getting started. Asked for an explanation, he pointed out, "I'm waiting for them to start themselves. I get most of my work from people who are halfway through."

∴

A city kid, visiting a farm for the first time, reached out to give a lamb a tentative pat. "Hey, Pop," he called out delightedly, "they make them out of blankets!"

∴

From the examination paper of a nine-year-old Chicago hopeful named Larry Wolters: "Nathan Haley said, 'I only regret that I have but one life to give for my country.' This has come to be known as Haley's comment."

∴

Mama Buttenheimer was reciting nursery rhymes to her young son, and came to "The Queen of Hearts, she made some tarts." The young son interrupted to ask, "And what was the King of Hearts doing?" "Basing my conjecture on the behavior pattern of your father," answered Mrs. Buttenheimer grimly, "I'd say he was doing precisely the same thing."

⁛

Letter received by an elementary school teacher in the Bronx: "Please never hit our Sylvester again. He's a delicate, sensitive boy and is not used to corporal punishment. We NEVER hit him at home except in self-defense."

⁛

There's a student at a very exclusive and expensive private prep school in the Murray Hill sector of New York who's obviously very angry at one of his teachers. Outside the door of the teacher's classroom he pinned a sign the other morning that reads, "Dr. Jekyll is not himself today."

⁛

If you care to believe Jean Bach, a lad in the Yorktown Heights elementary school was asked to use the word "Rotterdam" in a sentence. His answer: "This morning my kid sister swiped my candy bar, and I hope it'll Rotterdam teeth out."

⁛

Six-year-old Heathcote watched tearfully while his father changed from a business suit to his tuxedo. Finally he burst out, "Daddy, PLEASE don't wear that suit. It always gives you such a headache the next morning!"

⁛

I like Betty Le Gere's story about her little boy who was passionately attached to his toy soldiers and Indians, and played with them endlessly until his eleventh birthday. Then he swept them all into a big box and carried them up to the attic. "Why don't you like to play with them any more?" inquired Mrs. Le Gere. The boy explained soberly, "They don't talk back to me any more."

∴

Note left by a ten-year-old and found by his mother: "I have a terrible headache and stomach ache so I've taken two aspirins and a glass of milk and have gone to the park to play football."

∴

There's a kid in the fifth grade at a St. Petersburg, Florida, school who has taken to writing compositions the way a duck takes to water. His teachers expect him to be another Jerry Weidman. He's always waiting to see the comments written atop his pieces, too, when they come back to him.

One afternoon he came home from school to find a note from his mother reading, "I must attend a meeting over in Tampa this afternoon which may last for hours. Instead of our eating home this evening, therefore, I'll take you out for dinner and possibly a movie if we can find a good one. So be sure to put on a clean shirt and comb your hair properly. Love, Mother."

Across the top of the note the kid wrote, "Excellent—but your handwriting could stand improvement."

∴

At a Little League ball game in Chappaqua, the catcher of one team asked for time out to clean his mask. "What happened?" asked the ump. The catcher explained, "My bubble gum exploded."

∴

Young Eustace, Jr., had participated in his first Little League baseball game that afternoon, and lost no time in making a report when Eustace, Sr., got home from the office. "I was the star of the game, and hit two home runs," boasted Eustace, Jr.—no blushing violet he. "Great," approved Eustace, Sr., "and did you win?" "No," admitted Eustace, Jr., suddenly deflated. "We lost, eleven to nothing."

∴

Nobody could convince little Stanley's slightly discombobulated great-aunt Flora that she didn't possess extraordinary supernatural powers. Certainly little Stanley believed her when she told him, "Keep a close eye on your father tomorrow, my boy: I feel it in my bones that he's going to pass away before nightfall." Little Stanley never let his dad out of his sight the next day. He went to the office with him in the morning and out to see the Mets perform their daily miracles in the afternoon. Not one thing out of the ordinary happened all day. When little Stanley and his father returned home at 6 P.M., however, they found Stanley's mother in a highly emotional state. "A frightful thing happened here this morning," she sobbed. "The iceman dropped dead in the kitchen."

∴

Two very small boys were playing marbles together when a very, VERY pretty little girl walked by. One of the boys exclaimed fervently, to his pal, "Brother, when I stop hating girls, she's the one I'm going to stop hating first!"

3. *Taking Care of Same*

At a Georgetown home, a visiting couple writhed with boredom while the overvivacious hostess raved on and on about her two-month-old baby. Finally, however, she gave her guests an unexpected break. She rose abruptly and rushed upstairs to change the subject.

∴

A well-upholstered housewife at a family reunion declined a before-dinner drink from her gracious hostess. "I don't believe in drinking when the children are around," she explained. "And when they're not around—who needs it?"

∴

Advice to mothers from Dan Greenburg: "Unless you deliberately set aside a little time for regular relaxation, you will not be able to efficiently care for your family. Therefore, plan to relax a minimum of an hour and a half every fifteen years."

∴

The mother of a family of twelve in Santa Clara dresses all the kids alike. "When we had only four," she explains, "I dressed them alike so we wouldn't lose any. Now that we have twelve, I dress them alike so we won't pick up any that don't belong to us."

∴

A sociologist, embarked on a book exposing the troubles resulting from overlarge families, interviewed one mother of fourteen. In the course of the interview he asked, "Do you think all children rate the full, impartial love and attention of a mother, or do you, for instance, catch yourself loving one of them more than the others?" "There's always one I love best," admitted the mother. "Which one?" asked the sociologist. The mother answered, "The one who's sick—until he gets well; or the one who's away—until he gets home."

∴

Mr. and Mrs. Collins had had six children—all boys. When number seven arrived, the youngest of the six burst excitedly into the dining room of the family next-door and cried, "Come over and see our new baby! He's a GIRL!"

∴

A woebegone lady clad in a suit jacket and sheer slip pushed ahead of the line at a department store's lost-and-found window and inquired anxiously, "Has anybody turned in a black skirt with four children from two to five hanging on to it?"

∴

Mothers in overcrowded cities who cart their young off to the country so they can breathe a little fresh air run risks in other directions. Two Manhattan-bred youngsters, for example, were playing in the garden of a rented Connecticut manse when their horrified mother overheard one of them warning the other, "Better not eat that one, Timmy. It has wings on it!"

∴

With high-rise condominiums popping up all over the country nowadays, you can believe the story of one city youngster challenging his mother, "I'll bet you don't know what happened in fourteen ninety-two," with Mom answering patiently, "How can I? We live in the penthouse!"

∴

A young grade school teacher had just handed out report cards and awards to a class of obstreperous brats, and sent them off to their summer vacations. Now she leaned back in her chair and sighed, "I guess teaching school is pretty much like having a baby. Each takes nine months, and the last week is the worst!"

∴

A substitute teacher in a downtown public school surveyed her class the first morning she was assigned a job and sent a hurry call for the principal. "HELP!" she demanded. "They're all here!"

∴

From exam papers by the special kind of students who gravitate to the studio of Art Linkletter:

1. There's a big difference between *M* and *N*. Take the word "Acme." With three loops you're at the top, but with two loops you only have pimples.

2. Some wine is made by stomping on grapes. This kind of wine is called squash.

3. A prune is a plum that didn't take care of itself.

4. Obstetriks is a disease my ma catches every year.

5. The Indians never smiled at White Men, but they had plenty of fun in their teehees.

6. Bison roamed the great plains for years under the name of Buffalo. Despite this trick they were practically extincted.

7. The War of 1812 was fought between American and England in 1776.

8. French policemen often disguise themselves as gendarmes.

9. Trousers is an uncommon noun because it is singular on top and plural on the bottom.

10. Napoleon wanted children, but since Josephine was a baroness, she couldn't bare any.

∴

Kids no longer chalk up the old four-letter obscenities on walls and subway posters. That's considered very, very old hat these days—and disgustingly unsophisticated. Instead, you can find startling inscriptions like the following:

1. Oswald cannot relate to his environment.

2. Judge Crater, please phone your office.

3. Snow White is a junkie.

4. Millard Fillmore was a Commie fink.

5. Leda loves swans.

The handwriting, summarizes Warren Boroson, is obviously on the wall.

∴

The kids at a prep school in West Palm Beach have a sense of humor. A new teacher, determined to impress the boys with the fact that he meant business, wound up his first session by reminding them, "It's going to take more than just the proverbial apple a day to get by in THIS class." So the next morning they brought him a watermelon.

∴

A famous child specialist addressed a women's club recently in Indianapolis. During the question period that followed the lecture, one lady asked, "Doctor, what do you find is the principal ailment of children today?" The specialist answered promptly, "Mothers."

∴

A typical example of the new breed of self-reliant, completely independent young men of the new generation—aged fifteen—told his father in ringing tones, "Pop, it's time that I stood on my own two feet and made my own way—but I'm never going to be able to do it on my present allowance."

∴

Mrs. Rome complained to the school principal that her thirteen-year-old son seemed to be spending most of his time staring at the girls in their summer miniskirts. "Don't worry," were the principal's reassuring words. "He's just going through a stage that won't last more than the rest of his life."

4. *In Which the No-Longer-so-Little Boys and Girls Discover One Another*

An ardent young Lothario in Westminster, Maryland, sent his best girl a five-pound box of candy for her birthday with this note enclosed: "To Irma, with all my allowance."

∴

An exasperated mother finally found the way to keep her teenage daughter from hogging the telephone and messing up the house. She threatened her, "Get on the ball, my girl—or I'll let down all your hems!"

∴

The teacher of a high-school class in the fundamentals of economics led the discussion around to the population explosion. "Certain levels of our society reproduce much more frequently than others," he pointed out. "What people would you guess reproduce the most?" One bright student answered, "Women."

∴

The natural instincts of an attractive female manifest themselves at an extremely early age. Take the case of three-year-old Gloria, whose aunt arrived for a weekend bearing two big gift boxes for her niece and nephew. "Gloria," said the aunt, "you'll notice one of these boxes is red and one is blue. One is for you and one is for your brother Pulsifer. Since you're a girl, you can have first pick. Which do you choose?"

Without the slightest hesitation, three-year-old Gloria announced, "I'll take Pulsifer's."

∴

A chuckle-provoking cartoon in the *Saturday Review* recently pictured Jack forcing a reluctant Jill into his arms by the side of a well on top of a hill, expostulating, "You didn't think I'd climb all the way up here just for a lousy pail of water, did you?"

.˙.

About to be escorted to her first formal dance, a darling teenager, in a dither of excitement, whirled in to show her mother and father how she looked in her brand-new dress. "It must be all right," she reported later to her best friend. "Neither of them can stand it."

.˙.

A Radcliffe junior came home from a blind date and confessed to her roommate, "I had to slap him six times." "Was he fresh?" chuckled the roommate. "Not at all," corrected the junior. "I thought he was dead."

.˙.

A gay young blade hoisted his date into one of those rickety carriages that park opposite New York's Plaza Hotel one starry night and ordered the hackie, "Drive us to Staten Island." "Nothing doing," demurred the hackie. "That means a long ferry ride over and back—and my horse gets seasick."

.˙.

The sentimental Henny Youngman recalls the evening he first met his future bride. "Right away," he sighs, "I felt a lump in my throat. She's a karate expert."

.˙.

"Whaddya mean, I'm paying too much attention to the cigarette girl?" grumbled a Princeton senior to his date at a swanky night club. His date was about to apologize when the scantily clad cigarette girl paused at their table. The Princeton senior, a bit upset, airily ordered "a pair of cigarettes."

∴

An enterprising lad and his date were progressing swimmingly in the living room, but the date's father wasn't too happy at the head of the stairway above. "It's past midnight," he growled to his wife, "and I'm going down and throw that fresh twerp out." "Oh, Milton," she begged. "Don't be so harsh. Don't you remember how we used to act?"

"I certainly do," nodded the father. "That's why I'm going to throw him out."

∴

Undergraduates at a southwestern college claim that one member of the current sophomore class is unquestionably the world's greatest Romeo. As proof they exhibit his little black book—alphabetically arranged. The fifty-third entry is Alice Aaronson.

∴

A few of the lads were downing some liquid cheer at Casey's pub when a fire engine and hook and ladder pulled out of the firehouse across the way, and went dashing off with sirens sounding. "Time for me to go," exclaimed one of the lads, making for the exit on the double. "What's the hurry?" jeered a pal. "You're not a fireman, are you?" "Not me," called back the departing one happily, "but my girl friend's husband is."

∴

Once upon a time there was a chaste, unkissed young lady whose boyfriend finally rebelled. "Just one kiss here in the moonlight," he begged at the end of her senior prom. "I can't here," she demurred. "Somebody would be sure to see us."

"Then let me come to your room for a moment," he pleaded. "Oh, I couldn't," she parried. "My roommate would resent that."

"Do you really contend," asked the boy angrily, "that your roommate would take umbrage if I had just one sweet kiss from those innocent, ruby lips?"

"I sure do," she assured him. "He's terribly jealous."

∴

The father of an eighteen-year-old co-ed phoned her at her dormitory one night at about ten to remind her that the next day was her mother's birthday, and was shocked, to put it mildly, when a male voice answered the call. "Don't be so upset," counseled the male voice. "We've been meaning to tell you. Your daughter and I are engaged."

"In what?" roared the father.

∴

Riding to work aboard a crowded bus one morning, a young bank clerk came suddenly to life when a beautiful young lady, clad in a tight and revealing costume, came aboard. Just after she had deposited her fare, she lost her balance, and lurching for a strap, gave our banker an unintentional but reasonably painful whack across the forehead.

Obviously embarrassed, she started to apologize, but the banker cut her short with, "Don't concern yourself, my dear. For what I was just thinking, I deserved it."

The two left the bus together, and disappeared down a side street arm in arm.

∴

This really is a sad, sad little tale. A young cavalier was told repeatedly that the best way to meet pretty girls in New York was to buy a dog—a big, shaggy one if possible—and walk him in the park. Available damsels, he was informed, seldom failed to stop to pet the dog and ask his name—and the cavalier could take it from there.

So he bought a Great Dane pup, led it to Central Park, and turned it loose to gambol on the green. Sure enough, a beautiful girl arose from a bench, made a beeline for him, and murmured, "Is that your dog?" The cavalier gave her a warm smile and boomed, "It sure is." "Then here's a summons for letting him run loose in the park," said the girl—a lady cop with a heart of stone.

∴

Randall was obviously not himself when he reported late for work one morning. "Brother," sympathized a co-worker, "you must have had a pretty wild time last night." "Honestly," explained Randall, "I didn't touch a drop. But there was this gorgeous blonde beating on my door clear through till dawn." "Why didn't you get up and see what she wanted?" asked the co-worker. "What would have been the point of that?" demanded Randall wearily. "I know what she wanted, all right. She wanted to get out!"

∴

A starlet with a superb sense of double-entry bookkeeping finagled a date with the most eligible bachelor in town. She returned from the date with spirits high and reported to her roommate, "We're off to a promising start. I had to say 'no' to him from the minute we climbed into his car. He kept asking, 'Do you mind if I do this?' and 'Do you mind if I do that?'"

∴

A snappy young man visited a jewelry shop in Seattle in search of an engagement ring. "What sort of setting do you have in mind?" asked the jeweler. The young man looked startled for a moment, then said, "Well, probably her living-room couch."

∴

After going the bachelor route for many long years, a successful manufacturer of men's hats met a girl who struck his fancy, wooed her, and won her. The day after the engagement was announced, the hat maker danced delightedly about his office and cried to his partner, "Max, I've never been so happy! I'm on Cloud Seven and an Eighth."

∴

A wealthy old codger eyed an aspirant for his daughter's hand with ill-concealed suspicion. "In the unlikely event that I consent," he harumphed, "I take it you'll be expecting a handsome dowry. May I inquire what you propose to offer in exchange?" The aspirant answered hopefully, "How about a receipt?"

∴

A seductive young siren from a night club chorus line suddenly added to her equipment a very big, very authentic, very expensive diamond ring. "It IS a beauty," she agreed with admiring cohorts, "but I'm afraid it carries the Slibovitz curse." "That's one curse I never heard of," admitted the wardrobe mistress. "What is it?" The siren eyed her ring sorrowfully and explained, "Slibovitz comes with it."

∴

Complained a frustrated, lovely would-be bride of twenty: "I'm afraid my boyfriend has an aggravated case of cold feet." "Goodness," exclaimed her grandmother. "In my day we didn't learn that until after we were married!"

∴

Maintained a confirmed bachelor, "You won't catch me getting hitched until I discover a girl just like the girl who married dear old Granddad." "Forget it," chided a friend. "They don't make girls like that any more." "The heck you say," chuckled the bachelor. "Granddad married this one a week ago Tuesday."

∴

Guggenheim was a sight to behold when he staggered into his office two hours late: a black eye, three front teeth missing, his left arm in a sling. It was all because, he explained, he had kissed a beautiful bride after the ceremony. "That groom must be a monster," sympathized a pal. "Doesn't he know that's an accepted practice?" "I can't imagine what got into him," sighed Guggenheim, "unless because it was six years after the ceremony."

5. *College Days*

Home from graduate school with his roommate for a weekend vacation, a student informed his parents that he never had slaved so continuously in his life. "I bet it's rugged," sympathized the father. "How large are those graduate classes of yours?" "They're limited," was the reply, "to six fellows and three or four non-fellows." "Before you start feeling too sorry for your overworked son," volunteered the roommate, "let me explain that ordinary people call those non-fellows 'girls.'"

∴

When an irate father demanded to know why a professor had flunked his son, the professor replied, "In his final examination for my course, your son answered correctly eleven questions out of a hundred. You may be interested to know that on the same test, a baboon answered twenty-four."

∴

Debonair Rutgers Professor Ira Freeman has organized a group of convivials who love the classics but abhor the mere thought of any form of physical exercise. Needless to add, they call themselves the Adipose Wrecks.

∴

Up at Dartmouth, an English professor suddenly surprised a confrere writing on a washroom wall. "Elmer!" gasped the prof. "Don't tell me you're the kind of fellow who writes on washroom walls!" "Stuff and nonsense," huffed the confrere. "I'm merely correcting the grammar."

∴

The University of Oregon chess club was having some difficulty recruiting new members, until its ingenious president inserted this classified ad in the campus daily: "DO YOU KNOW HOW TO MATE? If not, come to Room 15 in the

Student Union this Thursday at 6:00 P.M. and learn the basic positions."

The response was electrifying.

∴

George Jessel tells about his recent lecture at a college in the deep South, and the reception accorded him at its conclusion. Commented the outspoken George, "The student body here seems to consist exclusively of fallen women and football players." "I heard that," cried out the dean from the other side of the punch bowl, "and I'll have you know that my wife attends this college." "What do you know?" responded Jessel hastily. "What position does she play?"

∴

"I understand, Mr. Cole," remarked an associate at a staff luncheon, "that you have a son at Princeton. Is he going to become a doctor, or a lawyer, or a publisher like you, perhaps?" "I don't really know," admitted Mr. Cole quizzically. "Right now the question before the house is: Is he going to become a sophomore?"

∴

In a college history class a notoriously dilatory student was asked to name the date on which the Thirty Years' War ended. After a considerable pause, the student declared, "Sixteen forty-eight." "Correct," rasped the professor, "but unless my ears deceive me, I distinctly heard that date whispered to you from the rear of the room." "Your ears didn't deceive you, Professor," the student told him solemnly. "This was just one more instance of history repeating itself."

∴

A hygiene instructor at an upstate college for girls had sneaked so many off-color stories into his lectures, that the girls decided to walk out of the classroom en masse the next time he began one. The instructor got wind of their plan, so the very next morning he began his talk with, "I understand that there is suddenly a shortage of ladies of easy virtue in Paris. . . ." The girls jumped to their feet, and headed angrily for the exit. "Ladies, ladies," the instructor called after them cheerfully. "There's no rush necessary. The next plane doesn't leave until tomorrow morning."

∴

World chaos is proving a boom to at least one group: history professors. Every six months they can bring out a revised edition of their textbook and flunk any student who doesn't buy a copy.

∴

When the late, famed poet Robert Frost was lecturing one summer at the Breadloaf School he passed out sheets of paper just before he left on which he asked, "What good did these talks do you?" Most students rhapsodized, but one maverick admitted, "Not one dam bit." Frost's reaction was, "That boy is honest, at any rate. I'd mark his paper ninety per cent." "Why not a hundred while you're at it?" chuckled a confrere. Frost explained, "He left the N off damn."

∴

Incidentally, it was of Robert Frost that James Reston reported, "Every time he visits the capital, the Washington Monument stands up a little straighter."

∴

At a girls' college in Indiana some years ago, dates were permitted only on Friday and Saturday nights, but one brash young suitor, sorely smitten by Miss Susan Swanson, popped up on Tuesday, saying it was imperative that he see Miss Swanson immediately. "You must know our rules," the dean reprimanded him. "What's this great emergency?" "I can't even tell you," said the suitor. "You see, I want to surprise her. I'm her brother."

"She'll be surprised, I reckon," said the dean. "But how do you think I feel? I'm her mother!"

∴

Because of hopeless overcrowding, the dean of a southwestern college found it necessary temporarily to house both male and female students in the same dormitory, the while strictly forbidding any male to step over an imaginary line to the female section. Student Penrose was the first offender apprehended. "Mr. Penrose," the dean intoned sternly, "this first offense will cost you one dollar, the next, two dollars, and so on until the fine reaches ten dollars." Mr. Penrose, unabashed, demanded, "What would you charge me for a season ticket?"

∴

"There's one great thing to be said for a college education." muses Joan Welsh. "It enables you to worry about things all over the world."

∴

A history professor at a university in Philadelphia is so meticulously fair that before marking an examination essay, he always turns back the outside blue cover so he cannot know the student's name, and possibly be unconsciously influenced in some way. His wife, however, taking his course, knows his habits backwards and forwards. She signs every examination at the bottom of the last page, "I love you. Sue."

∴

During the registration period at the opening of the summer semester in a top California university this year, the expected rush of pretty, miniskirted seventeen-year-olds took place under the sign reading "All Freshman women sign in here." One young man stood at the end of the table handing the girls as they were leaving Xeroxed forms asking for their names, addresses, phone numbers, and favorite recreations. At the end of the day, he gathered in his stack of completed forms and proceeded back to his faternity house, where he received the hero's welcome he had earned.

∴

A local businessman spent the better part of a Spring morning calling all of his friends in the hope that one of them could find some kind of summer job for his rock-'n'-rolling freshman son. One friend finally commiserated, "Are you having some financial crisis, Sam?" "Not at all," maintained the businessman. "We're having our biggest year ever. But if I don't get my kid a summer job, we'll have to take him to Europe with us."

∴

The McGill *News* recalls a time when humorist Stephen Leacock taught in a small Canadian college for the princely sum of $700 a year. Even in those good old days he had a tough time keeping body and soul together on a salary like that, so he finally wrote a letter to the college trustees saying, "Unless you can see your way clear to increasing my stipend immediately, I shall reluctantly be compelled to"—and here it was necessary to turn the page to read the conclusion—"continue teaching for the same figure."

∴

A Wall Street sage points out that if a three-year-old becomes uncontrollable, and destroys things, it's called a temper tantrum. But when an eighteen-year-old college student does it, it's called "a justified demonstration against the establishment."

∴

A group of disorderly undergraduates, smoking marijuana in a dormitory, heard the police closing in, and vamoosed forthwith, leaving the registered occupant of the premises to stash the incriminating evidence in the back of a cuckoo clock on the mantel. The raiding officers were about to give up their search in vain when the doors of the clock flew open, the cuckoo staggered out, and piped shrilly, "Hey, amigos, anybody know what time it is?"

∴

Things being what they are in the collegiate world, you can understand an old grad's uncertainty when his wife asked if he proposed attending his thirtieth reunion. "My going," he told her, "is dependent on just one thing: if the college is still there by Commencement Day."

∴

In the middle of a class in short-story writing in a Missouri institution of higher learning, the comely young teacher stopped her lecture on technique abruptly when a stalwart gent burst into the room, swept her into his arms, kissed her soundly, and exited happily without uttering one word. The lovely young teacher brushed back her hair, and in a slightly shaken voice told her bug-eyed students, "Well, kids, there's the last paragraph of a happy love story for you. Let's see you write the beginning!"

6. *Campus Wits*

How much has campus humor changed in the past four or five decades? Well, of the following twenty-five bits of dialogue, four appeared in the Columbia *Jester* and the Penn *Punch Bowl* in the early twenties, the others in various college comics within the past four years. I defy you to tell me which are which. (The answers follow No. 25.)

1. First Nurse: "Why is that crazy doctor hollering, 'Tetanus! Typhoid! Smallpox!'"

Second Nurse: "He's calling his shots."

2. She: "You remind me of Don Juan."

He (flattered): "Tell me just how."

She: "Well, for one thing, he's been dead for years."

3. Doctor (in the middle of the night): "Don't you know that my hours are only from two to five P.M.?"

Patient: "Yes, but the dog that bit me didn't."

4. Teacher: "Sam, can you name the fiftieth state?"

Sam: "Huh? Why—uh . . ."

Teacher: "Correct!"

5. Cop (catching up with elderly lady driver he's chased for three blocks): "Didn't you hear me yelling to you."

Driver: "Indeed I did, officer—but I thought it was somebody I'd run down."

6. Clerk: "Here's our latest card with a touching sentiment: 'To the only girl I ever loved.'"

Purdue junior: "Great! I'll take twelve of them."

7. "How's your wife?"

"Not so well, she just had quinsy."

"Good grief! How many have you now?"

8. Male: "How can I believe you, Beulah? That child doesn't even look like me."

Female: "You're looking at the wrong end, stupid!"

9. Customer: "How much are your tomatoes today?"
Grocer: "Thirty cents a pound."
Customer: "Did you raise them yourself?"
Grocer: "Yes, they were twenty-eight cents yesterday."

10. Husband: "It must be time to get up."
Wife: "How can you tell?"
Husband: "The baby has fallen asleep at last."

11. Traffic cop: "I'm afraid your wife fell out of your car about a mile back."
Driver: "Thank God! I thought I'd gone deaf!"

12. Indian chief: "Where's that paleface I just killed?"
Indian warrior: "Right over yonder. Just follow the arrow."

13. Patient: "Hey, doc, I'm coming apart at the seams. What do you prescribe?"
Doc: "A tablespoonful of glue three times a day."

14. Irate traffic cop: "Why do you keep sounding your horn that way?"
Fun-loving motorist: "I can't help it. I have honk-honk flu."

15. "What would you do if you had all the money in the world?"
"Pay my wife's bills—as far as it would go."

16. Junior: "Your grandfather's rather deaf, isn't he?"
Soph: "Is he though! Last night he led the evening prayers while kneeling on the cat."

17. Cannibal Cook: "Shall I stew both these navy cooks?"
Cannibal King: "No. One's enough. Too many cooks spoil the broth."

18. First Colorado frosh: "I'm majoring in ancient history."
Second ditto: "So am I."
First again: "Well, we'll have to get together and talk over old times."

19. Patient: "Did you bring me here to die?"
English nurse: "No. We brought you here yesterdie."

20. "Say, Joe, how did you get that swelling on your nose?"
"I was bending down to smell a brose in my garden."
"Silly fellow! There's no *B* in a rose."

"There was in this one."

21. Man to magician: "What happened to that sawing-a-woman-in-half trick you used to do?"

Magician: "My assistant walked out on me. She moved to Philadelphia and Seattle."

22. Mother: "Why do you say you'll never go out with that attractive ventriloquist again?"

Daughter: "Because last night he sat me on his knee and you should hear the things he made me say!"

23. "Did you give Miss Barber an aptitude test?"

"Yes—and for your information, she's not apt to."

24. Lieutenant: "Beg pardon, Colonel—the troops are revolting."

Colonel: "Well, you're pretty repulsive yourself."

25. Bellboy to alligator registering at a hotel: "Carry your suitcase for you?"

Alligator: "Yes—but be careful. It's my wife!"

(The four gems from the 1920's are numbers 7, 15, 20 and 24.)

7. Silver Threads

A curvaceous, robust young bride of twenty-seven brought her seventy-year-old husband to their doctor, complaining that the old boy seemed to be losing his vim and vigor. After a brief checkup, the patient asked anxiously, "Well, what's the score, Doctor? Am I overweight?" The doctor stole a look at the bride and answered, "No, not overweight. Just overmatched."

∴

Have you heard about that ninety-five-year-old die-hard who married a lady aged ninety-three? They spent the first two weeks of their honeymoon climbing into their automobile.

∴

An elderly gent, after a complete checkup, is told by his doctor, "You're sound as a dollar. You'll live to be ninety." "But I am ninety," splutters the gent. "See?" beams the doctor. "What did I tell you?"

∴

"Were I to lose all my money," demanded a seventy-five-year-old moneybags of his nineteen-year-old bride, "would you still love me?" "I certainly would," she assured him warmly—"and I'd miss you terribly."

∴

One of the late James Thurber's funniest stories concerns his grandfather, who fought as many as a dozen Indians barehanded—to hear him tell it—and vanquished them all. On his deathbed, he was asked by his minister, "Have you forgiven all your enemies?" "Haven't got any," maintained the old man.

"Remarkable," enthused the minister, "but how did a red-blooded, two-fisted old battler like you go through life without making any enemies?" Thurber's grandpop explained casually, "I shot 'em."

∴

A trusted old employee had been kept on by his firm years after his usefulness had ended, but when he began to be a serious nuisance to everybody around him, he was persuaded to "retire" on his eightieth birthday. At a farewell dinner, his associates pulled out all the stops to extol him, the Chairman of the Board (a frustrated thespian) actually breaking into tears as he ticked off the old man's accomplishments and virtues.

The old man was bowled over. "I had no idea I was so essential to the business," he quavered when it was his turn to speak. "Under the circumstances, I cannot let you all down. I withdraw my resignation. I shall stay with you!"

∴

"Yes, siree," cackled a peppery old codger between shuffleboard games at St. Petersburg one morning. "When I was in the service, I sure told those generals and admirals where to get off!" "What was your position?" asked an impressed tourist. The old codger answered reluctantly, "An elevator operator in the Pentagon."

∴

At a sales conference in Chicago, a usually staid office manager downed two full pints of whiskey and immediately became as skittish and frisky as a sub-debutante. "Be your age," chided a companion. "How can two measly pints of whiskey have such an effect on you?" "You seem to forget," chirped the office manager, as he leapt nimbly over a desk and took after a pretty girl who was passing by, "that two pints make one cavort."

∴

Old Mr. Altoid Gotrox, still fairly spry for an octogenarian, felt it necessary, nevertheless, to resist the determined advances of an impoverished but lusty widow of thirty-two. "Mother and Father both are against it," he explained to her. "You're not going to tell me your mother and father still are alive," she scoffed. "I am referring," he concluded loftily, "to Mother Nature and Father Time."

∴

A pompous old windbag put a nickel into one of those weighing machines that tell your fortune as a bonus. He proudly read the card he got aloud to his wife. It said, "You are brilliant, witty, and irresistible to the opposite sex." His wife nodded grimly and snapped, "It's got your weight wrong, too!"

∴

One of the decrepit guides at the Palace of Versailles never fails to inform tourists that he's the only one still alive in those parts who saw Napoleon with his own eyes. "Do you remember how he looked?" prodded one skeptical visitor. "Of course, I do," countered the guide impatiently. "He was six-foot-six and had a flowing red beard."

∴

A young lady expressed consternation at the news that her wealthy eighty-year-old grandfather had up and married his twenty-two-year-old secretary. "I can understand," she told her husband, "what December can see in May—but what, I ask you, is May going to find in December?"

Her husband answered, "Christmas."

∴

Paper tycoon Sam Himmell encountered an old retainer in an Alabama hamlet who remained continually cheerful despite a variety of afflictions and bad breaks that would have shattered an ordinary mortal. "How do you manage to keep so happy and serene?" marveled Himmell. "I'll tell you, Boss," grinned the old man. "I'se just learned to co-operate wid de inevitable."

∴

A socialite octogenarian wriggled angrily in an easy chair in his exclusive Park Avenue club and informed a reporter, "I know nothing, sir, about what you are pleased to call my generation gap. I don't even know anybody with hair!"

∴

In the middle of the Negev Desert, in a dilapidated shack, dwelled a holy man bent with age, pitifully emaciated, but with eyes still filled with hope and defiance. "How can you survive in this miserable place all by yourself?" an American tourist asked him. The holy man replied slowly, "It's a lucky thing for me that my religion demands that I fast four days a week. Otherwise, I'd starve to death!"

∴

A reporter was trying to get a human interest story out of an old, old man at a state-supported home for the aged. "Pop," asked the brash reporter, "how would you feel if you suddenly got a letter telling you that a forgotten relative had left you five million dollars?" "Son," came the answer slowly, "I'd still be ninety-four years old!"

WEDDED BLISS

A magazine offered a prize to the reader who came up with the best way to hold a wife. An entry that unfortunately was not awarded first place came from a subscriber in a state penitentiary. It read, "I found the best way was around the neck, but the operation should not be overdone. Please note change of address."

∴

Amy Lehman, irked by her husband Charles's frequent charge that she was a sloppy housekeeper, went over the whole apartment one day with a mop and dust-rag. That evening she had a moment of unalloyed delight. Her husband called out petulantly, "Amy, where's the dust on your bedside table? I had a phone number written on it."

∴

A sad-faced man limped into a doctor's office, and with a grimace of pain laboriously removed his shoes and socks, revealing shins that were black and blue. "You've certainly been banged up," commiserated the doctor. "I presume you're a professional hockey or football player?" "Certainly not," sighed the man. "All I play is bridge, with my wife as a partner."

∴

Arriving for her first sitting with a noted portrait painter, a wealthy Wilmington socialite told the artist, "I own very little important jewelry, but I want you to depict me wearing a marvelous three-strand string of pearls, a huge diamond brooch, and a spectacular pair of earrings." "But if you don't own such jewels," spluttered the puzzled artist, "why do you want them in your portrait?"

"It's in case I die first," explained the lady, "and my husband takes it into his fool head to get married again. I want his second wife to go crazy trying to find out what happened to them."

∴

The wife of a successful, dignified, middle-aged television producer met him at his sumptuous office one afternoon and headed him for a brief shopping trip. On the way down, a high-powered, beautifully attired secretary boarded the elevator, gave the producer a friendly jab in the solar plexus, and murmured, "Hello there, Cutie Pie." The producer's wife, seemingly unperturbed, answered sweetly, "Hello yourself. I'm Mrs. Pie."

.·.

Marvin Mandelbaum, the gate keeper, was reading his evening paper when his wife, an inveterate bargain hunter, arrived home with a big package under her arm. "Marvin," she exulted, "I picked up this gorgeous bridal gown at a clearance sale for only twelve-fifty!" "What earthly use have you for a bridal gown?" groaned Mr. Mandelbaum. "Don't you know we've been married already forty-four years?" "Of course I know," snapped Mrs. M. undeflated. "But for twelve-fifty it can hang in the closet!"

.·.

A traveling salesman was boasting to his cronies that he had his wife perfectly trained. "She knows she can't put anything over on me," he crowed. "Every time I come home from a trip, I buy a baseball bat, then slip stealthily into the house by the back door. And I haven't missed the man I caught her with once in the past twelve times!"

.·.

"My life has not been an easy one," a gentleman draped over a bar informed an acquaintance he just had picked up. "I've been widowed three times. The first two wives died of eating poisoned mushrooms. The third, poor thing, passed away as the result of a concussion."

"A concussion, you say?" murmured the new acquaintance. "How did THAT happen?" "A very sad case," sighed the widower. "I couldn't get her to eat the mushrooms."

.·.

Two old friends, who hadn't seen each other in years, had an unplanned reunion in the steam room of a Turkish bath.

"Morris," enthused one, "how's that beautiful wife of yours?" "Not so beautiful any more," sighed the other, "and, furthermore, I wish she'd stop nagging me all the time." "Is it money that bothers her?" asked the first. "No," was the answer, "it's my health. The minute it gets a little cold outside, she's pestering me to put on long underwear. All winter she's at me morning, noon, and night. So just to shut her up, I put on the long underwear today. And you know what? It's the first time I've been warm in fifteen years!"

∴

A lady lecturer, hotly defending women's rights, thundered, "Is there one man in this audience chicken enough to let his wife be slandered without protest? If there is, I dare him to stand up!" A measly little Milquetoast promptly arose. "WHAT?" sneered the lecturer. "Do you mean to tell me you would let your wife be slandered and say or do NOTHING?" "I'm sorry," he apologized, resuming his seat, "I thought you said slaughtered."

∴

A wealthy New Yorker took unto himself a ravishing blonde night club dancer as a bride, and drove her to Gettysburg for their honeymoon. At the top of one of the town's rolling hills he told her, "One of the Confederacy's finest and bravest regiments stormed this hill but only a handful of the gallant lads reached the summit." "No wonder," nodded the blonde sympathetically. "All these damn monuments!"

∴

A palmist told an eager young girl, "You will wed a very stingy man and for the first two years of your married life you'll be miserable." "And after that?" prompted the young girl. "After that," concluded the palmist, "you'll get used to it."

∴

SHE SAID . . .

1. An unsophisticated Main Line bride's face fell when she spotted twin beds in her bridal suite. "What's wrong, my darling?" queried the solicitous groom. "Oh, Joe," she wailed. "I certainly thought we were going to have a room to ourselves."

2. An ecstatic young bride staggered into the new apartment, dumped eleven big packages on the davenport, and threw her arms around her husband's neck. "Darling," she cried, "I had NO IDEA you were such a good credit risk!"

3. A winsome young Richmond matron was asked, "Do you ever talk to your husband while you're being embraced?" "No," she answered after a moment's reflection, "but I could if I wanted to. I have his telephone number."

4. "How are you so sure," a kindly boss asked his worried right-hand man, "that your wife insists upon a vacation abroad?" "Well, for one thing," the right-hand man reported, "she phoned me this morning from Rome."

5. "That new psychiatrist is working wonders with my hus-

band," reported Mrs. Collins to her bridge cronies. "He was always so obnoxious and arrogant. In two weeks he's become just the opposite. Now he's arrogant and obnoxious."

6. An angry lady demanding a divorce gave as her reason that her husband had insisted on washing her face. "What's wrong with that?" queried the judge. "Cleanliness is next to Godliness." "You didn't let me finish," maintained the wife. "Then he ironed it."

7. "I'll never forget the morning we arrived to see Niagara Falls," confided Mrs. O'Connor. "My husband's face dropped a mile." "You mean he was disappointed by that glorious sight?" demanded Mrs. Boyle incredulously. "Not at all," Mrs. O'Connor assured her. "He fell over the rim."

8. A Detroit lady was shocked to discover that one of her very closest friends was sporting a four-star, triple-A black eye. "I got it from my husband," volunteered the friend. "Your husband!" echoed the Detroit lady. "I thought he was at a convention in San Francisco." "So did I," agreed the victim.

9. "I have eleven children," wailed an unhappy wife to her lawyer, "and I've just discovered the so-and-so has never really loved me." "There, there," soothed the lawyer. "Think of the fix you'd be in today if he had!"

10. "Darling," apologized a husband over the phone, "the boss is making me work late again tonight, so don't wait up for me." Back came Friend Wife's gentle voice, "Get out of that bar at once, you big bum, and come home. This is a recording."

.:.

HE SAID . . .

1. A jaded Wall Streeter was explaining why summer is his favorite season in the year. "Just last August," he explained, "I took the little woman to the seashore. First, she buried me in the sand. Then I buried HER in the sand. And this coming August, come hell or high water, I'm going back and dig her up!"

2. Mrs. Spritzwasser complained so bitterly about various aches and pains that her husband reluctantly sent for the doctor, who arrived in due course and jammed a thermometer into Mrs. Spritzwasser's mouth. "Keep absolutely quiet for five minutes," warned the doctor—and Mrs. S. obeyed meekly. "Doctor," asked Mr. Spritzwasser reverently, "what will you take for that thing?"

3. Most trusting husband in all New York is probably a Mr. Ridgeley Twilling, who was heard to confide to a commuting companion, "My wife must be a great cook. I came home unexpectedly last night and found a two-hundred-and-forty-pound truck driver eating there."

4. There was a judge in Los Angeles who ceased doling out justice long enough to observe, "I've been married thirty-six years, and I don't regret one day of it. The one day I don't regret was August second, nineteen thirty-six . . ."

5. A henpecked editor checked into the Crowell-Collier office last week with a king-sized bump on his noggin. "You guessed it," he told his confreres sourly. "My wife bopped me with a lamp again this morning." "Why didn't you duck?" asked one friend. "I did," mourned the editor, "but she allowed for it."

6. A tearful woman had a strong case when she sued her brawny husband for divorce. "He beat me up three times a day, your honor," she wailed. "He beat me after breakfast, before dinner, and before bedtime regular as clockwork." "Don't believe a word she says, Judge," interrupted the husband. "She's punch-drunk!"

7. "I'm truly distressed that my wife should have come bothering you with her imaginary troubles," a husband told a marriage counselor. "The only complaint What's-her-name keeps charging me with is that I don't pay enough attention to her."

8. A very tipsy character staggered into a police station to confess, "I just shoved my wife out of the fourteenth-story window." "Did you kill her?" demanded the lieutenant. "I don't think so," said the character. "That's why I want to be locked up."

9. Mr. Dugan staggered home at 4 A.M. and was met at

the door by his outraged wife. "What excuse have you for getting here at this outrageous hour?" she demanded. His answer was right on the button: "Breakfast!"

10. "Those are pretty potent sleeping pills you're purchasing there," warned a good Samaritan in a drugstore to a wispy little customer. "Oh, they're not for me," was the hasty explanation. "They're for my wife. She thinks they're aspirins."

∴

Zsa Zsa Horntoot's husband arrived late at a country club dance and discovered that in emerging from his Rolls, he had torn one knee of his trousers.

"Come into the ladies' dressing room with me," suggested his resourceful Zsa Zsa. "There isn't a soul there and I'll pin it up for you." It developed, however, that the rip was too large to be pinned. A maid furnished needle and thread and was stationed at the door to keep out all and sundry, while Mr. Horntoot removed his trousers.

Suddenly a bevy of formidable matrons shoved the maid aside and demanded immediate admittance. "Quick," Zsa Zsa commanded her mortified spouse. "Get into this closet." She pushed him in just in time, and slammed the door.

No sooner had she admitted the matrons, however, than Mr. Horntoot began screaming, "Open this door IMMEDIATELY." "But the girls are in here now," Zsa Zsa reminded him. "To heck with the girls," cried Mr. Horntoot. "I'm out in the main ballroom."

∴

When, in 1950, the famous wit Dorothy Parker married fellow-writer Alan Campbell for the second time, she telephoned an old friend in New York: "Lilly, the room was filled with people who hadn't talked to each other in years—including the bride and bridegroom!"

∴

Young Trowbridge found his bride sobbing convulsively when he came home from the office. "I feel terrible," she told him. "I was pressing your suit and I burned a big hole right in the seat of your trousers." "Forget it," consoled Trowbridge. "Remember that I've got an extra pair of pants for that suit." "Yes, and it's lucky you have," said the little woman, drying her eyes. "I used them to patch the hole."

∴

What had begun as an office flirtation ripened into abiding love, and a boy and girl who worked for a big bank on Park Avenue rushed down during their lunch hour to get a marriage license. "Look," said the girl angrily, "they've jacked the price of a license up to four dollars!" "Think nothing of it," consoled the love-sick groom-to-be. "They're just trying to keep out the riffraff."

∴

A beautifully brought-up, sheltered little debutante eloped with a stalwart he-man, who, unbeknownst to her, was one of the leading mobsters on the eastern circuit. That night a rival "businessman" threw a bomb into the mobster's domicile, blowing out every window in the building, and destroying the basement completely. "What was THAT?" shrieked the terrified bride. Her husband hastily reassured her, "MICE."

∴

A sorely pressed newlywed sought valiantly to console his little bride, who sprawled, dissolved in tears, on the chaise longue. "Darling," he implored, "believe me. I never said you were a terrible cook. I merely pointed out that our garbage disposal has developed an ulcer."

∴

A man who had gone bankrupt chose a sure but arduous path to repair his fortune. He married a rich but very ugly and very nasty spinster fifteen years his senior. In the middle of the honeymoon, he received a wire telling him he had won a hundred thousand dollars in a state lottery. "Just my miserable luck," he mourned. "THREE DAYS TOO LATE!"

∴

The minister, casting an appraising eye over the bridal couple before him and the goodly crowd come to witness the ceremony, intoned, "If there is anyone here who knows why these two should not be joined together in wedlock, let him speak now or forever hold his peace."

"I've got something to say," a voice rang out bold and clear.

"You shut up," snapped the minister. "You're the groom."

∴

A father had just given the hand of his only daughter in matrimony to a brash Yale graduate named Michael, and said to her just as she was ducking out for her honeymoon, "Well, now I've set your young man up in a business of his own. Is there anything else I can do for you?"

"There IS one thing," murmured his daughter with just a trace of diffidence. "Michael would like you to buy him out."

∴

"Ingabord," a house owner informed his cook earnestly, "my mother-in-law flies in this afternoon for a two-week stay with us, and I've made out for you this list of all her favorite dishes."

"I got it," nodded Ingabord.

"Furthermore," continued the house owner, "if you serve a single one of these dishes while she's here—you're fired."

∴

Here's a mother-in-law story with a difference.

A young couple from upstate decided to spend their holiday in New York City, and it was the young husband who insisted that his mother-in-law be included in the party. The wise lady protested that she would be "excess baggage," but once persuaded to join the young folks, she had every bit as good a time as they did, seeing shows, ball games, museums, and dancing into the wee hours of the morning.

In her mailbox when she returned home was a postcard her son-in-law had sent her while they all were together at a Broadway night club. It read, "Having wonderful time. Delighted you are here."

∴

A disturbed young bride wrote a syndicated matrimonial consultant:

"I'm afraid I married a sex maniac. My husband never leaves me alone. He makes love to me all day long, while I'm in the shower, while I'm cooking breakfast, while I'm making the beds and even while my back is turned to him. Can you tell me what to do?

[Signed] Exhausted.

P.S. Please excuse the jerky handwriting."

.·.

At a cocktail party, two young matrons who had met for the first time and had liked each other at sight, were chatting happily in a corner. "See that rather attractive man over there?" asked one. "He was flirting outrageously with me a little while ago, but suddenly seemed to lose interest in me. I wonder why." "Perhaps," suggested the other, "he saw me arrive. He's my husband."

.·.

"Come quickly, madam," the upstairs maid beseeched her mistress. "Your husband is lying unconscious next to a big oblong box with a piece of paper clutched in his hand."

"Goody, goody," cried the mistress ecstatically. "My new sable coat has arrived."

.·.

Grandma had already extended her unannounced visit for three weeks, and her daughter-in-law and son were slowly going crazy. Finally they concocted a scheme: they would fake a fight and the one with whom she sided would tell her the other was so insulted that she'd simply have to leave.

So that night the wife deliberately spilled a plate of hot soup down her husband's neck. "You're the clumsiest, ugliest, stupidest clunk I've ever seen," roared the husband. "And you," shot back the wife, "are the laziest, demandingest, meanest poop in the world. What do *you* say, Grandma?"

"I'm not saying a word," replied Grandma cheerfully. "I'm staying two more months."

∴

Ad in a North Carolina paper: "My wife's too fat. You can have my 1965 Volkswagen very cheap." Ad in the same space in the following morning's issue: "For sale at tremendous bargain: 1965 Volkswagen and 1939 husband—both slightly dented."

∴

At the golden anniversary of a noted Glencoe couple, the peppery wife was asked, "At any time during your long married life, did you ever even consider divorcing your husband?" After a moment's reflection, she answered, "Divorcing him, no. Killing him, yes!"

∴

Murgatroyd Bopkin was the kind of honest—and fearless—husband who confessed to his wife that a red-headed dancer in a nearby night club was making his heart go pitty-pat. The understanding wife demanded that he take her to inspect this new light of his life. So he did. "It's that gorgeous blonde third from the left," he told her proudly. "And see the little redhead next to her? That's our neighbor Sussman's girl."

The wife studied the two coryphées for a moment, then announced firmly, "I like ours better."

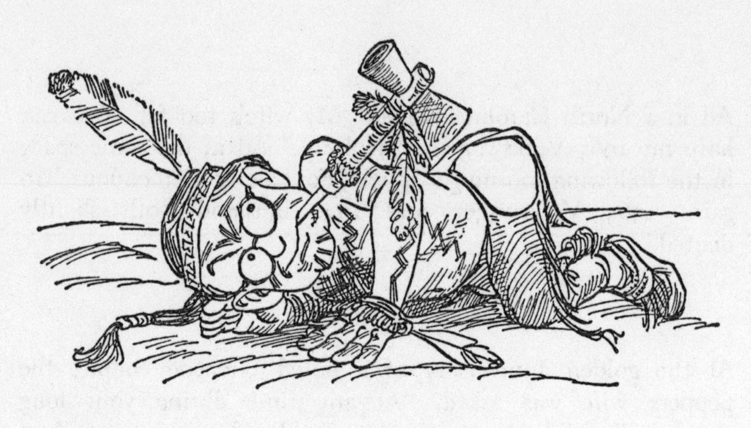

OVERHEARD

Alexander Graham Bell's first words: "Hello. Hello. Dammit. HELLO!"

⁘

Husband calling his wife to the phone: "Darling, somebody wants to listen to you."

⁘

Mrs. Paul Revere (overheard by a neighbor): "I don't care WHO is coming. I'm using the horse tonight!"

⁘

Manhattan banker to would-be borrower: "Honestly, sir, if the President of the United States were to march through that door this instant, we'd charge him the same outrageous rate of interest we're asking from you."

∴

Near-sighted bandit holding up a bank: "On the double, now, everybody get your hands up. . . . Are they up?"

∴

Hospital director to new trustee: "We now are entering the quiet zone of the hospital. Please try not to make any nurse."

∴

Man showing doctor his wife's injured hand: "She did it getting dinner ready last night. It must be frostbite."

∴

In a club car: "My wife doesn't care how good-looking my secretary is—as long as he can type."

∴

Psychiatrist to patient: "You're quite right. A man IS following you constantly. He's trying to collect the two hundred dollars you owe me."

∴

At the Raffles Club: "When I got the bill for my operation, I found out why they wear masks in the operating room."

∴

Internal Revenue agent to agitated taxpayer: "Yes, Mr. Heimerdinger, I'm afraid we DO want to make a federal case out of it."

∴

At a boss's desk: "Well, sir, I wouldn't ask for a raise when I know you only have one yacht, but somehow, my kids found out that other families eat three meals a day."

∴

Cannibal chief to a reporter on safari: "I never yet have met a woman I didn't like."

∴

Moth, surveying a topless bathing suit: "Somebody's stolen half my lunch."

∴

One pig to another: "If I had my way, EVERYBODY would be Orthodox Jewish!"

∴

Absent-minded professor's wife: "Hubert, are you sure you've forgotten everything?"

∴

Small boy to slightly smaller girl: "Are you the opposite sex, or am I?"

∴

On the 8:27: "I'm beginning to wonder if it was such a good idea to give our son one of those rockets that blasts off for his ninth birthday. As of today, we've got the only cat in Bedford who knows what our house looks like from three hundred feet up!"

∴

Triumphant father to mother watching their sixteen-year-old son mow the lawn: "I told him I lost the car keys in the tall grass."

∴

High-school girl to classmate: "I wrote to eleven colleges and this one had the best rating: 1522 boys and 177 girls."

∴

Professor to dean: "Of course I remember Wimpfheimer. He took my course for his first siesta here."

∴

At a fraternity smoker: "That girl in the corner has broken every date she's had. She goes out with them."

. .
.

Father welcoming his daughter's date for the evening: "She'll be right down. How about a couple of games of chess?"

. .
.

At a big college football game: "Will the person who owns the Cadillac convertible with the cowhide seatcovers please hurry to the parking lot? There's a bull attacking the back seat."

. .
.

Alluring damsel at a cocktail party: "No more for me, thank you; I'm being driven home."

. .
.

Weary gent at the same party: "I'm exhausted. I think I'll start flirting with some miniskirted debutante so my wife will drag me home."

. .
.

At a men's luncheon club: "Boy, am I in a fine pickle! Our maid caught me kissing my wife this morning!"

. .
.

Lady with several bundles at the entrance to Marshall Field's: "Did you by any chance notice a very angry man in a blue sedan drive by here nine or ten times?"

∴

Lady to pollster: "My opinion is that whoever is elected, my husband will be furious."

∴

Advice from a marriage counselor: "The best way to cure your wife's nagging is by affection, understanding, tolerance —and stuffing a pair of old socks in her mouth."

∴

Insurance salesman: "My greatest success was with a young housewife who wasn't adequately covered."

∴

At a tea shoppe: "Anne is one of those quiet, unassuming girls. You know what I mean: a real phony."

∴

Lady driver: "The thing I dislike most about parking is that noisy CRASH!"

∴

Night club habitué, gazing fondly at an old friend in the chorus line: "She's the best thing that never happened to me!"

∴

"The tree overhanging our lawn has five hundred thousand leaves. Every fall it sheds two million of them into our swimming pool."—Donald Klopfer

∴

At the Dallas Airport: "We're going to put up a REAL skyscraper in this town. Just to give you an idea of how high it will be, the elevators will show movies."

∴

Father blocking the screen of a TV set: "Now, Junior, if you don't obey your mother immediately, we won't let you stay up till two A.M. tonight to watch the drama that's listed as unsuitable for children."

∴

Complaint of a teacher in a progressive high school: "The little monsters take everything I say with a grain of LSD."

∴

On the Columbia campus: "I'm not sure yet what I'm going to take next semester: the dean's office or the Library."

∴

Overheard at an Internal Revenue office: "You'd better start figuring again. This return you handed in blew three tubes in the computing machine."

∴

Publisher to novice author: "I predict a most successful career for you. You write beautifully, your characters are clearly delineated—and you have a filthy mind."

∴

One astronaut in orbit to another: "Hey, look, Pat! We're flying right over the Empire State Building, Westminster Abbey and the Taj Mahal!"

∴

Mother to six-year-old son in a New York sidewalk restaurant: "Finish your milk, Milton, before it gets dirty!"

∴

Disdainful lecturer at Hunter College: "The subject of my talk this afternoon is Air Pollution—sometimes known as Television."

THE PRINTED WORD

1. *Authors*

Henry Fielding, the great English novelist, way back in the 1740's anticipated the seeming trend of fiction in the 1970's. In his still widely read *Jonathan Wild*, for example, there occurs this memorable sentence: "He in a few moments ravished this fair creature, or at least would have ravished her, if she had not, by a timely compliance, prevented him."

∴

Maybe the picture you have in your mind of the kind of writer who goes in for sports reporting will undergo a slight change if you glance through Arlott and Daley's new book, *Pageantry of Sport*. For here you will find, of all people, William Wordsworth glorifying ice-skating, Izaak Walton rhapsodizing over fishing, novelist Henry Fielding on hunting, diarist Samuel Pepys describing a hot tennis match, and Mark Twain giving a vivid description of a mule race in New Orleans!

∴

In Stephen Birmingham's *Our Crowd,* he tells of the time the affluent Wall Street banker Joseph Seligman hired none other than Horatio Alger, Jr., to tutor his five unruly boys—hoping that they would acquire all those red-blooded American standards of such heroes of his books for the young as Tattered Tom, Ragged Dick, and Paul the Peddler. Alas, in real life author Alger turned out to be a timid, easily intimidated Casper Milquetoast, and when the Seligman small fry deviled him, he'd cry, "Oh, Lordy Me," and run to the cook for help.

∴

Mr. Alger may have been a failure as a tutor, but at least he gained one very tangible reward from his experience. Banker Seligman took charge of his investments and made a fortune for him.

∴

Jerry Mangione, a scarred but stalwart survivor of the depression-motivated Federal Writers' Project in the 1930's, likes to recall the vicissitudes that attended the production of guide books for every one of the states, churned out by thousands of worthy young writers who, but for this government help, might actually have starved.

The national director of the project was a worthy but excitable gent named Henry Alsberg, sometimes referred to as "a colossus of chaos," who was usually on the long-distance phone frantically demanding, "Get me Florida," and then conducting a long conversation under the impression he was getting a hot-off-the-griddle report from Honolulu.

The first guide book to come off the presses was Idaho's—because its editor, Vardis Fisher, did the whole book by himself. ("Heck," he explained, "there weren't any writers in Idaho but myself.") His guide was published in 1937. Others were delayed as late as 1942. By the time the series was completed, incidentally, 335 cities claimed to be "the crossroads of America" and the stories of forty-two began, "Our town, like Rome, was built on seven hills."

∴

When it came to absent-mindedness, the late G. K. Chesterton took the cake. On one occasion he had a date to meet his publisher and felt he wouldn't be able to keep it, so he dashed off a note, extending his apologies and suggesting a meeting a week later. He then took the note personally to the publisher's office, arriving at exactly the time of his appointment.

∴

One of Washington's loveliest hostesses boasts of the day, just after her presentation at Court, when she found herself seated next to the bewhiskered George Bernard Shaw at dinner. She murmured to him, "Mama says I should steer clear of the question of your age." "Is that so?" nodded Shaw. "Well, how old would you say I am?" "Eighty-eight?" she hazarded nervously. Shaw reached under the table, pinched her knee sharply, and chuckled, "I am, am I?"

∴

At the famous Algonquin round table one lunchtime some years ago an unusually subdued Dorothy Parker reported sadly, "My old cat that I've loved so dearly has grown so feeble and helpless that I'm simply going to have to have him put away. I've been wracking my brain over what would be the most humane way to do it." Playwright George Kaufman reflected respectfully for a moment, then inquired, "Have you thought of curiosity?"

It was Kaufman, too, who announced without preamble one evening that he was thinking of killing *himself*. Duly shocked, Edna Ferber gasped, "How, George?" Kaufman answered amiably, "With kindness."

∴

Miss Parker's legion of admirers like to recall the day she slapped down one of the most arrogant, self-satisfied celebrities of our day. Said celebrity announced, "I make it a point always to be especially gracious to my inferiors." "How wonderful," gurgled Miss Parker. "But tell me—WHERE DO YOU FIND THEM?"

∴

A very famous author's wife, asked how it felt to be married to a man who had won both the Pulitzer Prize and a National Book Award, admitted, "Nothing really exciting has happened around our ivory tower since the morning he got his beard caught in his typewriter."

∴

In his highly diverting new book, *How Many Miles to Galena,* Richard Bissell, of *Pajama Game* fame, tells of an hour he spent in the Mark Twain Cave. "Would youse like to see a bat?" a guide asked him. "Might as well go all the way," conceded Bissell. "Well, there's one in that crevice," pointed out the guide. "He's just a young, little feller now. He don't know the score yet." "He looks pretty terrible," shuddered Bissell. "Will he look any better when he gets to know the score?" "Nope, worse," answered the guide.

∴

Back at his hotel, Bissell ran into poet Carl Sandburg in an elevator. After Sandburg had stepped out, Bissell said to the elevator operator, "Do you know that that was the famous Carl Sandburg?" The operator was not overly impressed. "Yeah," he nodded carelessly, "we get a lot of them here!"

∴

Gertrude Stein is remembered today as a brilliant but often totally undecipherable essayist and novelist—her oft quoted "a rose is a rose is a rose" being a fair sample of her tantalizing prose. Miss Stein was, in fact, a shrewd, stout-hearted lady, with superb taste, and the ability to speak or write with perfect clarity when it suited her purpose. I know because I was her publisher for years in America. Nobody possibly could misunderstand Miss Stein, for instance, when, in the mid-thirties, after her first visit home in twenty years, she declared, "America seems to me to be getting too old to become young again. Employees are getting to feel themselves employed and no longer are able to see themselves as potential employers."

Taken to her first football game, Miss Stein opined that the players "do what red Indians do when they are dancing.

When they lean over and when they are squatting they are like an Indian dance. The Russians squat and jump too but it looks different, but the Americans and the red Indians had the same so how could they not be the same, the country is large but somehow it is the same and if it were not it would not remain our country and that would be a shame. I like it as it is." Now isn't that all just as clear as day?

∴

Dick Rowan tells about an author who tried to interest a publisher in a short but revolutionary new book he had written entitled *Should Women Have Children After 35*. The publisher recoiled, then threw the author out of his office with a decisive, "Thirty-five strike me as more than enough."

∴

George Orwell, author of the memorable *1984*, once told an interviewer that the principal reason he wrote books was that his old fifth-grade teacher might see his work and be remorseful that she'd misjudged them.

∴

After Moss Hart had made a fortune with a series of Broadway hits, he, too, journeyed up to the Bronx to show his old public school principal (a man who had predicted nothing but disaster for him) how wrong that estimate had been. The principal recognized him at once. "Ah, Hart," he rasped. "What are you coming round here for again? You're wasting your time. I won't lift a finger to help you."

∴

Moss Hart was a particularly happy man when his superb autobiography, *Act One*, hit the top rung of the nation's best-seller lists. He loved signing copies for people, too, whether he knew them or not.

One afternoon he was sauntering up Madison Avenue when a dear little old lady hove into view, a copy of *Act One* tucked closely under her arm. Certain he was going to delight her, Moss Hart stopped her, pulled the book away from her, and told her, with his most charming smile, "I am Moss Hart and I'll be delighted to autograph this copy of my book for you."

The dear little old lady did not react as expected. She yanked the book back from Hart and informed him tartly, "Young Man, if you don't stop annoying me instantly, I shall call for a policeman!"

∴

Are you one of those people who are constantly wringing their hands over the way the world is going? Remember, then, what Ralph Waldo Emerson said to just such a lady three generations ago. "I've decided to accept the universe," she said finally. Emerson told her, "You'd better!"

∴

In Marcia Davenport's book of reminiscences *Too Strong for Fantasy*, she devotes a few words to Alexander Woollcott, as ill-mannered and snobbish a celebrity as ever gushed into a microphone. "While I was still at school," recalls Miss Davenport, "I used to come in on winter afternoons to find my mother and Woollcott playing backgammon. I was gauche and timid and loaded with every disadvantage of my age, including bands on my teeth and corrective spectacles. My mother would greet me lovingly and say to Woollcott, 'You know my daughter Marcia.' And time after time he would glance at me without recognition and say, 'Disaster, isn't it?' If my mother had realized how I felt she would have ordered him out of the house, instead of thinking the brute funny."

.:.

Like most famous writers in the thirties, John O'Hara would trundle off to Hollywood whenever the urge to collect some of that easy money out there became too strong to resist. Don Schanche recalls one time when O'Hara, for purposes of research, he explained, conned producer Lewis Milestone into giving him a small acting part in a film then being made called *The General Died at Dawn.*

The star of the picture was O'Hara's close personal friend Gary Cooper. John enacted the role of a foreign correspondent downing a drink or two in the diner of a Chinese railroad train. His one line was to say, "Oh, hello, O'Hara," Cooper's film name, as the star walked down the aisle. They had to reshoot the ten-second scene six times, because every time John delivered his epic line, Cooper stopped cold, turned to Milestone, and said, "But Millie, HIS name is O'Hara."

"Gary," producer Milestone finally exploded, "you've now been playing O'Hara in this film for forty-three days. O'Hara is YOUR name! Get on with it."

.:.

In the James Joyce Museum in Sandycove, near Dublin, Ireland, is a photograph of the author of *Ulysses* when he was a young, impetuous, and penniless scrivener. In his later years, Joyce was asked what noble thought had wrinkled his brow while he posed for the picture. "I was thinking," answered Joyce, "of asking the photographer if he could loan me five pounds."

.:.

The late Sinclair Lewis had invited actor Jean Hersholt to dinner one evening, and, in a playful mood, had a shingle hung outside his door reading "Paul Christian, M.D."—the name of the doctor Hersholt portrayed on his long-running radio series.

The joke, unfortunately, misfired. The Hersholts arrived, saw the sign, exclaimed over the remarkable coincidence and drove back five miles to their hotel to discover where their directions had gone wrong. They finally landed at Lewis' a full hour late. The dinner was ruined and Lewis, of course, blamed it all on poor Hersholt.

∴

Sinclair Lewis spent his last night in America at my house. At dinner, he explained to my wife and myself that he would have to retire early, since he was scheduled to board his boat for Italy at eight the following morning.

While we were having coffee, the phone rang. It was William Faulkner, arrived unexpectedly in New York. "Can I ask Bill to come over?" I inquired of Lewis. "No, you cannot," snapped Red. "Haven't you been a publisher long enough to know that you don't bring two of your big authors together at one time? This is MY night. Tell Faulkner you'll see him tomorrow."

That's how it was arranged. Soon after Lewis went upstairs

to bed, about an hour later, my wife and I were alarmed to hear him shouting, "Bennett! Bennett!"

I rushed into the hall to call up, "What's the matter, Red?"

"Nothing at all," he answered mollified. "I just wanted to make sure you hadn't sneaked off to see Faulkner!"

.˙.

There's an author of a formidable string of best sellers who fancies himself as a Great Lover. What's more, he cashes in on each big romance by turning it into a short story he sells to the slicks for whopping prices. A San Francisco reporter once asked him, "Who was that lady I saw you with last night?" The author answered agreeably, "That wasn't no lady. That was my next short story."

.˙.

In his rollicking autobiography, *Fun While It Lasted*, Barnaby Conrad tells a story of a gay young blade in Spain who spied a beautiful maid named Carmen through the bars of her small window one afternoon.

She was lovely, irresistible, and soon they became sweethearts. But never would she meet him in some other setting, more suitable, perchance, for lovers. Her excuse: her family was too strict.

Finally, however, his insistence was rewarded, and she reluctantly agreed to meet him the next day in the park. And indeed that's where he saw her waiting for him on a bench when he hurried to keep the tryst. She was a midget! She didn't see him. He stole silently away, and left Spain that very evening.

.˙.

Amy Vanderbilt, whose book on etiquette has made even Emily Post take a back seat, found herself sitting next to a man she never had seen before at a dinner party one evening. Along about time for the main course, he turned to her and said, "The lady on my right says you're Amy Vanderbilt. She's kidding, isn't she?" "No, I'm Amy Vanderbilt all right," laughed Miss V. "In that case," said the man sharply, "what are you doing eating my salad?"

∴

Jean Kerr, a wonderful girl and an amply proportioned one (she's the author of the fabulously successful *Mary, Mary* and *Please Don't Eat the Daisies*), takes a dim view of that shapeless splinter of a model, Twiggy, and others of similar slenderness. "Oh, for the days of girls with hips and things," sighs Jean—"and all the other items that used to be standard equipment before the roof fell in on the fashion industry—or, to be precise, the bottom fell out."

∴

Leo Rosten, *Look* editor and author of *The Education of Hyman Kaplan*, was confronted by a very angry son one evening, who accused him, "Do you know what you've become, Pop? REQUIRED READING!"

∴

St. Louis-born poet T. S. Eliot, after he graduated from Harvard, moved on to Oxford and soon became so English that even Englishmen found it hard to understand him. Before writing *The Waste Land* and becoming one of the world's greatest poets, he toiled briefly in Lloyd's Bank, where he appeared invariably impeccably attired in black coat, striped trousers, bowler, and tightly wrapped umbrella. One slip: he developed a fondness for a music hall ditty entitled "Too Many Gins Give the Ladies Double Chins" and hummed it so incessantly that the bank manager, if ever so diffidently, had to ask him to desist.

While a member of the British publishing firm of Faber and Faber, the formidable Mr. T. S. Eliot was fond of handing other authors exploding cigars and cushions that gave forth a rasping Bronx cheer when sat upon.

∴

H. Allen Smith tells of the day his Uncle Fred climbed a tall mountain and found a huge rock poised at its crest. He worked with might and main for hours and finally dislodged it. It went hurtling down the mountainside, headed straight for town, crashed through the supermarket and the First National Bank, and finally came to rest against an oak tree in the rear of that institution.

Folks came rushing from all sides to see what all the excitement was about, but Uncle Fred, arriving on the double, pushed them aside to scrutinize the rock carefully through a magnifying glass. Finally he straightened up, and announced, "Nope. No moss."

∴

Almost everybody knows that lions travel in prides, that pups come in litters, that elephants en masse are referred to as herds, and that fish navigate in schools. But you'll have to dig into James Lipton's unique book *An Exaltation of Larks* to find that in their time and fashion, good folks have referred to an ostentation of peacocks, an impatience of wives, an unction of undertakers, a sneer of butlers, a twinge of dentists, a tantrum of decorators, an indifference of waiters, a descent of relatives, a no-no of nannies, and a babble of barbers. If the game appeals to you, you might strike out on your own!

∴

Dan Greenburg, self-confessed chronic worrier (see his book *How to Make Yourself Miserable*), was upset one day when he noticed how much radium there must be on the dial of his wrist watch. He had no rest until he could locate a jewelry store, where he ordered the clerk on duty at the watch counter to scrape the radium right off the hour marks on the watch.

"For heaven's sake, WHY?" demanded the mystified clerk. "It's dangerous having radium so near the body," explained Greenburg. "Look at what happened to Madame Curie." "Nuts!" snorted the clerk. "There's more radiation coming out of the stone lions in front of the New York Public Library than in that watch!"

Did this end Mr. Greenburg's fears? Not on your life! Now he never will go near the New York Public Library!

∴

Somerset Michamud sat happily typing the final pages of his new novel. In the yard, his six-year-old son had just tripped over a tree root and broken his leg. The boxer puppy had chewed up Mrs. Michamud's best curtain, the twins had spilled a can of paint in the parlor and were now trying to pull each other's hair out, and the nurse had given notice. Mrs. Michamud called out to her husband, "Lunch is almost ready. How far have you gotten with your manuscript?" Mr. M. answered, "It's going like a house afire. The hero is just proposing to the heroine."

"Give it a happy ending," begged Mrs. M. earnestly. "Have her say 'No.' "

2. *Books*

Some of the most famous books of all time were turned down by as many as a dozen publishers before somebody could be found willing to sponsor them. *The Good Earth*, *The Four Horsemen of the Apocalypse*, and *No Time for Sergeants* are cases in point.

Marc Connelly tells a story about Longfellow's *Evangeline* that may or may not be true. According to Mr. C., the manuscript of *Evangeline* was once rejected with a letter explaining, "Your poetry is good enough, but Fenimore Cooper has written so much about Indians already that we feel the market is exhausted."

∴

In Pocatello, Idaho, a couple browsing in a bookshop came upon ten copies of Homer's *Iliad*. "Wonder why they stock that book so heavily?" mused the wife. The husband surmised, "Probably a local author."

∴

A distinguished book publisher, driving with the top of his convertible down, was wearing vermilion pants, a green shirt, a canary yellow tie, and a Sherlock Holmes hat. A motorcycle cop drew alongside and ordered him to the curb. "But I was only going thirty miles an hour," protested the publisher. "I'm not going to give you a ticket," the cop reassured him. "I just wanted to hear you talk!"

∴

By this time, it's a safe estimate that at least 80 per cent of the literate population of the U.S.A. has either read *The Wizard of Oz* or seen it on TV—or both. Frank Baum's wonderful creation sells thousands of copies year after year—yet I wonder how many people know where the name "OZ" comes from. According to the late author's own autobiography, he had outlined the story of Dorothy and the Tin Man and the Straw Man and the Cowardly Lion and all the others in his mind, but still had not hit upon a name for the magic land they were seeking, when his eyes fell on a filing cabinet in a corner of his office. The top drawer of this file was labeled "A–H," the second drawer, "I–N," and the bottom drawer, "O–Z." "That's it!" he cried delightedly. "OZ!" The rest, to coin a phrase, is history.

It was columnist Jerome Beatty who unearthed the fact that the full name of the Wizard of Oz was Oscar Zoroaster Phadriz Isaac Norman Henkle Emanuel Ambroise Diggs. Put the initials all together and they spell "Oz Pinhead." Mr. Beatty's source? Frank Baum himself. The disclosure is made in the fourth of the almost interminable series, *Dorothy and the Wizard of Oz.*

∴

There's a way-out little book on the market called *The Unofficial Horoscope*—and Lord help anybody who takes it seriously. Here are a few typical entries for the month of January: Jan. 4: Beware of low-flying butterflies. Jan. 9: Do something artistic today. Frame a friend. Jan. 15: Stop burning your candle at both ends. You're becoming a drip. Jan. 20: Somebody may recognize you today. Hide!

∴

Publisher Bill Jovanovich, in his book, *Now, Barabbas,* recalls the old days when a salesman was expected to pull out all stops for his product, with only scant regard for the truth. For example, when the binding glue on some sample copies of a new geography text gave off an offensive odor, the publisher's salesmen were instructed to inform finicky lady buyers. "Ma'am, if you smell something, it's not the book: it's me."

∴

David Randall, expert rare-book dealer, tells many fascinating details of his specialty in his new book *Dukedom Large Enough.*

In book auctions, he advises, "the bargains are most often at the end of a sale. That's when interest flags, most dealers have already overbought, people are exiting, the auctioneer is tired, and things slip through." When browsing in rare- and used-book shops, adds Randall, "Keep to the upper and lower shelves. Most people, even the shop owners, are too damn lazy to climb a ladder or stoop to their knees once the books are shelved, and that's where the bargains are."

∴

A Rolls-Royce pulled up in front of a Fifth Avenue bookshop the other evening and the chauffeur announced sheepishly, "My lady wants a couple of new murder stories committed by nice people."

∴

A group of teachers at a Westchester County school endeavored to discover how much books mattered to their students. The kids were asked to write essays on "A Book Is . . ." And here are a few of the answers they turned in: a tenth-grade girl wrote, "A book is two-faced. It can make you laugh or it can make you cry. Nothing in this world that is so small can do so much." An eighth-grader chimed in with, "Books can be written by people who are so rich they were millionaires when they were seven or by people who are so poor they were made in Japan."

A fourth-grader opined, "A book is a lot of paper with words on it. This morning I put two books in the washing machine and shot five holes in 'Alice in Wonderland' with my pellet rifle." And a seventh-grade girl stated that a book "is pretty dull, unless it's fiction. Who cares what happens to real life people? I have my own troubles!"

∴

At one of those sleazy bookstores in the Forty-second Street sector, a dubious customer picked up a paperback and asked the attendant, "Are you positive this is an unexpurgated edition?" He was assured, "Mister, that book is so unexpurgated it's even dirtier than when it was written."

∴

On the wall of a publisher's office hangs a quotation from Clarence Day that will bring cheer to everyone who loves to read good books:

The world of books
Is the most remarkable creation of man.
Nothing else he builds lasts.
Monuments fall, nations perish,
Civilizations grow old and die out
And, after an era of darkness, new races build others.
But in the world of books are volumes
That have seen this happen again and again
And yet live on, still young,
Still as fresh as the day they were written,
Still telling men's hearts
Of the hearts of men centuries dead.

3. *Magazines*

In the good old days of *The New Yorker*, when its brilliant founder, Harold Ross, was still running the show, James Thurber, who worked for the magazine as well as supplying it with his inimitable drawings, delighted in getting the Master's goat. It was not too difficult. One afternoon he burst into Ross's office to protest, "Some so-and-so around here has stolen my coat." "Get out," roared Ross. "Can't you see how busy I am?" Thurber retreated, but was back again five minutes later to report, "He's stolen my shirt, too!"

∴

It will be a long time before any new artist can duplicate the success of the late Peter Arno, whose racy, irreverent cartoons were one of the major reasons for the early success of *The New Yorker* magazine. Arno himself liked best his long-running, outrageous Whoop Sisters cartoons. Other of his personal favorites were: 1. A disheveled maid in a sailor shirt complaining to a bedazzled roommate, "He told me there was a storm coming up so like a fool I let him tie me to the mast"; 2. A tuxedoed old gadabout ogling a nineteen-year-old chorus girl and beseeching, "Tell me about yourself, your struggles, your dreams, your telephone number"; and 3. A pompous old Bostonian, confronted by a pennant peddler before a Harvard-Yale football game, gasping unbelievingly, "Which ONE? Great heavens, are you MAD?"

∴

The late Henry Luce, creator of one of the most powerful magazine empires in history, had his fair share of faults, but dodging issues definitely was not one of them. If you are fed up with weaseling editors and commentators who are continually apologizing for what's wrong with America, and ignoring all the things that make our country great, you will appreciate Luce's answer to a critic who damned him for his prejudices: "I am a Protestant, a Republican, and a free enterpriser, which means I am biased in favor of God, Eisenhower, and the stockholders of Time, Incorporated—and if anyone who objects doesn't know this by now, why the hell are they still buying the magazine?"

Luce's policies proved disastrous in many respects, but even detractors must admire a man who was willing to put his views so squarely on the line.

∴

After he had graduated from Yale in 1920, and before he teamed up with Henry Luce to start *Time* magazine, Briton Hadden applied to Herbert Swope for a job on the latter's glittering New York *World*. Swope said he had no opening. Hadden drew himself up and announced severely, "Mr. Swope, you are interfering with my destiny." Swope was amused—and gave him a job at twenty-five dollars a week.

∴

Remember that ritzy magazine, *Vanity Fair?* Bob Sherwood, Pulitzer Prize author, worked on it very briefly early in his career. When the editor of the regular feature, "What the Well-Dressed Man Will Wear," went on vacation, Sherwood filled in for him. Convinced that nobody ever read the column, Sherwood got going with "On dit that peg-topped pants and cloth-top shoes are coming back, also that the best-dressed man's waistcoat this season will glitter darkly with cut jade." It developed that one man read the column after all, and that was its regular editor. Mr. Sherwood was fired.

∴

The saddest hyprochondriac Morey Amsterdam knows tested every medical cure in a famous digest magazine—and died of a typographical error.

∴

An editor of a leading magazine for cat lovers has been casting his eyes over the subscription lists. He discovered there are two subscribers in Paw Paw, Michigan; three in Kitchel, Indiana; one in Catskill, New York; and two in distant Saskatchewan. Now he's trying to dig up a prospect or two in Mousie, Kentucky, and Rat, Missouri.

∴

They're still telling stories about George Horace Lorimer, long-time editor of the *Saturday Evening Post* in the days of its glory. Lorimer knew exactly what he wanted—and what his readers did, too—and woe betided any author who tried to tamper with his formula. The author who probably sold Lorimer more stories than any other three *Post* contributors combined was Clarence Budington Kelland. Kelland met Lorimer one day at lunch and told him, "I'll have my new serial ready to deliver to you in two weeks." "Good," enthused Lorimer. "Don't go changing that plot."

∴

Referring to a notoriously stingy magazine magnate, a disgruntled member of his underpaid staff reported happily to his cohorts one morning, "The old so-and-so's about to announce his engagement, but he met with an unfortunate accident yesterday while buying his girl a ring. He got his fingers crushed between two pushcarts."

∴

At the spring sales conference of a great publishing combine, the San Francisco manager cried out in anguish, "Lock every door! I've lost my wallet with a hundred bucks in it. To the honest man who returns it, I'll give a five-dollar reward." From the back of the room came the call, "I'll make it fifteen!"

∴

An aging newspaper hack, famous for his continuous name-dropping, told one gathering he had been an intimate of the Barrymores, the Crosbys, the Marx Brothers, the Trumans, and the Astaires. "I'll bet you also know the Lunts," prompted one listener, tongue in cheek. "Of course I do," was the modest reply—"and the Fontannes, too."

4. *Newspapers*

James Gordon Bennett, high-living old tyrannical owner of the once fabulously successful New York *Herald*, was accustomed to having his every whim gratified instanter. Arriving for a spot of luncheon one day at a little restaurant in the hills above Monte Carlo, he found the table he fancied occupied by some unknown bounders. (A bounder to Mr. Bennett was anybody who had the audacity to get in his way.) He angrily sought out the owner of the restaurant, bought it on the spot for $40,000 in cash, threw every patron out of the place, and had his luncheon in solitary grandeur at the table he favored.

Furthermore, when his meal had been finished off with a couple of snifters of cognac, Bennett casually made a gift of the entire establishment to the waiter who had been lucky enough to serve him that day. The waiter's name was Ciro, incidentally, and he used his jackpot to open a restaurant of his own—Ciro's of Monte Carlo—that in time became more famous than James Gordon Bennett ever had been.

∴

One of publisher Bennett's strange and unreasonable rules was that every reporter in his employ use the word "night" instead of "evening." "Night," he explained testily, "is a more exact term." The rule, however, was abruptly suspended when a mischievous society editor, reporting the crowning event of the season, noted that, "The hostess looked ravishing in a pink silk night gown."

∴

William Randolph Hearst, an inveterate collector of Old World treasures, once acquired an antique Greek swimming pool—complete with a floor of inlaid gold foil and a surrounding complement of life-sized statuary. Hollywood wit Charles Lederer was showing the pool to visitors at the famous publisher's California retreat one day and told them, "Mr. Hearst bought that complete in Athens one day. There still were people swimming in it when the deal was consummated. They were sore as Hell!"

⁘

The late Herbert Bayard Swope, famous and flamboyant newspaper editor in the twenties and thirties, is the subject of an exhaustive biography by E. J. Kahn, Jr. Kahn quotes Pegler's description of Swope: "All gall, divided into three parts: Herbert, Bayard, and Swope."

In one of his innumerable house parties, Swope once included two men named Stephen. His wife had a vastly higher opinion of one than of the other and persisted in referring to them as "the two Steves—common and preferred."

That same weekend, Swope, who was always outrageously late for every appointment, kept six rather important gentlemen waiting over an hour to join them in a trip to the race track. One finally burst into his private apartment to see what was holding him up. He returned, apopleptic, to report, "You know what the so-and-so is doing? COUNTING HIS SHIRTS!"

⁘

Not every newspaper editor, testifies author Dick Schaap, is precisely a mental giant. Take the one, for example, who sent a reporter to cover the local post office and cook up a story on how much fuss was being kicked up by the rise of first-class postage stamps from five to six cents for ordinary mail. The reporter came back, chuckling, to tell about the lady who was buying all the five-cent stamps she could afford before the price went up. The editor pondered momentarily, then said, "Go back to that post office and pick up ten dollars' worth of those five-cent stamps for me!"

Schaap remembers two other stories about alert editors-in-chief. One scanned a drama critic's review in which, because of a typographical error, the word "brilliant" came out "grilliant." "Grilliant, eh?" beamed the editor. "I like that fellow's vocabulary. We need more fresh, punchy words like that in our copy." The other editor sneered at by-lines. "Who cares what author wrote a story or a book?" he demanded. "For instance, who remembers today the names of the men who wrote those Horatio Alger or Rudyard Kipling stories?"

.˙.

Alice Albright Hoge, in her lively biography of her highflying grandaunt Cissy Patterson, tells of the severe winter when Cissy learned that the ducks in Washington's Rock Creek Park were starving. With appropriate front-page tub-thumping in her Washington *Herald*, Cissy hired a helicopter to drop bundles of food to the famished birds. The packages, unfortunately, hit the closely gathered ducks squarely amidships and wiped out the flock.

.˙.

A small-town editor had repeated so often to his eager but inexperienced new assistant, "Always remember that names make news," that on his next assignment, his report began, "Fire last night destroyed Farmer Alvin Heimerdingers' barn, claiming the lives of three cows named Bossy, Bessy, and Gertrude."

.˙.

Edward Barrett, who was the dynamic and popular dean of the prestigious Pulitzer School of Journalism for twelve years, came naturally by his love of the newspaper business. His father was the editor and publisher of the Birmingham, Alabama, *Age-Herald*, and Barrett has said that he learned about the power of the press almost before he learned to walk.

One of the many nationally famous men Barrett met in his boyhood was Circus-man John Ringling, who made the mistake of challenging Barrett's father to a domino match and wound up losing the largest of the circus elephants in the process. Barrett, Senior, claiming immediate possession, proudly marched the elephant home and led him into the garage—which the elephant promptly demolished. Mrs. Barrett thereupon gave her mortified husband exactly six hours to get the elephant off the premises.

This was the moment when young Edward Barrett showed his first flash of genius. "Convince Birmingham that it needs a zoo," he suggested. Papa Barrett's resultant editorial was so convincing that the city fathers voted a zoo forthwith. Its first acquisition was a magnificent elephant—courtesy of the Barrett family.

Barrett's credo: "The key journalist of the future must be able to relate today's event to yesterday's fact in a way that helps indicate tomorrow's meaning."

∴

When Kin Hubbard was a cub reporter, he turned in at least five news items a day. Some of them were legitimate, but his hard-hearted editor wouldn't go for one that began, "While feeling his way carefully along an ear of corn at the Gem Restaurant last night, Eugene Whipple, a steel worker with a large mustache, lost his balance and fell off his stool."

∴

The answer man on a metropolitan newspaper was stumped recently by two questions submitted by teenage readers: 1. Is it true that goats' right legs are shorter than their left legs so they can stand on hillsides? (He took a chance and answered "Nonsense!") And 2. Which way does a dog wag his tail: right to left, or left to right? (He answered, "I guess it depends on which way the wind is blowing.")

∴

One reader in Ossining wrote to inquire, "What is the average height of fences in Ossining, New York?" The answer man responded, "We decline to reply on the grounds that your address in Ossining seems to be Sing Sing Prison."

∴

H. Allen Smith recalls the time a reform mayor of Gotham initiated a big clean-up campaign. One of his stunts was to set up a special trash can in Times Square and wire it for sound. A small transmitter-receiver was hidden in the can, with an operator with a mike stationed in a window overlooking the square.

Several intrigued reporters were watching when a lady threw an old newspaper on the sidewalk. The trash can admonished her, "That's not the way to keep New York clean, lady. What's your name?" The lady shot one startled look at the can, then snapped, "I don't talk to trash cans"—and strode away.

∴

A determined lady phoned the city desk of a Des Moines paper to order her husband's name inserted in the obituary column the following morning. He was shot, she explained, when discovered in a compromising situation with his seductive secretary. "When did your poor husband pass away?" asked the city editor. Replied the caller, "He starts tomorrow."

∴

According to the author of the engaging lyrics for "Little Green Apples," it may not rain in Indianapolis in the summertime—but that didn't prevent a typographer at the local *News* plant from perpetrating a lulu there recently. The mayor of the city elected one day to inspect the trash-disposal areas. Reported the *News*: "Our mayor spent several hours checking rumps."

∴

Four memorable typographical errors ferreted out recently by *Editor and Publisher*, the news magazine of the newspaper business:

1. From a New Jersey paper: "No governor in many years has been able to love on the salary paid him."

2. From a New England daily: "An event for the ladies bound to attract many entries will be a petting and approach contest on the golf course."

3. From a Kansas journal: "Mrs. Blank was overcome by gas while taking a bath this morning, but owes her life to the watchfulness of the janitor."

4. From the woman's page of a southwestern weekly: "The spring gowns in the Paris collections are so sheer that every wearer will have to have a slap of some sort underneath them."

∴

Small-town newspapers aren't the only ones who are guilty of occasional typographical errors! Dig this item, for instance, that was printed by the august Chicago *Tribune:* "Mrs. Carlisle circulated her navel unsuccessfully among various motion picture producers." And it was none other than the New York *Daily News* that told its readers that a certain distinguished lady "made her statement as she received 'The Woman of the Rear' award."

∴

Three nuggets unearthed in the classified ad columns:

1. From Minnesota: "Adolph, please come back home. The children miss you, the lawn hasn't been mowed in three weeks, and the garden needs a worm like you. Your loving wife, Gretchen."

2. From North Dakota: "Wanted: Husband for beautiful blonde, 18. Must have income to support her in style she believes she was born to—including minks, caviar, and diamonds. Applicant please write 'Desperate Father, Box 44.'"

3. From Salt Lake City: "Live stock for sale: Mexican burro, very gentle, friendly. Can be seen at Creek Road in Union, or heard within a radius of three miles any morning from 6:00 A.M."

∴

Respectable elders in the Fort Lauderdale sector, weary of the wicked ways of local and imported hippies and pot-smokers, have approved an ordinance by the City Commission banning obscenity in books, magazines, and phonograph records. Caskie Stinnett uncovered this hilarious feature of the ordinance: it is so specific in describing acts and language that are banned that the local newspaper didn't dare to reprint it in full!

∴

An Ohio editor defines a "square" as "anyone old enough to remember when dirty jokes, books, and movies were known as dirty jokes, books, and movies."

∴

At a country club, a member came over to the owner of the city's most prosperous newspaper and told him, "Say, I owe you a vote of thanks. Your paper proved just the thing to stop my kids from raising a racket while I was trying to sleep a little longer Saturday morning." "I'm glad to hear that," boomed the publisher, highly pleased. "Which particular article or editorial did the trick?"

"Oh, it was nothing IN the paper," the member hastened to explain. "I just rolled it up and whacked them with it."

THEM AS HAS

The Very Rich

Well-brought-up young ladies in the 1870's learned their good manners from the pages of a book that is unbelievable by present-day standards. It was called *Hill's Manual of Social and Business Forms* and it has just been republished under the slightly updated title of *Never Give a Lady a Restive Horse.*

Professor Hill gave strict orders to young ladies just climbing out of bed in the morning. "Take a complete bath at once," he commanded, adding, "A simple washing out of the eyes will not do at all." In the chapter headed "Errors to be avoided," Professor Hill brooked no nonsense from male readers, either. "NEVER," he ordered, "allow butter, soup, or other food to remain on your whiskers." There are forty-one other "nevers" listed by Professor Hill, including things not to be done in hansom cabs and other horse-drawn vehicles. Unfortunately, the good professor departed this vale of tears before being up to telling us how to get in and out of those damnable undersize taxicabs.

∴

Two of New York's "beautiful people" took their maid with them when they went to New Mexico for a winter vacation. The maid soon thereafter came running to her mistress with news of their nearest neighbor's religious affiliation. "Look out for that lady," cautioned the maid. "I hear she's a Seventh Day Adventuress!"

∴

A professional fund raiser complained to Arthur Godfrey that he had ignored several letters inviting him to join this and that honorary committee. "All your mail," explained Godfrey, "was on stationery emblazoned 'From the desk of So-and-so'—and I never correspond with furniture."

∴

A bejeweled dowager's town car broke down one afternoon and, unable to spot an empty taxicab, she went home by subway for the first time in her life.

That evening she described her grim ordeal to her husband. "My dear," she exclaimed, "you have no idea how crowded those subway cars are. Why, the people are packed into them like caviar!"

∴

A strikingly beautiful debutante had an unnerving experience at a dinner party recently. Attired in an expensive, very fancy evening dress, she noticed that her entrance created a strange stir among the guests already arrived. The reason: the furniture in the drawing room was upholstered in the identical material of her costume!

On the way home that night, her escort remarked, "I've never seen you so lively before! You were hopping about like a kangaroo." "I had no choice," she admitted ruefully. "If I remained still, I was afraid somebody would sit on me!"

∴

In the last years of his life, showman Billy Rose's proudest possession was a small island off the shore of Connecticut, where he imported a weird assortment of ostriches, snakes, and other wildlife that terrorized houseguests. One day a wild turkey suddenly attacked the bantam-sized Mr. Rose and sent him fleeing for the sanctuary of the kitchen. As he scurried into the doorway, Rose turned on the turkey and snarled, "The next time we meet, you so-and-so, there'll be a plate of cranberry sauce beside you!"

∴

A wealthy manufacturer regarded the young man pleading for his daughter's hand with deep suspicion. "I wonder," he mused, "if you'd be so anxious to marry my Rosalie if I didn't have a penny?" "I think I'd love her twice as much," vowed the suitor fervently. "Get out," cried the manufacturer. "We've got enough idiots in this family already!"

∴

Cleveland Amory tells a story of the time when Newport, Rhode Island, was the summer mecca of high society. An elegant gentleman and his wife were lounging on the beach when an unfortunate who had ventured too far out in the surf suddenly began to shout "*Sauvez moi! Sauvez moi!*" "That fellow," pronounced the elegant gentleman, "is either a Frenchman or a snob." While the two of them debated the proposition, the shouts ceased, for the swimmer obligingly drowned.

⁂

In his absorbing book *The Founding Father*, author Richard Whalen tells this revealing story about Joseph P. Kennedy, multimillionaire father of the late President Kennedy. In Joe Kennedy's final year at Harvard, in 1911, the precommencement festivities were highlighted by the traditional Harvard-Yale baseball game. Kennedy was on the Harvard squad, but when the ninth inning of this game rolled around, had not yet gotten into the line-up. Unless he did, he would not win his coveted "H." Aware of this, the Harvard captain, Charles McLaughlin, gave Kennedy a break. Harvard had the game sewed up, so with Yale down to its last batter in the ninth inning, McLaughlin installed Kennedy at first base to help rack up the final out and thus win his letter.

The Yale batter hit a routine grounder and was out at first. Captain McLaughlin, in accordance with time-honored protocol, wanted the ball for his trophy room, but young Kennedy blandly refused to give it to him.

"I made the put-out, didn't I?" pointed out Kennedy—and stuck the ball into his pocket.

⁂

Truman Capote, aboard film tycoon Sam Spiegel's sumptuous yacht, swears he heard the genial host tap a Palm Beach banker friend on the arm and propose, "Fifty thousand dollars for your thoughts!"

⁂

In the cabin of Frank Sinatra's luxury cruiser is a wooden plaque that quotes these words of a former boat owner who has learned by experience: "A boat is a hole in the water surrounded by wood into which one pours money."

∴

The late Lucius Beebe was fond of a story concerning an imperious Pittsburgh steel baron of the old school who booked passage on a liner bound for the Caribbean. The master suite proved too confining for his lordship, so he had it summarily enlarged by knocking out all adjacent partitions and converting half the deck into his private domain. The impromptu carpentry so weakened the structure of the already aging vessel that it sank on the way back to New York.

∴

In circulation there's a delectable tale about one of those well-heeled scalawags who like to cheat the United States Customs Service. This particular culprit was a vulgar, very rich dowager with three daughters who, in the course of a European tour with them, acquired three valuable old tapestries. Determined to pay no duty on the tapestries, she hired a dressmaker at considerable expense and had them made into three bulky dresses, which she insisted her daughters must wear the day they landed in New York. The girls protested bitterly, because they looked frightful in the dresses, but mama won out. Furthermore, her stratagem worked brilliantly.

At least she thought it had. Back home, she discovered that there IS no duty on old tapestries!

∴

In home construction circles they're still telling the story of the newly crowned king of finance who was showing his ultramodern push-button country home to a friend. "Here's the neatest gadget of the lot," he exulted. "After a night on the town, I sometimes feel like stepping into a nice hot bath right here without the trouble of going to the bathroom. I just press this little button. . . ."

He pressed the button and in rolled the bathtub, full of nice hot water—and the king of finance's wife.

∴

Chung Foo Wong was the perfect Chinese houseboy in every respect but one: he could not seem to remember to knock on the door before entering a room. As a result he had embarrassed his comely employer time and again by barging into her boudoir when she was in various stages of undress.

She finally threatened him with instant dismissal if ever again he repeated his offense—and a whole month went by without one intrusion by Chung Foo. "See?" beamed his employer. "It's easy enough to respect my privacy if you only put your mind to it. How have you remembered?" "Velly simple," answered Chung Foo. "Before me come in, me look thlough keyhole. If missie no dlessed, me no come in."

∴

The son of wealthy parents, dining with his mother just before graduating ceremonies at his college assembly hall, begged her please not to interfere when he sallied forth into the business world. "Remember, Mom," he cautioned her, "I'm determined to become the boss's son on my own."

∴

One of the country's leading insurance salesmen finally has solved the years' old mystery of the disappearance of a beautiful, fragile chair, a priceless eighteenth-century antique from France, from the drawing room of a wealthy old socialite.

Said socialite had asked her insurance agency to send out its brightest young man to talk to her about a new policy, and our hero won the assignment. While waiting nervously for her in the parlor, he plunked himself onto the delicate antique and shattered it into a hundred pieces. Horrified at the thought of facing the bereft owner, he hastily gathered up the priceless fragments and pitched them into the fire smoldering in the parlor grate.

When her ladyship entered the room, she nodded approvingly, and commented, "That's the first decent fire my fool butler has whipped up all winter," and, her weary bones thawed out by the blaze, allowed herself to be talked into the biggest policy ever written up by the agency. The young salesman dates his sensational rise from that day—and now, thirty years later, feels it's safe to divulge the details.

∴

Freddie Brisson knows a boulevardier who took out a ravishing American debutante in Paris and kept her out until the oui hours of the morning.

∴

Another of his rakish intimates was escorting a girl in Hollywood when they drove by a revival meeting where a bearded evangelist was exhorting onlookers, "Repent, ye sinners, repent!" The reprobate nudged his companion slyly and murmured, "I'm game if you are, baby—but let's do it in style. How about the repenthouse at the Beverly Hilton?"

∴

"There are no such things as decorum and good manners in society any longer," wailed a Boston hostess recently. "At my last dinner party, one of my guests launched forth on a decidedly off-color story and I told him he could just get his hat and leave my house."

"Good for you," enthused her even more straitlaced friend. "What happened?"

"All my other guests went with him," wailed the hostess, "to hear the rest of the story."

∴

Junior was extremely clever at appearing in the parlor at the very moment his older sister was about to embark on a heavy petting party with her current boyfriend. The favorite of the moment, hoping to win the little pest's indulgence, asked him one evening, "Hector, what do you want for Christmas?" Hector answered promptly, "I wanna watch."

So they let him.

∴

A very rich lady, widely known for her penury, called up a New York real estate agent recently and said she had decided to move. "What I need," she went on, "is a rent-controlled apartment of eight or nine large rooms with four baths; on either Fifth or Park Avenue; and I'm perfectly willing to pay up to three hundred dollars a month if you find a place I want."

There was a dead silence on the agent's end of the phone, and the lady finally demanded, "Are you looking through your files?" "Not exactly," admitted the agent. "We're just removing your name from them."

∴

"Daughter," commanded a father sternly, "I want you home tonight by eleven o'clock." "But, Father," she protested, "I'm no longer a child." "Precisely," nodded father. "That's why I want you home by eleven."

∴

On the late financier Bernie Baruch's ninety-fifth birthday, an insensitive reporter asked him, "Mr. Baruch, do you think there's as much love in the world today as there was years back?" "Of course there is," was Baruch's unhesitating reply, "but there's another bunch doing it!"

∴

Mr. and Mrs. Hubbard's sixteen-year-old daughter was out at her first dinner dance, and when her escort hadn't brought her home by 11 P.M., they were frantic. They knew the dance was being hosted by a lady named Jones, but there were fourteen Joneses listed in the phone book so they scarcely knew where to begin. They chose one Jones at random and dialed the number. A lady answered. "Pardon me," said Mrs. Hubbard, "but might you be the Mrs. Jones who is giving a party this evening for teenagers?" "I am not," was the decisive reply. "I am the Mrs. Jones who was taking a bath two flights up when you called."

∴

A snooty, irritating wife of a brand-new millionaire had bored all the other ladies at a dinner party with tales of her wondrous new jewels, furs, gowns, town house, etc., etc., but finally she gave the hostess an opening. "How many bathrooms have you in this quaint little place?" she asked. Snapped the hostess, "We can seat eleven."

∴

One of those newly rich conglomerate wizards with an income of about a million dollars a month bought himself a co-op apartment on Fifth Avenue. Six months after he took possession, he opened the door of what he had thought was a coat closet and found nine rooms he didn't know he had.

∴

A party of society folk decided to do a bit of slumming one evening recently and had their Rolls deposit them at the corner of Delancey Street and the Bowery. "I presume," one lady in the party remarked to a newsboy stationed there, "that we are now in the authentic Lower East Side." "Well, one thing I'll tell you, lady," answered the newsboy, "Marlboro Country it ain't."

SOUL SUPPORT

Religion

The gentle art of press agentry goes all the way back to the days of the Old Testament—if this story can be believed. It seems that Moses' crack publicity man—on the edge of the Red Sea—urged him to build a bridge across so his people could escape the wrath of the Egyptians. "We haven't time for that," demurred Moses. "Instead, I figure I'll order the Red Sea to part and just lead my folks across. How does that notion strike you?"

The press agent, visibly impressed, told Moses, "You do that, Moses, and I'll guarantee you at least two full pages in the Old Testament."

∴

An inveterate pickpocket finally breathed his last, and prostrated himself before St. Peter, craving admission through the Pearly Gates. St. Peter heard him through courteously, but then decreed, "It's Hades for you, my boy—and meanwhile, kindly give me back my watch."

∴

A survivor of the Johnstown Flood who had told the story—with trimmings of his own added from time to time—to a thousand bored relatives and friends over the years, finally died of old age and went to Heaven. Settled there, St. Peter stopped by to ask if everything came up to expectations. "It's great," was the enthusiastic response, "but I'd sure like to tell some of these angels about the Johnstown Flood!"

St. Peter obligingly assembled an audience for the old boy, and just before the recital began, he whispered in his ear, "I think I'd better warn you: Noah is in your audience."

∴

"And what," inquired the kindly Sunday School teacher, "do we learn from the story of Jonah and the whale?" "We learn," maintained little Ronald, "that people make whales sick."

∴

A distinguished biblical scholar is positive that what one of the Three Wise Men in Bethlehem really said was, "When we announce this, can you imagine what it's going to do to Christmas week business in the theater?"

⁘

Of all definitions of eternity ever attempted, CBS's Philip Sterling prefers this one by an old Baptist minister: "Brethren and sisters, if a single sparrow hopped from the Atlantic Ocean to the Pacific Ocean, one hop a day, with a single drop of water in his bill, and then hopped back at the same speed and kept this up until all the water in the Atlantic Ocean was in the Pacific Ocean, then, brethren and sisters, then it would be only daybreak in eternity."

⁘

Henry Cadbury, the Quaker biblical authority, tells about the small boy who, when asked which story in the Bible he liked best, replied, "That one about the multitude—you know, the multitude that loafs and fishes."

⁘

Supreme Court Justice Tom Clark tells about a lady who was a paragon of virtue on earth, but upon her death, was dismayed to find herself ticketed for Hell. She phoned St. Peter, who begged her to be patient, because Heaven was temporarily so overbooked he couldn't make room for her.

Two weeks later she buzzed St. Peter again, warning him that they were teaching her to drink, and smoke. Patience and fortitude, counseled St. Peter; he would soon be able to accommodate her—but not just yet.

A fortnight later, the paragon of virtue made a final call: "Hi there, Pete? FORGET IT!"

∴

An elderly sinner renounced the world and sought sanctuary at a Trappist monastery, though he was warned by the Master of Novices he couldn't speak for five solid years—and then would be permitted only two words. At the end of the five years he reappeared before the Master and spoke his two words: "Hard beds!" Another five years drifted by, and now his two words were "Terrible food." At the end of the third five-year period, he announced, "I quit." "It's about time," nodded the Master of Novices. "All the time you've been here, you've done nothing but complain!"

∴

A Long Island church has installed a big TV set so that members of the flock can follow Sunday professional football encounters. One Sunday, a wife told a business associate seeking to contact her husband by phone, "He's at church." "Goodness," exclaimed the associate. "I didn't realize he's that religious." "Oh, yes," said the wife. "He's a devout Jet fan."

∴

Herbert Tarr, author of *For Heaven's Sake*, received a letter from a Long Islander stating that her church was in a hopeless financial mess. "We've tried bingo games, grab-bags, box socials, benefit movie openings—everything," she complained. "Can't you suggest something, no matter how drastic, to keep our church afloat?" Mr. Tarr answered, "Try religion."

∴

Kelly Fordyce has encountered a church sexton who appreciates a bad pun when he hears one. "This job of mine is a push-over," he explains. "All I have to do is mind my keys and pews."

∴

A firm believer in seat belts, a Mr. Koshland of the Southampton Koshlands drove to church one recent Sunday morning, jammed into the one remaining space in the parking lot, hurriedly unbuckled his belt, stepped out of his car—and his pants fell off.

∴

A handsome but bashful young man from the Bible Belt was recently hired by a firm of certified accountants. Shortly thereafter, he reported to the office manager, "I must tell you that some of the young ladies in your employ are tempting me sorely." "Stand firm, young man," the startled manager told him, resisting a smile, "and you'll get your reward in Heaven."

A week later the young man was back. "It's that beautiful redhead, sir! She's pursuing me relentlessly. I don't think I can resist her—but if I do, what do you think my reward will be in Heaven?" The office manager informed him, "A bale of hay, you jackass!"

∴

Ten-year-old Ralph was instructed to escort his sister Rosalie, two years his junior, to Sunday School, and each was given a dime to contribute to the library fund. Back home, Ralph was asked if all had gone according to plan. "I gave my dime, all right," reported Ralph, "but Rosalie couldn't give hers. She swallowed it."

∴

A reader from Lamar, Maryland, sends in a story of a cordially detested old harpy who finally gave up the ghost after snarling at everybody in town for eighty years. Just as the funeral services ended a sudden storm blew up. There was a blinding flash of lightning followed by a terrific clap of thunder. From the group of soaked mourners came a voice: "Waal, she's GOT there!"

∴

The distinguished Arkansan, Brooks Hays, told of the new preacher assigned to a piddling backwoods church. His first sermon, condemning horse racing, fell flat as a pancake. A deacon admonished him, "You reckless young fool, this area is noted for its fine horses and many members of this very congregation earn their livelihood in the sport of kings." The next week, the new preacher enlarged upon the evils of smoking only to incur the wrath of tobacco growers thereabouts. And the third Sunday, when he ranted about the evils of whiskey drinking, he discovered there was a big distillery less than five miles from his church.

Frustrated, he wailed, "What CAN I preach about here?" "Preach agin them heathen witch doctors," advised the deacon. "There ain't one of them within a thousand miles of us!"

∴

Young Rabbi Shmool finally summoned courage to complain to the richest member of his congregation, "I hesitate to bring this up, but do you always fall asleep while I'm preaching?" "Look," was the consoling reply. "Would I sleep if I didn't trust you?"

∴

A favorite story in church circles when our parents were young concerned a young pastor who had dabbled with the theater before entering divinity school, and wanted to give his first sermon in a new church a dramatic send-off. Noticing that there was a scuttle in the roof above the pulpit, he deliberately chose as his text "The Holy Ghost descended in the form of a dove," then arranged to have the sexton open the scuttle at just the right moment, releasing a white dove which the pastor had trained to light on his shoulder.

On the evening of the service, he led carefully up to his climax, dramatically intoning, "And the Holy Ghost descended in the form of a dove"—but nothing happened. Louder—and angrily—he repeated his text—with which the scuttle door opened slightly and the voice of the sexton was heard by the whole congregation wheezing, "Your Reverence, the cat ate up the Holy Ghost. Shall I let down the cat?"

∴

The Rev. Martin hired for himself a sleek young secretary who just had resigned from a job at the Pentagon. She promptly relabeled the two baskets on Dr. Martin's desk "Sacred" and "Top Sacred."

∴

A minister, anxious to please a new parishioner, enthused, "What a lovely place you've fixed up here, Mrs. Cooper! And in such a few days, too! But what is that I see in that stunning vase atop the TV set?" "My husband's ashes," explained Mrs.

Cooper. Overcome with embarrassment, the minister stammered, "But nobody told me Mr. Cooper had passed away." "He hasn't," said Mrs. Cooper grimly. "He's just too lazy to look for an ashtray."

∴

Dr. Leo Green tells about an architect who promised to build a badly needed new auditorium for the church if he could be allowed to keep the construction plans a secret until the inaugural ceremonies. A record crowd turned up for the opening. The preacher, scheduled as usual to speak only until noon, was, as usual, just getting warmed up when he should have signed off.

But that's when the new plan became operative. At 12:03 sharp, a trap door opened, the preacher dropped into the basement, and the happy congregation went home to Sunday dinner.

∴

Mr. Logan found himself trapped with the nine-year-old son of his minister, Dr. Glenn, and to kill time asked the lad, "Does your father ever preach the same sermon twice?" "Does he ever," was the emphatic reply, "but my pop has what it takes. He hollers in different places!"

∴

We don't know what it was, but down on earth, hard-drinking, two-fisted legal light Gallagher must have done something right, for when he breathed his last, he was admitted forthwith within the Pearly Gates. Unfortunately, though he searched high and low, he couldn't find a single old companion on the premises, and soon became so bored that he wangled a weekend pass to the nether regions.

Down below he found countless convivials, and was treated

to a series of wonderful parties in air-conditioned halls, with tempting victuals and beautiful girls. Heaven seemed more dreary than ever after these activities, so he got a pass for the next weekend, too, and had an even more exhilarating two days in Hell.

The third week he decided to move to Hades for good. "Here's your exit visa," a heavenly attendant told him, "but I hope you realize you never, never can come back here again." "Who wants to?" taunted Gallagher—but this time, after entering the gates of Hell, he found himself enveloped in flames, with four nasty devils prodding him unmercifully with their pitchforks. "How come?" he wailed piteously, "that you torment me this way, when the last two times I was here you treated me magnificently?"

"Ah," chuckled one of the devils. "The last two times you were here you were a TOURIST."

∴

The daughter of a famous clergyman, according to one of Adlai Stevenson's favorite stories, was busy with her crayons one day when her mother paused to ask whose picture she was drawing. "God," she replied.

"But, my dear," remonstrated the mother, "nobody knows how God looks." Totally undiscouraged, the daughter answered, "They will when I'm finished."

∴

Father Kelly, a golfer of sorts, was 160 yards from the seventh green, and was advised by his caddy to use a number three iron. "I believe I can make it with a four," insisted the good father—but his ball landed woefully short in a deep sand pit. "Confound it," grumbled Father Kelly, "I guess the good Lord didn't hear me."

"He probably heard you all right," conceded the caddy, "but in my church when we pray we keep our heads down."

∴

A conscientious minister decided to get acquainted with a new family in his congregation, and called on them one spring evening. After his knock on the door, a lilting voice from within called out, "Is that you, Angel?" "No," replied the minister, "but I'm from the same department."

∴

Elmer Engstrom tells of the country parson who decided to buy himself a horse. The dealer assured him that the one he selected was a perfect choice. "This here horse," he said, "has lived all his life in a religious atmosphere. So remember that he'll never start if you order 'giddyap.' You've got to say, 'Praise the Lord.' Likewise, a 'whoa' will never make him stop. You've got to say, 'Amen.'"

Thus forewarned, the parson paid for the horse, mounted him, and with a cheery "Praise the Lord" sent him cantering off in the direction of the parson's parish. Suddenly, however, he noticed that the road ahead had been washed out, leaving a chasm two hundred yards deep. In a panic, he forgot his instructions, and cried "Whoa" in vain several times. The horse just cantered on. At the very last moment he remembered to cry "Amen"—and the horse stopped short at the very brink of the chasm. Alas! That's when the parson, out of force of habit, murmured fervently, "Praise the Lord"—and bingo! Into the chasm plunged rider and horse!

∴

During a sermon in Sussex, a baby started to wail and his angry mother carried him toward the exit. "Stop," commanded the minister. "Come back. Your baby isn't disturbing me a bit." To which the mother called back, "Oh, 'e ain't ain't 'e? Well, you're disturbin' 'im!"

∴

A wise old bishop in Virginia once urged a newly elected Congressman to go out in a pouring rain and cast his eyes heavenward. "It will bring a revelation to you," he predicted.

The Congressman did as bidden, and came back soaked to the skin. "Look at me," he wailed. "I didn't get any revelation. I only felt like a blithering idiot."

"Not bad," chuckled the bishop. "Don't you think that was quite a revelation for a first try?"

∴

Charles Vaughan tells about a rural minister who was calling on a member of his congregation one afternoon when the young son of the house burst in holding a rat by the tail. "He's dead," he assured his mother. "We clobbered him and stamped on him till . . ." At this moment he spotted the minister and concluded in a subdued voice, "Till God called him home."

∴

When an American destroyer laid over for a weekend in Swedish waters, two praiseworthy gobs aboard decided to go to church. Unable to understand one word of Swedish, they resolved to play safe by sitting behind a solid-looking citizen and doing whatever he did.

In the course of the service, the pastor paused to make some special announcement, whereupon the citizen leaped to his feet. The two sailors promptly did likewise, whereupon the entire congregation dissolved into a gale of laughter.

Later the sailors learned the cause of the merriment. The pastor had announced a baptism and requested the father of the baby to rise.

∴

A very wise minister surprised his congregation one sweltering midsummer Sunday morning with this announcement: "Friends, I have here in my hands a hundred-dollar sermon that lasts ten minutes, a fifty-dollar sermon that lasts twenty minutes, and a twenty-dollar sermon that lasts a full hour. We will now take up the collection and see which one I will deliver."

∴

They tell about a wise old rabbi in the heart of Russia whose advice was slavishly followed by the members of his synagogue. One morning he was cornered by a troubled follower who explained, "I invested all my savings in two hundred chickens. When I went out to the coop this morning a hundred of them had died. What should I do?"

"It is the voice of the Lord," quoth the rabbi. "Say a prayer. Then double the sales price of the chickens you have left and you will not have lost a single kopek."

But the next morning the villager was back to report, "Another fifty of my chickens perished last night."

"The ways of the Lord are sometimes mysterious," said the rabbi. "The fifty chickens that have survived are obviously the finest and most valuable of the flock. Say another prayer of thanks."

Alas! The next morning the last fifty chickens had bitten the dust. "Now what should I do?" wailed the villager.

"My son," quoth the rabbi. "I have lots more invaluable advice I could give you—but what use would that be to you? You have no more chickens!"

THE GOOD LIFE

1. *Merry Christmas!*

There's one specialist in New York who has played the role of Santa Claus for a leading department store for twelve successive years. One day, just before the holiday season opened, he came home to find his wife in tears. The couple's three little boys, aged five, six, and seven, respectively, had discovered Pop's Santa regalia in a closet, and were moping disconsolately in a corner.

"Now, don't take on this way," implored the wise father. "You boys have found my suit, and now you've got to know. Nobody lied to you when you were told there was a Santa

Claus. The only thing different is that *I* am the REAL Santa Claus."

Then Pop made his three boys happier still by appointing them his official elves!

∴

Clipped from the classified ad section of a Dayton newspaper: "Lost: my wife's charge plate. Reward—if returned AFTER Christmas."

∴

A dear, trusting little girl walked up to a department store Santa Claus and said, "Hello, Mr. Claus." Santa answered sourly, "Go way, little girl. I'm not on till the afternoon shift."

∴

Another department store Santa Claus steadfastly refused to take off his beard when the holidays were over. When he still sported it at the opening of the baseball season, the boss finally said, "Unless you give me a sound reason for keeping that thing on, you're fired." "Well, for one thing," admitted Santa reluctantly, "if I take it off, I'm afraid I'll look too much like my picture at the post office."

.:

Gordon Comay reports that he was wandering through the toy department of a big store one day during the holiday rush when the loudspeaker announced: "Mrs. Arthur Jones reports that her seven-year-old son, Spike, has been lost. Will Spike Jones please come immediately to the manager's office?" A small boy inspecting an electric train display alongside Mr. Comay was visibly depressed by this announcement.

"Damn it," he grumbled, "I'm lost again!"

.:

The gardenia-adorned floorwalker of a Detroit store discovered another yuletime juvenile standing near an escalator with his eyes glued upon the moving handrail. "Something wrong, sonny?" asked the floorwalker. "Nothing to worry about," the boy assured him. "I'm just waiting for my chewing gum to come back."

.:

Intent upon buying himself a gift ball-point pen, a holiday shopper tested several brands by writing "*E Pluribus Unum*" with them on a scratch pad. Finally, the impatient temporary clerk behind the counter produced another tray of pens and suggested, "Maybe one of these will satisfy you, Mr. Unum."

.:

A Broadwayite with a predilection for practical jokes came up with one a month before Christmas that worked out very nicely for him. He phoned the secretaries of every one of his male friends and told them, "I've got to have your boss's collar size before the day is over." The secretaries not only got him the required information, but advised their bosses, "So-and-so is obviously going to send you some fine shirts for Christmas, so you'd better buy him something, too." The Broadwayite thus ended up with a lot of pretty good loot. As for his friends—well, each one at Christmas time received a card reading, "Here's wishing a happy holiday to the grandest guy who ever wore a size sixteen [or whatever size the secretary had divulged] collar."

∴

From the Wolf Envelope Company comes this touching story of a father, designated "dead letter man" in a post office, who had been sorrowful and withdrawn from his family since the sudden death of his young son. Then, at Christmas time there fell into his hands this letter, addressed to Santa Claus by his little daughter:

> Dear Santa Claus:
>
> We are very sad at our house this year, and I don't want you to bring me anything. My little brother went to heaven last spring. All I want you to do when you come to our house is to take Brother's toys to him. I'll leave them in the corner by the kitchen stove; his hobby-horse and train and everything. I know he'll be lost up in heaven without them, most of all his horse; he always liked riding it so much, so you must take them to him, please, and you needn't mind leaving me anything but if you could give Daddy something that would make him like he used to be, make him smoke his pipe again and tell me stories, I do wish you would. I heard him say to Mummie once that only Eternity could cure him. Could you bring him some of that, and I will be your good little girl.
>
> *Marian*

2. *Artists and Models*

A young artist embraced his undraped model ardently and murmured, "You're the first model I ever kissed since I took up painting!" "How many models have you had?" panted the suspicious object of his affections. "Four," said the artist. "An apple, an orange, a cauliflower—and you!"

∴

One of the year's best cartoons was drawn by Ruge and appeared in the *Saturday Review*. It showed a young lad hopelessly entangled in one of those sculptural pieces hacked out of old window sashes, scrap iron, and aluminum foil in a modern art museum. The caption has the lad's mother frantically imploring him, "Bertram! Get out of that masterpiece this instant!"

∴

Merle Haas has just added to her art collection a watercolor that she describes as "an authentic masterpiece." It is, too. It's signed "By Pablo Masterpiece."

∴

Jim Fosburgh, distinguished artist, encountered an old moonshiner in the Tennessee hills whose profile fascinated him. "I'll give you twenty-five dollars," proposed Fosburgh, "if you'll let me paint you." When the moonshiner hemmed and hawed, he added, "Remember: twenty-five dollars is a lot of money." "There hain't no question 'bout the money," the moonshiner told him earnestly. "I was jist wonderin' how I git the paint off afterward."

∴

An artist whose paintings are attracting more and more attention these days specializes in landscapes of wild storms at sea, oncoming hurricanes, and the like. A young female student came to his one-man show in Cleveland recently, recognized him from the newspaper pictures, and came over to tell him, "I think you're wonderful—but what a shame you've had such rotten luck with the weather!"

∴

An art connoisseur made the mistake of taking a prominent contender for the world's heavyweight boxing title to a show of Picasso paintings recently. A reporter, astounded to see the prize fighter in an art gallery, asked him, "Do you mean to say you appreciate pictures like this?" "Coitinly not," replied the indignant pug. "I don't even know where I am!"

3. *Loud Speakers*

A fancy and huge dinner party was given in the grand ballroom of the Waldorf Astoria in honor of a visiting dignitary who, unfortunately, when called upon to speak, pulled a thick manuscript out of his pocket and began to read it in a dull and interminable monotone.

The M.C. could do nothing about guests at the rear tables who began sneaking through the exits, but he was really embarrassed to discover that an important guest on the dais, only two chairs down from the speaker, had fallen sound asleep. He reached over behind the speaker and hit the sleeper soundly on the head with his gavel—not once but twice. The second blow caused the sleeper to jerk his head up, and survey the scene in obvious confusion. Then he realized where he was, heard the unsuspecting speaker droning on, and pleaded in a voice that could be heard ten rows back, "Hit me again, I beg you. I CAN STILL HEAR HIM!"

∴

An old stratagem of beleaguered plutocrats trying to avoid testimonial banquets at from twenty-five to fifteen hundred dollars a plate is to send laudatory telegrams, hoping that the toastmaster will read them to the suckers in attendance. This doesn't happen, however, when George Jessel, world champion M.C., is in charge of affairs. He usually picks up the sheaf of wires at his place, tears them to shreds, and announces, "To heck with them! Let them come here and fork over fifteen hundred bucks apiece like we had to!"

(Jessel adds that there's only one sure way to stay awake during an after-dinner speech or lecture and that's to deliver it yourself.)

∴

Guests at a banquet honoring one of the leading citizens of an Oklahoma community got a surprise when the citizen's wife demanded that she be allowed to introduce him. Nor did her introduction contain usual phrases like "It is our privilege to honor tonight . . ." or "There is no need to tell this audience of the outstanding virtues and accomplishments . . ." No indeed! She simply turned to him and commanded, "Get up, Eustace!"

∴

A perennial master of ceremonies at testimonial banquets surprised and delighted one audience by taking only twelve minutes to introduce the guest of honor. It turned out later that ten pages of his speech had fallen to the floor during dinner, and the waiter had carried them off with the remnants of the main course.

∴

The shortest introduction on record, by the way, was made once by the usually verbose Jawn Charles Daly. That was the night he announced, "Our speaker this evening requires no introduction. He failed to show up."

∴

The next time some pompous, long-winded ass bores the daylights out of you going on and on pontificating at a banquet in his honor, you might care to remind him that the Declaration of Independence contains only 300 words, Lincoln's Gettysburg Address, 226, and the Lord's Prayer only 56!

∴

If you'd like some help in phrasing an introduction for the guest of honor at a banquet, Joey Adams proffers these suggestions in his *Encyclopedia of Humor:*

1. Here's the man about whom the President once said, "Who on earth is that?"

2. When our honored guest first came to this city, he was flat broke. Today he owes over three hundred dollars.

3. In his last appearance he drew a line three blocks long. Then they took his chalk away.

∴

Impressario Sol Hurok observes that people who cough incessantly never seem to go to a doctor. They go to banquets and concerts.

∴

A controversial Senator, shy of funds for his re-election campaign, did a little moonlighting as a lecturer for a few weeks after Labor Day. His first Sunday on tour, he went to church, his car flanked by motorcycle cops, security guards, and TV experts.

As he walked up the aisle of the church at the conclusion of the services, a small boy tugged at his sleeve and whispered, "Are you the guy that came with the police?" "Yes, son," chuckled the Senator, "I am."

"Well," nodded the boy, "you better duck out the side door. They're still waiting for you."

∴

Dr. Harry Fosdick told about a lecturer who built up a great reputation as an expert on child education, though he never had married himself. The title of his lecture was "Ten Commandments for Parents." Then he met the girl of his dreams, married her, and became a father. Shortly thereafter he changed the title of his talk to "Ten Hints for Parents." He was blessed with a second offspring—and his talk was relabeled "A Few Tentative Suggestions for Parents."

When his third child arrived, he quit lecturing altogether.

∴

On a somewhat disappointing lecture jaunt, Mark Twain, tired of his manager's continual beefing, exclaimed impatiently, "Yes, I know. We've had our trials and troubles—but so has everybody else. The Lord has given us both vinegar and honey, but let's always remember that He has given us the vinegar with a teaspoon, and the honey with a shovel!"

4. *Food and Drink*

A lady who simply could not resist nibbling fruit, candy, and nuts between meals finally got so fat that a desperate remedy seemed called for. She elected to paste inside her refrigerator door a cut-out of a slender, perfectly built, unclad nymph.

The reminder worked like a charm. In one month she lost eleven pounds. Unfortunately, during the same period, her husband peered inside the refrigerator so often, HE gained twelve.

∴

Milt Kamen encountered a stoutish character in a health food store who announced that he was on a new reducing diet: he only ate things that swim. "That means, I guess," ventured Kamen, "that your whole menu must consist exclusively of fish." "Not at all," countered the stoutish one. "I just teach things to swim—then I eat them."

∴

Pat Henry details the sad fate of a fat friend whose diet included a substitute for sugar. After observing this diet for two years, he died of artificial diabetes.

∴

In Leo Rosten's wildly successful *The Joys of Yiddish*, he tells of a Mr. Sokoloff, who had been dining regularly at a certain restaurant on Second Avenue, beginning each meal with a dish of chicken soup. One night Mr. Sokoloff called out to his waiter, "Come back here and taste this soup." "After twenty years," demurred the waiter, "you question the perfection of our wonderful chicken soup?" "Come back and TASTE IT," repeated Mr. Sokoloff. "All right, all right," conceded the waiter. "I'll taste it—but where's the spoon?"

"Aha!" cried Mr. Sokoloff.

∴

Overheard by Leo Rosten in Miami Beach: "Darling, you look wonderful. How have you done it?" "S-s-sh, I'll tell you a big secret. I'm having an affair." "How marvelous! Who's catering?"

∴

Sinking rapidly, old man Mandelbaum detected the aroma of strudel coming from the kitchen. "Mama's baking a strudel," he whispered eagerly to the son at his bedside. "Go out to the kitchen and tell her if there's one thing I want to do before

I go, it's to eat a piece of her wonderful strudel." The son did as he was bidden, but returned empty-handed, reporting, "Mama says it's for the folks who come in later."

∴

M. André Simon, one of the greatest experts on fine wines, sometimes goes into such ecstasies in print over a favorite vintage that his audience wonders whether he's talking about a wonderful wine or a wonderful woman. Gently emphasizing this point while introducing Monsieur Simon at a wine-tasters' festival one evening, the master of ceremonies, author Charles Morgan, read off this paragraph by Simon, "changing," he explained, "nothing but a pronoun."

"Somewhat short in the nose, she gave more than she promised—a good fault. Full of life, silky, serious, robust and elusive; refined and expanding; she left behind, as she departed, a sense of complete gratification without the least feeling of satiety."

"Really," concluded Morgan to the great amusement of the company, "what ARE you describing, M. Simon? Chateau Ausone 1909 or Cleopatra?"

∴

There's a circuit judge in Mississippi who knows exactly how he feels about whiskey and, furthermore, has the vocabulary to make his sentiments crystal clear. "If," he declares, "when you say whiskey you mean the devil's brew, the bloody monster that defiles innocence, dethrones reason, takes the bread from little children and topples men and women into the bottomless pit of degradation and despair, then certainly I am against it. BUT—if when you say whiskey you mean the oil of conversation, the brew that puts a song in our hearts and laughter on our lips, that puts the spring in an old gentleman's step on a frosty morning and pours into our treasury millions of dollars to cut down our deficit, then, fellow citizens, I am for it body and soul. That's my stand, and I will neither retreat from it nor compromise!"

.:.

A questionable character stopped a lady on Madison Avenue to solicit a contribution for a proposed home for incurable alcoholics. "Come up to my apartment this evening," suggested the lady, "and you can have my husband."

.:.

A judge glared at a drunk in the line-up and commented, "You've been popping up before me in this court regularly for over twenty years." The drunk answered, "Can I help it if you don't get promoted?"

.:.

An exhausted business executive gratefully climbed into his bed in a Washington hotel at midnight, looking forward to a solid nine-hour sleep. At 2 A.M., however, a loud banging on his door awakened him. It was a semi-coherent drunk, angrily declaring, "Thish ish my room. Get out!" It took the executive twenty minutes to get back to sleep. Once more he was awakened by the same drunk an hour later, who still claimed the room was his.

When the drunk woke him up a third time, the executive literally blew his top—but this time the drunk got in the first words. "So it's you again!" he screamed. "Damn it, are you occupying EVERY room in thish hotel?"

.:.

A man arrived at a famous North Westchester restaurant several minutes before his wife to instruct the head waiter,

"No matter what kind of soup I order, fill the tureen with martinis. My wife has a fit if I order even one little drink."

His instructions were carefully followed out, and then the head waiter was summoned once more. "I'll have some more soup," announced the flushed customer, "but this time make it extra dry."

∴

There's a bar in Las Vegas that consistently reports higher profits than a dozen just as ornate on the same street. This bar is painted silver—and drinkers can't find their change on it!

∴

A palpable loser drifted into a midtown bar and braced the proprietor for a handout. He whined that his wife was sick, his daughter didn't have a dress to graduate in, he himself was suffering from arthritis and rheumatism, and the whole family was facing eviction from their tenement flat. All the time he talked he was fiddling with a silver dollar in his hand. "Why don't you buy something with that dollar you already have?" queried the proprietor. "Not on your life," replied the loser angrily. "That's my good luck piece!"

∴

A grizzled old codger from Kentucky consumed two quarts of high-proof bourbon every day of his adult life and lived to be ninety-two. At his cremation it took three days to put out the fire.

∴

A visitor to a midtown bar ordered a manhattan. When it was placed before him, a sprig of parsley floated therein. "What's that THING in my manhattan?" he demanded angrily. The quick-thinking waiter answered spryly, "That, sir, is Central Park."

∴

A millionaire bootlegger was breathing his last—though the prohibition blight still hung heavy over the land. Summoning his favorite son, he whispered weakly, "Before I pass on, my boy, I have one last secret to divulge to you: wine may also be made from grapes."

∴

They tell one about a kindly bartender who whispered to a customer, "Don't look now, but there's a fellow walking out of here wearing your hat and overcoat."

∴

Another tapped a drinker on the arm and apologized, "Excuse me, mister, but if you're the palefaced runt who looks like a lop-eared rabbit, I'm to tell you your wife got tired of waiting and drove the car home without you."

∴

"I have finally persuaded my husband not to drink when he's the host," boasted a watchful wife. "I made him realize that once he's had a few himself, he starts bringing out the good stuff!"

∴

A prisoner at the bar was charged with being intoxicated—and it was quite obvious the charge was justified. "I note by your record," said the judge severely, "that you've been arrested for being drunk eighteen times in the past six months. Are you going to do nothing to try straightening yourself out?" "Yes, I am," pledged the prisoner. "I'm going to get me a new wife." "What good will that do?" asked the judge. "A lot," the prisoner replied. "Every time I drink, this one has me arrested."

∴

A character who obviously had barely survived a hard, hard night, stepped up to the bar at the Regency and told the bartender, "First, a couple of aspirins. And don't slam the lid of the box!"

∴

A tipsy guest accosted his hostess to inquire, "Do lemons have legs?" "Lemons with legs!" scoffed the hostess. "You must be out of your mind." "Oh, dear," sighed the guest. "In that case I'm afraid I've just squeezed your canary into my martini!" (Sick, sick, sick!)

∴

A pair of inebriated gents wobbled into a neighborhood saloon. "Give me," demanded one, "a horse's neck." Added the other (a frugal soul), "I'll take a horse's tail. No point in killing two horses."

∴

An elderly couple, visiting Florida, paused at a Miami street corner where a soap-box orator was expounding to a sparse handful of passers-by on the dread effects of the Demon Rum. "While liquor ruins your health," he thundered, "who lives in the lap of luxury? Who owns the biggest co-op, the most expensive automobile? Whose wife wears the most priceless jewelry? It's the SALOON KEEPER, my friends—prospering from your misery."

Some days later the elderly couple ran into the orator again, and thanked him for putting them on the right track. "I'm deeply gratified," he beamed, "that I've persuaded you both to stop drinking."

"We didn't mean that at all," said the elderly gent. "You see, we came down here looking for a good real estate investment. After hearing your talk, WE BOUGHT A SALOON."

∴

"No more hard liquor for me," vowed a reformed book salesman. "The last time I succumbed I was so plastered I lost my balance taking off my pants and fell head over heels." "What's so terrible about that?" deprecated his seat-mate. "Lots of people have done that."

"What?" demanded the reformed character. "In the LINCOLN TUNNEL?"

∴

Jackie Gleason is purported to have stepped up to a bar in Miami Beach's Fontainebleau Hotel and demanded a martini compounded of twenty-four parts gin, one part vermouth. The bartender, startled but game, said, "Coming up. Like a slice of lemon peel twisted in it?" Snapped Gleason, "If I want a lemonade, I'll ask for it."

∴

Enthused a lady who simply loved to cook, "I soaked my chicken all night in brandy, basted it with sherry, sprinkled it with vermouth, and put rum sauce in the dressing." "Yum,

yum," nodded her friend. "How was it?" "Believe me, Norma," declared the lady cook, "this was the first time in all my experience that a chicken ever climbed out of the oven and tried to join Alcoholics Anonymous!"

150—QUICKIES—150

—Rivals for the hard luck championship of Minnesota are Mr. A., who received a bottle of irresistible "Come and Get Me" perfume from his best girl one Monday and was drafted into the Army on Tuesday, and Mr. B., who moved to a suburb of St. Paul and was promptly run over by a Welcome Wagon.

—Herb Caen insists that conditions have become so chaotic in one midwestern community that the police department now has an unlisted telephone number.

—Bob Hope told Anita Gillette, "You sing like a canary—and your bird cage is mighty good, too."

—A little girl describing her appendectomy: "They told me it wouldn't hurt, and then they stuck a needle in my arm and I DISAPPEARED!"

—Absent-minded professor taking a shower: "Now let me see: which pocket did I put that soap in?"

—Conceded an irascible businessman: "I'll give my wife credit for one thing. She's always ready to listen to both sides of an argument—so long as it's in the next apartment."

—Paul Goetz complains that his hometown TV station owner has cut down so sharply on expenses that now even the weather reports are reruns.

—A Hollywood star, famous for his capacity for overdrinking, told his new lady love, "I've put your picture in the one spot I'm sure to see it every night: under the table."

—A harassed housewife tells about a rascal who broke into her car and pilfered thirty-five dollars worth of groceries—out of the glove compartment.

—Asked to name three great inventors, a brilliant student in Wisconsin proposed, Thomas Edison, Alexander Graham Bell, and Pat Pending.

—The wife of a young man just graduating from college admitted that his senior year was the toughest. "That's the year," she sighed, "we got an M.A., a B.A., and a B.A.B.Y.!"

—A regular patron at Shnops' bar reports that he and his girl can't seem to agree on wedding plans. "She wants a big church wedding with ushers and bridegrooms—and I just don't want to get married."

—Shed a tear for the respected doctor who squandered every cent he owned playing the horses and had to rob a bank. But none of the tellers could read his handwriting on the demand note.

—Have you heard about the sultan who left a call for seven in the morning?

—They say a key man at the Income Tax Bureau is writing a potential best seller called *How We Collected $1,800,000 from the Fellow Who Wrote a Book About Making $2,000,000 in the Stock Market.*

—Then there was the dog who went to the flea circus and stole the whole show.

—How to keep your teenage daughter out of hot water: put some dishes in it.

—An eye specialist in Kansas City has just been granted the auto license number he craved: 2020.

—A crystal gazer informed a male customer, "I see a buried treasure." "I know," nodded the customer wearily. "My wife's first husband."

—Paul Allen observes that the revolutionary fathers made it tough for actors. They only provided thirteen states where they could run for governor.

—A surgeon, reporting to an anxious wife, assured her, "The operation was a complete success, madam—until your husband fell off the table."

—The leader of a famed highland bagpipes band was asked why his aggregation always paraded while it played. His explanation: "It's harder to hit a moving target!"

—Bowlegged cowboy, completing army physical: "Well, doc, how do I stand?" Doctor: "That's what I'd like to know."

—A beautiful but slightly discombobulated young woman stormed into police headquarters to inquire, "Where do I apologize for shooting my husband?"

—A maker of eyeglasses has just moved his shop to an island off Alaska, and is now known as an optical Aleutian.

—A happy vacationer, fresh out of ready cash, sent a check to a bank where he already was overdrawn with this accompanying note: "Having wonderful time. Wish you would clear."

—A New York lawyer, questioning a bank teller in a forgery case about a check allegedly signed by a Mrs. Achilles Katz, brought down the court, judge included, when he demanded, "Look at this check carefully, sir. Do you or do you not recognize the signature on the bottom of Mrs. Katz?"

—Mrs. Blanchard saw a pair of acquaintances in the lobby at an opening night and remarked to her husband, "Now THAT looks like a happily married couple." Replied Mr. Blanchard warily, "Don't be too sure, my treasure. They're probably saying the same thing about us."

—Wife to husband on their twenty-fifth wedding anniversary: "This year let's give each other sensible gifts—like neckties and sable coats."

—Joan: "Is that all there is to the story?" Edie: "I guess so. I've already told you more than I heard."

—A boastful father, defending a shiftless son, insisted that it had taken the boy only three terms to finish his first year in high school. Turned out he was referring to the terms of Dwight Eisenhower, Jack Kennedy, and Lyndon Johnson.

—Short-haired girl to long-haired lad: "Of course Daddy doesn't mind our being alone together every night. He thinks you're a girl!"

—A Cambridge tailor with a Harvard education has a sign in his window reading, "We shorten miniskirts."

—Call from a bride, just finished cooking one of her very first meals: "Dinner's ready, darling. Come and guess it."

—One wife's definition of retirement: "Twice as much husband on half as much income."

—Pat Henry is extolling a wonderful new drink: nine diet pills dissolved in a triple order of straight Jack Daniel's whiskey. "In less than a fortnight," boasts Pat, "I've lost fifteen pounds and my drivers' license."

—Did you hear about the pioneer in the Dakotas in the 1870's whose horse came to a sudden stop? Injun trouble.

—A city kid saw a peacock for the first time and exclaimed, "Look, Mom: this chicken is in bloom!"

—Dr. Cecil Doolittle claims that one section of a big Alaska city is known as Dogless. This enables the residents to insist they live in Dogless Fairbanks.

—Little Rosemary's alibi for missing school for a week was not convincing, but at least it was original. She explained to her teacher, "I had intentional flu."

—"I'm in real trouble," a little man confessed to an analyst. "I can't rid myself of the conviction that I'm a dog." "Jiminy!" exclaimed the analyst. "How long has this been going on?" The little man answered, "Since I was a puppy."

—Wally Bruner's latest dream: he met a teacher in a see-through dress and she persuaded him to join the Transparent Teachers' Association.

—Have you noticed that the perforated area of our postage stamps is stronger than the stamps themselves?

—A Hollywood starlet's explanation of why she was divorcing her husband: "After three drinks he turns into a revolting beast—and after the fourth, I pass out altogether."

—New hit song at the Mt. Kisco post office: "To each his zone."

—Elderly Texan, dictating his will, "To my no-good son I leave five million dollars—and he's mighty lucky I didn't cut him off entirely."

—Winston Churchill once was asked if he knew any professional women. He answered promptly, "I've never met any amateur ones."

—At a party, there are two kinds of people—those who want to go home early and those who want to be the last ones in the place. The trouble is they're always married to each other.

—Late September, asserts Gilbert Vail, is the time of year when the owner of a swimming pool discovers he's not as popular as he thought he was.

—In Las Vegas, the owners of the posh and crowded Caesar's Palace are very annoyed—but very—with the fresh kid who's opened an orange juice stand nearby. He's calling it Squeezer's Palace.

—A papoose strapped to his Indian mother's back leaned out of his shelter and called to another papoose being carried in similar fashion, "How's your old woman on hills?"

—Discouragement: watching your secretary yawn while typing one of your most amusing letters.

—Have you heard about the motorist who inadvertently barged into a nudist camp—and stripped his gears?

—There's one bus driver on the Madison Avenue route who has hung one of those shrunken heads over his coin box. He explains to curious passengers, "He wouldn't move to the rear of the bus."

—A convict serving a life sentence in a Wyoming jail writes

a weekly column for the prison newspaper. He calls it "Here Today, Here Tomorrow."

—The town eccentric has bought an old double-decker bus to go to drive-in movies. "I like," he explains, "to sit in the balcony."

—A lady doing her Christmas shopping asked a clerk, "What can you suggest for a man of fifty?" The clerk answered, "A girl of eighteen."

—In a radio audience-participation show in New York recently a Long Island housewife was asked by the M.C., "How do you feel about Flushing, Long Island?" She answered innocently, "I think it's a wonderful idea."

—A Dallas oil tycoon just shelled out an even two million clams to an interior decorator. He'd installed well to well carpeting.

—When a very, very fat lady barged into a midtown restaurant recently, another patron exclaimed wonderingly, "That gal has more chins than a Chinese telephone directory."

—The head of New York's auto license bureau received his first thank-you card in the mail the other day. It was from the husband of a wife he'd flunked.

—There's a dog kennel up Greenwich way that calls itself Chock Full O'Mutts.

—A bee's stinging apparatus measures less than one thirtieth of an inch. The other two feet are pure imagination.—Will Rogers

—Clayton Fritchey's brush-off of a rather pathetic politician who runs for President every four years but gets nothing but horselaughs for his efforts: "He passed out three campaign buttons—and his shirt fell off."

—"Tell me, Mr. Sussman," a doctor asked an irritable patient. "Did you wake up grouchy this morning?" "Not today," answered Mr. Sussman. "I let her sleep."

—Oldsters agree that no two children are exactly alike—especially if one is yours and the other one isn't.

—A teenager called her legion of boyfriends so steadily that when she finally got married the grateful telephone company retired her number.

—And speaking about all these marriages of high-school kids, one elderly gent of twenty swore he attended one wedding ceremony where the bridegroom wept for two hours. It seems the bride got a bigger piece of cake than he did.

—It was a wise and experienced mother who announced to a gaggle of young fry at her son's birthday party, "Now remember, kids, there will be a special prize for the little boy who goes home first."

—Buzz Wheelock claims that you can tell a man's real age by the pain he feels when he gets a new idea.

—There's an actor at the Friars Club who's given up drinking for good. Reason: he did it for the wife and kidneys.

—Dick Cavett dismisses most of those new family serials infesting TV as "the bland leading the bland."

—One of Houston's more enterprising auto dealers has a pile of small foreign cars in the center of his showroom with a sign: "Take one!"

—There's a famous publisher in New York who goes in for purple shirts, yellow ties, and magenta pants. He's in a clash by himself.

—A star fullback in Oklahoma has been an undergraduate now for eleven years. He can run and tackle like an All-American—but he can't pass.

—It was so cold in the deep South last spring, grumbles Jerry Mitchell, that six enthusiasts went out to water-ski and came back as popsicles.

—Blossoming sub-deb to an about-to-be ex-boyfriend: "Let me explain it to you this way, Myron: if our romance was on TV, I'd be switching channels."

—Notice at the counter of a car rental agency in a popular resort area: "We're Number Three. We don't try AT ALL."

—A close friend of Zsa Zsa Gabor reports that the first three words of English she ever learned were Van Cleef and Arpels.

—Al Hirt tells about a strong-minded wife who flatly refused to take the pill. Her husband had her pinched for practicing license without a medicine.

—A visitor from Edinburgh explained, "I hate always to eat and run, but the way I tip it's the only safe procedure."

—There was a good reason for Leonardo da Vinci's bad humor one morning in Italy, says Ben Ridder. He caught Mona Lisa humming, "I'll Never Smile Again."

—Lewis Young brings to mind one of Groucho Marx's asides in *Coconuts* that merits revival: "This is a gala night—and a gal a night's too much for any man."

—When an old TV star's show was canceled by the powers that be, a fan asked him, "Do you answer personally the hundreds of letters that come in every day demanding that your program be renewed?" He answered disarmingly, "Good Lord, no! I scarcely have time to write them!"

—Mike Morrisey has found a way at last to dissuade his neighbors—and their progeny—from coming over to swim in his pool. He's bought a pet shark.

—Andy Wimpfheimer spotted a woman ankling down Park Avenue with a mighty peculiar greyhound dog. It had a bus painted on its side.

—When lovely movie star Tuesday Weld wants to travel incognito, insists Ian Manson, she registers under an assumed day.

—"You'd be surprised," declares Joe E. Lewis, "how many New Year's resolutions are actually carried out—feet first."

—SHE: Did Daddy seem pleased when you told him about the thousand dollars you've saved up? FIANCE: He certainly did. He borrowed it.

—A grizzled New York taxicab driver surrendered his medallion after thirty-one years of bucking the traffic. He explained that all the fun had gone out of driving. There were too many inexperienced pedestrians.

—The wives of a progressive Indian reservation in New Mexico have taken to swapping husbands as a new weekend sport. They call it passing the buck.

—Boast of a new sunbathing pavilion in Sarasota, Florida: "We leave no stern untoned."

—There's a process server in Newark who's getting altogether too cocky to suit his cronies these days. They don't like the way he's been putting on the writs.

—A trigger-tempered boss caught an employee reading his newspaper during working hours, and barked, "When you get to the Help Wanted ads, start making notes."

—Donald O'Connor observes that when a teenager gets one of his infrequent haircuts these days, he tells the barber, "Just take off a little around the hips."

—You've got to keep your eyes open if you're a resident of Reno. A lady house owner there stepped out of a neighborhood Laundromat for less than five minutes—and somebody won her wash.

—A romantic sub-deb embraced her boyfriend passionately. "Isn't it wonderful?" she cooed in his ear. "We're just like Romeo and Juliet! My father says he's going to kill you!"

—A prominent San Diego surgeon is developing a serious inferiority complex. It's because he's always on the outside looking in.

—Following her marriage to an amorous old millionaire,

a show girl explained to her friend, "I just happened to have the combination that opened his safe: 40–26–36."

—Oscar Levant once challenged Mrs. George Kaufman, "Guess whose birthday this is." "Yours?" questioned Mrs. K. "No," replied Levant, "but you're getting warm. It's Shakespeare's!"

—A navy recruiter failed dismally in persuading a likely young prospect to sign up for submarine duty. "Thank you kindly," demurred the prospect, "but I ain't shipping out on any vessel that sinks on purpose."

—Pals of Wall Streeter Arthur Goodman claim he's now so wealthy he's hired a stooge to play golf for him.

—Years of intensive research in Rome have convinced Jimmy Schnozzola Durante that Italian women really know they're getting along in years when their shoes pinch them more than men do.

—There's a seafood place in Sheepshead Bay that advertises as "The House of Eel Repute."

—A girl in Nashville is convinced her beau in a hillbilly quartet is serious in his intentions. He gave her his guitar with no strings attached.

—One of those new far-out artists gave the most authentic one-man show of the season last month. Only one man showed up.

—Hen-pecked husband to his secretary: "Well, I got my wife the electric typewriter she's been craving. Now, if I could only find her a chair to match. . . ."

—On a TV show, Merv Griffin was asked by a guest, "Where's a good place to go if you find yourself in New York in February?" Merv's prompt reply, "Barbados."

—Joe Cook once called a friend at three o'clock in the morning to demand (in a disguised voice, of course), "Do you have running water in your apartment?" "Yes, I have. What about it?" was the angry reply. "Well," countered Cook, "put her out. She's my squaw."

—Have you heard what happened the day after the walls of

Jericho came tumbling down? Four building contractors were indicted.

—The doorman of a nobby mens' club tripped on the entrance stairway, and landed in a heap at the bottom. "Careful, you fool," cried the club manager angrily. "They'll think you're a member!"

—"His widow's distraught," relays auto-race enthusiast Cliff Mackay, "and his kids are pappyless: he drove like he thought he was at Indianappyless!"

—Lon Tinkle knows a fellow-Dallasite who's so doggone rich he has a crew of landscape artists come to his home every Monday to spray his shoe trees.

—At the end of the sixth round, a battered heavyweight staggered back to his corner. "Hey, Killer," his disgruntled manager whispered in his ear, "I gotta great idea for the next round. Hit him back!"

—Have you heard about the fellow who never worried about his marriage until he moved from Chicago to Los Angeles and discovered he still had the same milkman?

—An Adirondack guide admitted to a party he had in tow, "We're lost!" "Lost!" echoed the man who had hired him. "You told me you were the most reliable guide in the whole state of New York." "And I meant it," insisted the guide. "But I've got a distinct feeling we are now in Vermont!"

—Paul Flanagan has discovered a sure-fire way to save money. He forgets who he's borrowed it from.

—"I'd like to marry your daughter," announced a young bank clerk to the president. "That is, if you have one."

—Flash from Phyllis Diller: "A Peeping Tom just phoned, begging me to pull down my shade."

—Goody Ace, who writes just about the best comedy routines seen on television—and gets paid accordingly—has invested part of the loot in common stocks. Now, he admits, he spends a great deal of time keeping up with the Dow Joneses.

—There was a bride in Great Falls who was so suspicious of her husband-to-be that she insisted upon having male bridesmaids.

—Sign on an interurban bus in cannibal country: "Take this bus and leave the driver to us."

—Bible specialist Robert Loomis has discovered what Eve whispered to Adam just after he had bitten into the forbidden fruit: "How do you like them apples?"

—Bob Ellsworth figures that New York's new helicopter taxi service must be a big success. One flew over his house the other day with an "Off Duty" sign on it.

—A Carolina genius has perfected a new baby food that's half orange juice and half garlic. It not only makes the baby healthier, but easier to find in the dark.

—Heard about a check Howard Hughes recently made out? It was so big, the BANK bounced.

—"What," asked David Frost of a guest on his TV show, "would you like to be remembered for?" The guest answered, "Ever."

—Bob Bernstein says he's tired of arguing with his kids about borrowing the family car. So, next time he wants it, he's just going to take it.

—In mid-Manhattan a brave man named Schusser challenged, "Show me a fellow who is over the hump and I'll show you a bareback camel rider."

—When a commuter was asked by an inquiring reporter, "Now that you've moved out of the city, what do you miss the most?" the unhesitating answer was, "The morning train."

—Brenda Vaccaro notes that the woods are full of girls who refuse to pet in parked cars.

—A frugal Vermonter complains that his grandfather preserved the first dollar he earned in a ten-cent frame. Now the frame's worth a dollar and the dollar's worth a dime.

—Steve Allen encountered a hopeful suitor who dropped into a computer-dating center and registered his qualifications. He wanted someone who enjoyed water sports, liked company, favored formal attire, and was very small. The computer operated faultlessly. It sent him a penguin.

—Arthur Schulte believes that the nearest to perfection most people ever come is when filling out an employment application.

—Earl Wilson is authority for the information that an enterprising 175-pound chicken has opened a roadside tavern along a main road in South Carolina and is doing a land-office business: southern fried colonel.

—"There's one insurmountable trouble with opera," complains Peter Ustinov. "There's too much music in it!"

—A psychiatrist was puzzled by disclosures made to him by a new patient. "Is there any insanity in your family?" he demanded finally. "There must be," nodded the patient. "They keep writing me for money."

—A new hotel in Honolulu is so elegant they've even air-conditioned the steam room.

—A stranded Martian came upon two young ladies at a nudist camp. He looked them over with obvious approval, then beseeched, "Take me to your tailor!"

—A lady explained to her local postmaster that she wanted to send a goldfish to her sister in London. "Regular mail?" she was asked. "No, no," she answered. "It's got to go air mail. This fish gets seasick."

—A Broadway playboy was rejoicing over the terms of his recently granted divorce. "My ex-wife got the car, the house, and custody of the four kids," he exulted. "I didn't get stuck with anything!"

—Bill Cosby ran smack into a very fat lady on Queens Boulevard, injuring his car more than the fat lady. "I saw her all right," admits Bill, "but I just didn't have enough gas to drive around her."

—A popular ballad singer was in the middle of his ninth song at a Catskill holiday show when his agent rushed up screaming, "You're in the wrong hotel!"

—Teacher: Use "conscience stricken" in a sentence. Pupil: "Don't conscience strickens before they're hatched."

—Comedian Henny Youngman, introduced to one-time fem tennis champ Alice Marble, remarked, "That's my game, too." "Tennis?" queried Miss Marble. "No," replied Youngman. "Marbles."

—A boastful golfer on the pro tour, accused of magnifying his triumphs, explained angrily, "I'm not a liar, sir. I just remember big!"

—"I'll tell you how awful my wife's cooking is," volunteers Jim Backus. "Pygmies come clear from Africa to dip their arrows in it."

—In Greenwich Village the other night, a hippie actually stole a fire truck. Passers-by didn't make a move to restrain the hippie, surmised Bob Sylvester, because they mistook him for a Dalmatian.

—Brand-new sign outside a fortuneteller's booth on the Asbury Park boardwalk: "We guess your sex—25 cents."

—Heartwarming words spoken by a journalist at services for a departed associate: "This was a man of few acquaintances: only friends."

—And from Norway comes an encouraging word: "Don't let them get you down," cables Herb Mayes. "In this country, at least, the pun is still mightier than the fjord."

SHOW BIZ

1. *The Players*

You never know about actors, pointed out the late, great novelist John O'Hara—who definitely did! Humphrey Bogart, for instance, began on Broadway as an effete "Tennis, anyone?" actor. James Cagney and Pat O'Brien were, believe it or not, chorus boys. Dick Powell warbled his way through all those Warner Brothers musicals on the *Flirtation Walk* pattern. And Gary Cooper and John Barrymore started out as cartoonists! One never can guess at the outset of one's career where it's all going to wind up!

Many of Broadway's most glittering stars credit their first big break to a stroke of sheer luck. Take Henry Fonda, for instance. Hank, fresh out of Princeton, heard that Marc Connelly was seeking a handsome young actor to play opposite June Walker in his 1934 production of *The Farmer Takes a*

Wife. He applied for the job, and Connelly, impressed with his looks, proposed, "Sit down, young man, and I'll read you a few pages of the play." Connelly, a ham of the first water, thereupon proceeded to read the entire play HIMSELF. Fonda didn't open his mouth. At the end of the recital, Connelly, vastly pleased with his own performance, informed him, "You're just right for the part. See my manager, Max Gordon, tomorrow and demand two hundred dollars a week. Don't take a cent less."

Fonda, who had been earning a princely thirty-five dollars a week in summer stock at Cape Cod, followed instructions to the letter—and a new star was born.

.˙.

It was columnist Jack O'Brian, incidentally, who stunned Henry Fonda by advising him to drink nothing but absinthe. "Remember," counseled O'Brian, "that absinthe makes the heart grow, Fonda."

.˙.

It is the eminent drama critic Walter Kerr's profound conviction that if the star of a Broadway show is famous and popular enough, he can flaunt every centuries-old theatrical tradition—even changing the dramatist's lines or plot to suit his convenience—and get away with it.

To prove his point, Kerr cites a night at New York's Winter Garden, where Al Jolson suddenly clapped his hands in the middle of a scene and announced cheerfully, "It's eleven o'clock, folks, and if we don't get this curtain down at once the stagehands will have to be paid overtime, so whoever stole those pearls better give them right back because this show is OVER." A luscious, giggling blonde, Claire Windsor, produced the pearls—and everybody went home happy!

∴

Theatrical folk, relates Helen Hayes, appreciate the story of the lad who was such a mathematical wizard that at the age of twelve he could do calculations in his head that had stumped Albert Einstein when he was forty. Unfortunately, this prodigy was so involved in equations that he had no time for anything else. In an attempt to divert him, his parents took him to an all-star revival of *Peter Pan*—and were delighted to note that he was utterly engrossed throughout the first act.

At the intermission, his father said cheerfully, "Well, son, I see you're enjoying the play."

"Do you know?" answered the son. "There were 71,832 words in that act?"

∴

Elliott Nugent still shudders at the memory of a pre-Broadway opening of a new comedy at which, soon after the first act got underway, a drunk in the audience began to grumble, "This is the worst piece of junk I ever saw in my life." He repeated his criticism at regular intervals—a little louder each time.

At the first intermission, the outraged female star of the production screamed at the stage manager, "Why don't you throw that objectionable bum out of the theater?" "I can't miss," mourned the stage manager. "He's the producer."

∴

A lady who ran a dairy farm near New Hope, Pennsylvania, grew increasingly dissatisfied with the price she was receiving for her eggs, and finally wrote on one of them, "I got only two cents for this fine fresh egg. How much did you have to pay for it?"

Some days later she received a reply—from an actor who

had played the lead in a stark drama in nearby Trenton. "My dear madam," he wrote, "while delivering my fine speech that brought down the second act curtain last night, I received your egg for nothing."

∴

During the first intermission of an outdoor performance of *Othello*, Sir Laurence Olivier was stopped at the door to his portable dressing room by a distressed lady who wanted directions to the New Haven-bound bus. "But why," asked Sir Laurence, "aren't you staying for the remainder of the performance?" "Frankly," explained the lady, "I saw it years ago in Brooklyn in Yiddish—and it hurts me to see what it loses in translation."

∴

Maurice Dolbier remembers the unquestioned highlight of a presentation of *Hamlet* by a group of college undergraduates. It was the entrance of the Ghost—who had, as the enraptured audience immediately discovered, forgotten to take off his spectacles.

∴

That reminds me of a recent *New Yorker* cartoon on the same subject, in which Hamlet spots the Ghost and gasps incredulously, "DAD!"

∴

Groucho Marx recalls that his father loved to make bets—especially when he was betting on a sure thing. One matinee he was watching his four sons clown on the stage when the man sitting behind him sneered, "Brothers, my eye! I know they're not. They don't even LOOK alike." Marx pere wheeled about and snapped, "I happen to know they ARE brothers." "Hooey," responded the man. "I'll bet you five dollars they're not!" The father of Groucho, Chico, Harpo, and Zeppo considered the proposition gravely for several seconds, then answered, "WHAT ODDS WILL YOU GIVE ME?"

∴

Groucho claims that he made extraordinary sacrifices to collect his *Groucho Letters*, published by Simon and Schuster: he had to turn down hundreds of beautiful girls whom he formerly turned up. Two of the biggest laughs he ever earned in vaudeville, says Groucho, were, one, when Zeppo emerged from the wings to announce, "The garbage man is here," to which he replied, "Tell him we don't want any," and, two, when Chico shook hands and said, "I'd like to say good-by to your wife," to which he snapped, "Who wouldn't?"

.·.

Laurette Taylor was a wonderful actress, but, by common consent, an annual sure bet for the "Worst-Dressed Star" award. Once the head of Bergdorf Goodman, prestigious Fifth Avenue fashion center, decided to take a hand in the proceedings, and designed for her newest play a beautiful dress cut in the newest fashion. The designer awaited her entrance on the opening night in a glow of anticipation. "What a time we had with her," she admitted. "But finally we got everything just right. Wait until you see her!"

Then Laurette Taylor strode on stage—and the designer let out a gasp of horror. "My God," she mourned. "She's got the damn thing on backwards!"

.·.

In a reminiscent mood, Bob Hope recalled one of his first real parts on Broadway—in the triumphant musical *Roberta*. "I'd have worked that show for nothing (almost)," nodded Hope, "just to be able to stand in the wings and thrill to Jerome Kern's great music. And what a cast: George Murphy, Tamara, Ray Middleton, Sydney Greenstreet—and Fred MacMurray! Fred, as a matter of fact, still owes me a hat and cane from that show, which he borrowed to do a screen test for Paramount. I remember thinking at the time, 'They'll knock his brains out.' Three months later he was co-starring with Claudette Colbert in *The Gilded Lily*!"

.·.

Critic John Chapman, waxing nostalgic, harks back to the wondrous first *Music Box Revue*, unveiled by Producer Sam Harris in 1921, with a score by Irving Berlin, and a great cast that included William Collier, Florence Moore, Clark and McCullough, Miriam Hopkins, Ivy Sawyer, Wilda Bennett, Joe

Santley, and Sam Bernard. That was the show that introduced "Say It With Music" and "Everybody Step" and where Sam Bernard sighed, "I remember when a man couldn't LIFT a dollar's worth of corned beef and cabbage!"

.:.

The one and only W. C. Fields used to explain that he acquired his jarring nasal drawl when he accompanied his father selling slightly spoiled fruits and vegetables to reluctant Philadelphia housewives aboard a rickety grocery wagon pulled by a decrepit nag named White Swan. While his father was short-changing occasional buyers, young Fields would chant in a sing-song snarl a list of vegetables that never were in stock. When housewives attempted to purchase these goodies, Papa Fields would explain that his son was an unfortunate half-wit —then clout him over the ear when they were out of sight.

.:.

One of Fields' more outrageous acts was to spike the morning glass of milk of his hated rival, six-year-old Baby Leroy, with straight gin. Then when the poor kid fell sound asleep in the middle of a scene, Fields exulted, "As I always have proclaimed, the kid's no trouper."

.:.

MAE WESTICISMS.

1. There are no good girls gone wrong. There are just girls found out.

2. I always say, keep a diary and some day it will keep you.

3. When they tell me ten stage-door Johnnies are outside waiting for me, I always tell my dresser, "I'm rather tired tonight. Send two of them home."

4. Never come crawling to a man for love. He likes to get a run for his money.

∴

When Tallulah Bankhead saw the movie based on Tennessee Williams' play *Orpheus Descending*, reports novelist Merle Miller, she consoled him with, "Tenny, darling, how awful for you. They've absolutely ruined your perfectly dreadful play."

∴

At the height of her career, the ebullient Tallulah acquired a highly questionable pet, a lion cub that she was pleased to name Winston Churchill. Winston was not nearly so docile and amiable as Elsa, the star of *Born Free*. Strong men quailed when Winston bounded in for a romp. Once he almost bit off Noel Coward's left hand. Tallulah thought that Coward's shriek of alarm was decidedly inappropriate. "Don't be a spoil-sport," she jeered. "Can't you see that Winston is just teething?"

∴

Knighted on his seventieth birthday, Noel Coward was given a series of galas in England and America that overwhelmed even him. As one London scribe lovingly reported, "Sir Noel, at one of these parties, possibly just a bit weary at four in the morning, turned toward us that extraordinary piece of land-scaping which he uses for a face and actually shed a tear, while royalty stood to acclaim him."

∴

Some years ago a well-publicized Hungarian troupe visited our shores to stage a revival of Lehar's famous operetta, *The Merry Widow*. A local addition to the production staff noticed that the leading lady was having trouble with her W's in her rendition of "Witch of the Woods." "She's singing it 'Vitch of the Voods,'" he told the Hungarian director. The director, unconcerned, queried, "Vell?"

.:.

Master comedian Joe Cook used to startle audiences by rushing onstage, interrupting a tender love duet, to inquire, "Is there a Mr. and Mrs. Jones in the audience? I've got a message from your baby-sitter. She wants to know where the fire extinguisher is."

.:.

Once there was a petite lady star who was supposed to suggest to her suitor, "Come, let us retire and seek a cozy nook." Alas, one evening she had a few too many before show time, and the way her invitation came out THIS night was, "Come, let us retire and seek a nosey cook."

.:.

According to Oscar Levant, Oscar Wilde once wrote a story, although Levant doesn't tell where, about an actor who was starring in a theater in which a fire broke out. Wishing to show anew what a consummate actor he was, he strode to the front of the stage and demanded silence. "Be calm," he ordered. "Everybody return quietly to your seats. Everything will be all right." He delivered these words with such authority that the entire audience obeyed him implicitly—and moments later were burned to death.

.:.

Sometimes dreams are better when they don't come true. Take a dream of Barbra Streisand's, for instance. "I always dreamed of a penthouse, right?" she grumbled to interviewer Rex Reed. "So now I'm a big star I got one and it's not much fun. I used

to dream about terraces, now I gotta spend $500 just to convert mine from summer to winter. Let me tell you, it's just as dirty with soot up there on the twenty-second floor as it is down there on the bottom."

Poor Barbra!

∴

An overenthusiastic booking agent sold a new crooner to an Adirondack resort proprietor for his Fourth of July weekend on the promise that he was "another Frank Sinatra." On July tenth, the agent called the proprietor again to tell him he just had signed up "another Sammy Davis." "All right," agreed the proprietor. "Send him up at once. We just fired Sinatra."

∴

An actor in the very low echelons beseeched his agent to find him a part—any part, anywhere—before he starved to death. The agent finally got him a small part in a stock company presentation in Butler, Pennsylvania, and wired him to report on Monday morning. The actor jubilantly wired back, "Butler, O. K." The agent replied, "Not Butler, O. K.; Butler, Pa."

∴

George Burns tells about a pair of veteran vaudevillians who realized a lifelong dream in the twilight of their careers. They were booked at the famous Palace Theater in New York! On the same bill with them was the great matinee idol, John Barrymore. They approached Barrymore diffidently after the Monday matinee, and invited him to have a drink with them. "Not today," Barrymore begged off. "I've lost my mother and I'm desolate."

"We know just how you feel," sympathized the female member of the team. "We just lost our trunk."

∴

The annual Christmas playlet was the order of the day at a fashionable private school and the coach chose an amiable, beautifully brought-up boy of seven to essay the role of the innkeeper at Bethlehem. He had trouble learning to turn away Mary and Joseph with a curt "There is no room at the inn," but had his part down pat by the end of the rehearsal period. Then came the big night, with his proud mother and father beaming at him from the first row of the orchestra. He boomed out his "There is no room at the inn" with great authority—but then he couldn't resist adding, "but come in, anyhow, and have some cookies and milk."

2. *The Playwrights*

John Barrymore was a recognized authority on Shakespeare, and frequently delivered lectures on the plays and career of the "bard of Stratford." He had just concluded one such talk at a girls' college and asked for questions, when one girl inquired, "Considering the extreme youth of Romeo and Juliet, do you think it possible that they had any actual physical relationship?" Barrymore answered promptly, "They certainly did in the Chicago company."

∴

Incidentally, there is no truth whatever in the story that *Romeo and Juliet* was turned down flat when Shakespeare first offered it to the tight-fisted manager of the Globe Theatre. "Come now, Will," this manager is reputed to have said, "do you really think sophisticated Londoners are going to pony up two pounds to see a couple of half-baked Italian kids moon over one another?"

∴

Shakespeare usually said it first! That's the message relayed by the Cleveland Public Library, with the following quotations appended to prove the point:

A fool's paradise (*Romeo and Juliet*)
The primrose path (the same)
It smells to heaven (*Hamlet*)
Method in his madness (the same)
Something rotten in the state of Denmark (the same)
Hearts of gold (*Henry IV*)

Better part of valor (the same)
Eaten me out of house and home (the same)
More sinned against than sinning (*King Lear*)
Throw cold water on it (*Merry Wives of Windsor*)
It was Greek to me (*Julius Caesar*)
A dish fit for the gods (the same)
The milk of human kindness (*Macbeth*)
Paint the lily (*King John*)
The green-eyed monster (*Othello*)

∴

In Helen Hayes' beguiling autobiography, *On Reflection*, she tells of the memorable day in her life when a Broadway theater was named after her. She was eager to learn how her brilliant but erratic husband, playwright Charlie MacArthur, would react to the news, so she rushed into his room to ask, "How does it feel to be married to a building?" "Charlie didn't seem to mind," recalls Miss Hayes. "In fact, he paid me a great tribute. He was on his way out and he had on his hat, but now he took it off. It was a pretty important occasion that could make Charlie take off his hat in the house."

∴

Probably the greatest hit the Marx Brothers scored on Broadway was *Coconuts*, with a book by George S. Kaufman and a score by Irving Berlin. Groucho Marx and author Kaufman had many a tiff, however, while the show was in rehearsal—mainly because Groucho was always trying to slip in material of his own when Kaufman supposedly wasn't looking. One line particularly annoyed Kaufman, who pointed out that it had not gotten a single laugh when Groucho introduced it at an afternoon run-through. "How can you tell what's going to make a particular audience laugh?" reasoned Groucho. "I understand crowds laughed at Robert Fulton when he introduced his steamboat." "Not at matinees," snapped Kaufman.

.˙.

Garson Kanin recalls another day when Kaufman was directing rehearsals of a play being produced under the aegis of Max Gordon. One of the actresses obviously was wrong for the part, but Gordon wouldn't assume the task of discharging her. "You are chicken-hearted!" declared Kaufman. "I'll fire her!" He thereupon picked up a phone and dictated this telegram: "Terribly sorry have decided you do not fit role and will have to replace you. Signed: Max Gordon."

.˙.

The late Russel Crouse, known as "Buck" to the people who loved and admired him (and this included everybody who ever met him), found time between writing hit shows with Howard Lindsay to answer a letter addressed to his nonexistent secretary. It came from the Kansas City *Star* and sought for its eighty-fifth anniversary issue a one-page biography of Mr. Crouse, listing his "key accomplishments and titles currently held." Pixieish Crouse answered in part: "Russel Crouse is the typical continental boulevardier type: handsome, dashing, and a little nuts. He is about two weeks younger than St. Augustine, Florida, flies his own plane, runs the hundred-yard dash in 1 hour, 17 minutes, and plays the glockenspiel. He paints pop-art, being known in his family as Pop, and loves operettas, particularly telephone operettas. He has a summer villa in Villadephia, and employs two valets, three butlers, and one footman or chiropodist . . ."

.˙.

Abe Burrows, early in his career, not only wrote additional bits of business for a Broadway-bound musical, but appeared personally in it as well. The opening night audience was so ecstatic that nobody had to wait for the reviews to know they had a big, fat hit on their hands. Burrows, bubbling with joy, collared the producer, and demanded, "I want a star on my door—and I don't care who she is."

.:.

George Axelrod, author of *The Seven Year Itch,* immortalized on the screen by Marilyn Monroe, was idling down Sunset Boulevard in his shiny new convertible when a reckless truck-driver crashed into him and reduced his new car to an irreparable wreck. Stunned, but undefeated, Axelrod rallied to observe, "Be it ever so crumpled, there's no plate like chrome!"

.:.

Giving a new twist to the time-honored problem of how boy meets girl is a major concern of every playwright who favors comedy, and Neil Simon, fabulously successful author of *Plaza Suite, The Odd Couple,* and *Last of the Red Hot Lovers,* is no exception.

Well, here's how playwright Simon met his own charming wife, Joan. The scene was a Pennsylvania summer resort named Taimiment, where young Mr. Simon was writing special material to keep the paying guests amused in the evenings. The year was 1953, and Simon, incidentally, was performing something of the same chore that Danny Kaye and Sylvia Fine (later Mrs. Kaye) had accomplished a decade earlier. Neil Simon saw his Joan for the first time munching a sandwich, and fell in love at sight. Too shy and bemused to introduce himself, he brushed by her as casually as possible, and murmured, "What lovely earlobes!"

And some eight weeks later they were married.

.:.

A Broadway character whose sole claim to fame is that he wrote a moderate hit about twenty years ago has been boring all and sundry with the details ever since. Jerome Weidman calls him "the well-known playwrote."

∴

Richard Rodgers has found a way at last to cope with that dreaded moment—occurring, sad to say, more and more frequently these days—when the final curtain descends on the opening night of what is obviously an unmitigated disaster, and you have to drag your reluctant feet backstage to do a little heroic lying to your close friends, the perpetrators. They have stationed themselves—author, stars, director, producer—in a solid phalanx where not one of them can be bypassed and await your malarkey with a heartbreaking look of desperation in their eyes. You haven't a prayer of escaping them.

Rodgers no longer even tries. He marches up to the chief culprit, and without venturing one word of criticism or commendation of his own, assumes an attitude of extreme anxiety and inquires, "Well, what do *you* think?" Taken by surprise, the victim addressed hesitates for just a moment, and by the time he's rallied sufficiently to reply, good old Dick is halfway over for a recuperative nightcap at "21."

∴

The heroes of this story are two gray-haired Middle European playwrights who have loathed and been insanely jealous of each other for years, but who embrace each other fervently and express undying love and admiration every time they meet. At one of these meetings Playwright One reminisced, "The crowning night of my life, I guess, came when my new drama opened during World War Two, and the first night audience stood and cheered me for a full hour after the final curtain fell. Did you happen to be there, my dear friend?" "No," answered Playwright Two reflectively. "Fortunately, at the time, I was in a concentration camp."

3. *The Producers*

Jerry Stagg's biography *The Brothers Shubert* chronicles the fantastic career of two men who ruled as virtually absolute monarchs of the world of the theater for a full fifty years. In one season alone they produced thirty plays on Broadway! Yet they did not even speak to each other for many of those years, but conducted their business through intermediaries.

Gypsy Rose Lee described Brother Lee as "a cross between a wooden Indian and a hooded cobra." Actor Walter Catlett once became so incensed at Brother J.J. that he knocked him clear off a rehearsal stage into the orchestra pit. J.J., though stunned, cried out, "You can't walk out on me! I'll hold you to your contract if I go broke suing you!"

A lady once sued the Shuberts claiming she had been scalded at the hot water tap in the washroom at one of their theaters. The case was laughed out of court. The whole world knew that only cold water was on tap in a Shubert theater!

∴

Even the greatest theatrical luminaries perpetrate a classic boner on occasion. Take the time the immortal song-and-dance man, George M. Cohan, was trying out a new play called *Gamblin'* in Atlantic City (where so many Broadway-bound shows opened in those days). Mary Phillips played the feminine lead in exemplary fashion, but Cohan decided that the newcomer opposite her had no romantic appeal whatever, and replaced him for the New York premiere.

The name of the actor replaced: Clark Gable.

∴

Cohan, like many other producer-playwrights, deeply resented actors who changed his lines or bits of business after a show had settled down for a long run. One night, Cohan dropped in unexpectedly on one of his hits that had been selling out on Broadway for six months. As the final curtain fell, he charged angrily backstage and pinned this notice on the bulletin board: "Rehearsal for entire cast at eleven tomorrow—to take out improvements."

∴

Back in 1944, Billy Rose put on an elaborate revue at his newly acquired Ziegfeld Theater called *The Seven Lively Arts,* starring Beatrice Lillie and Bert Lahr, and featuring a ballet specially written for the occasion by the great Stravinsky. After the premiere, Rose cabled Stravinsky, "Ballet sensational success. Would be even greater if you will reorchestrate it." Stravinsky cabled back, "Content with sensational success."

∴

Shortly after one of producer David Merrick's rare failures closed after a disastrous tryout in Boston, he was stopped by a lady selling raffle tickets who begged, "Won't you take a chance on a turkey?" Merrick assured her sadly, "I just did."

∴

Mr. Merrick dined alone one midday at Sardi's. At the next table an actor whom Merrick had fired a few days previous sat glaring at him. His luncheon consumed, Merrick told the waiter, "I believe I'll have a bit of cheese." The actor leaned over and hissed, "With crackers or in a trap?"

∴

A young man-about-town phoned a photogenic starlet and her mother answered the phone. "Barbara doesn't live here any more," reported the mother, "and I haven't the faintest idea where you can reach her—unless you're a producer or a director."

⁂

Veteran stage producer Max Gordon warns all aspiring playwrights, "The curtain goes up and two people are out on the stage, and somebody better say something pretty darn fast!"

⁂

Producer Leland Hayward once bought a play because he heard that superb actor Laurence Olivier reading it aloud to a group and found himself profoundly moved by it. It turned out to be one of the most dismal failures of his career. "This has been a great lesson to me," he confessed on closing night. "That's what I get for letting a seven-thousand-dollar-a-week actor read a drama to me, and getting a two-hundred-dollar-a-week actor to play it!"

⁂

There's an usher in a Broadway theater that hasn't housed a hit show in three years—just a dreary succession of "turkeys"

that close after five or ten dismal performances. "I'll tell you how bad it is," volunteers this usher. "I haven't had to change my flashlight batteries since nineteen sixty-five!"

∴

A pair of octogenarians were bemoaning the decline of the Broadway theater. "I remember," cackled one, "when no man or woman who counted would dream of going to an evening performance unless they were dressed for the occasion." "I remember even further back than that," sighed the other. "I remember when the actors and actresses dressed, too!"

∴

What will end this rash of nudity that is turning so much of the theater and motion picture world into a cross between a men's stag show and a medical clinic? James Edward has an interesting theory on what will bring back clothing to the entertainment industry: unions! "Once the costume designers band together and order a producer to buy clothes for his cast, whether they are used or not," he reckons, "some entrepreneur is going to say, 'By golly, if I'm paying for costumes, I damn well want to see them.'" By that time, too, producers may discover that it's even harder to find beautiful bodies than it is to find beautiful scripts.

4. *The Critics*

Irv Kupcinet tells about the veteran vaudeville monologist who was playing gin rummy at the poolside of a Miami Beach hotel when a tough old drama critic fell out of a window six stories above. As the critic catapulted downward, he spotted the vaudevillian below and hollered, "Catch me, Sam, catch me!" "Nothing doing," Sam hollered back firmly. "Did you catch me at Loew's Granada last week?"

∴

One of the best-known criticisms of a performance of *Hamlet* appeared in the London *Standard*. It concluded, "A debate for many years has raged as to whether William Shakespeare or Sir Francis Bacon actually wrote 'Hamlet.' After last night's performance it may be determined once and for all by digging up the two graves. The one who turned over during the night was the author."

∴

Herb Caen's capsule critique of a shoddy night club offering also bears reprinting: "The two aging stars appeared in a skit in which they were purported to be married as Mr. and Mrs. Show Business. The audience threw rice, orange blossoms, and up."

∴

Before George S. Kaufman became a famous playwright on his own, he served a long hitch as drama critic for a New York newspaper—and what a lambasting he could give to a play that failed to intrigue him! Reviewing one misbegotten "comedy," he concluded, "There was scattered laughter in the rear of the theater, leading to the belief that somebody was telling jokes back there." He was no kinder to his own first play. It was called *Someone in the House*. Kaufman's two-word summary was, "There wasn't."

∴

At a beauty contest in Phoenix to select the year's new Miss Arizona, an entry from Flagstaff proved too skinny to appeal to one demanding Phoenix reporter. He wrote, "Miss Flagstaff looked like she was at half-mast."

∴

CRITICS AT LARGE:

1. Bernard Shaw, reviewing the debut of an overpublicized violinist, wrote, "Herr So-and-So last night left not only his contemporaries but his accompanist far behind."

2. Billy Rose auditioned a singer for his production of *Jumbo,* listened patiently while he butchered three songs, then remarked, quietly, "I'd like to buy back my introduction to you."

3. An impossible-to-please agent, recalls Oscar Levant, patronized a certain Broadway restaurant regularly, and was loathed by every waiter in the place—with reason. One day a headline revealed that the agent had been caught in a crooked stock promotion and clapped into jail. "Hey, hey," rejoiced one of the waiters, "I'd like to see him send the pot roast back now!"

4. When a dreadful English actress named April Something-or-other opened in a clinker that ran one consecutive performance, courtly Brooks Atkinson murmured, "Oh, to be in England now that April's here."

5. David Lardner dismissed one lugubrious "comedy" with, "The plot was designed in light vein, which speedily became varicose."

6. John Mason Brown, reviewing Tallulah Bankhead as Cleopatra: "She barged down the Nile and sank."

7. Wolcott Gibbs: "Miss Mendelssohn, as the demented governess, gave a notable display of continental acting technique, which seems to have quite a bit in common with professional wrestling."

8. *Newsweek,* slaughtering an inept dramatization of a big best-selling book, reported, "The author, as a boyhood friend of the producer, played a dirty trick on him. He told him he had talent."

Dizzy from watching a succession of "daring" foreign films made by shoestring producers, a movie critic in New York was heard to mumble, "I'm beginning to realize what a great service is being performed by all those new schools that teach you to read faster. After a short course, you can often read the foreign subtitles before the heroine gets her clothes back on."

Critic George Oppenheimer complains that the typical biographical sketches furnished in theater programs these days are not only patently dishonest, but show no imagination whatever on the part of the jaded press agents who supply the inaccurate details. What George would like to read someday is a refreshing "Miss A. went on the stage despite strong parental misgivings which were proved 100 per cent correct," or "Mr. B. is known from coast to coast for his pathetic inability to remember lines," or "Young Miss C. was largely responsible for the flop of her last play because of chronic drunkenness, but has been given this one additional chance because of the generosity of the chief investor, who is also her boyfriend."

If George Oppenheimer has his way, theater goers are once more going to save their programs and keep scrapbooks!

5. *The Circus*

A story from the Dexter Fellows archives concerns a lion tamer who advertised for an assistant. A cocky young Irishman appeared who stated confidently, "I'm your man, boss. The lion doesn't live that could raise one hackle on my skin." "Good," nodded the trainer. "I'm looking for a brave lad like you who'll stick his head in the lion's mouth. Like to have a shot at it?"

"One thing bothers me," confessed the Irish lad, paling noticeably. "What happens if the lion suddenly decides to close his mouth?"

"In that case," the trainer assured him heartily, "you can take the rest of the day off."

∴

The fat lady at the Barnum Circus confided recently, "I've cut down to six cigarettes a day: one after each meal."

∴

The circus manager took rather a dim view of the insignificant shrimp who was applying for the job of wild animal trainer. "Ain't you kind of puny for a guy what's got to keep lions, tigers, and leopards at bay?" he sneered. "That's the very secret of my success," declared the unabashed applicant. "Those animals keep waiting for me to grow bigger."

∴

A ham actor was assuring an assemblage of barflies that he came by his great talent naturally. "My mother worked in the circus for years," he boasted, "and she never once used a net." "What did she do?" asked somebody. The actor reluctantly admitted, "She sold popcorn."

6. *Night Clubs*

Prohibition was a disaster for many, but the owners of night clubs in Manhattan never had it so good, either before or since. Consider the attractions they could afford to book—all in New York, and all flourishing at the same time: The Heigh Ho Club featured the dancing of Fred and Adele Astaire, plus the warbling of Rudy Vallee. Libby Holman starred at the Lido and Beatrice Lillie at the Sutton Club. At the Fifty-fourth Street Place, Helen Morgan held forth, and Sid Silvers and Phil Baker starred at the Little Club. Joe Frisco was the stuttering host at the Back Stage and Clayton, Jackson and Durante were smashing furniture at the Club Durante. Add to all these celebrities Paul Whiteman at the Frolic and Clifton Webb at Ciro's. Even Las Vegas never has had a line-up comparable to that!

Did the mobsters participate in the ownership of these glorified speakeasies? Well, one New York assistant district attorney was all but laughed out of the state when he cautiously testified in court that he had discovered that "gunmen were reputed to have a small interest in one of the clubs."

∴

Peter Lind Hayes discovered Joe Frisco, the unpredictable night club star, standing outside his hotel one morning feeding a policeman's horse one doughnut after another. "Are you trying to make that poor horse sick?" demanded Hayes. "Not at all," answered Frisco indignantly. "I j-j-just want to see how many d-d-doughnuts he eats before he asks for a c-c-cup of coffee!"

∴

A reckless young man-about-town romanced a shapely night club hostess for some months, then gave her the air, whereupon said hostess sued him for a hundred thousand dollars for breach of promise. Conceded the young man ruefully to his lawyer, "When I make a beaut, it's a mistake!"

∴

Joe E. Lewis, greatest of the night club comics, began his career in joints owned and managed by mobsters. "At the first place I worked," recalls Lewis, "the boss used to shoot you good night."

∴

Lewis pooh-poohs doctors who urge him to stop drinking. "Never," he vows. "I know lots more old drunks than I know old doctors."

∴

There's a noisy, arrogant night club "personality" who didn't realize how thoroughly disliked he is at his golf club until the day he drove out to it alone and sought to join a group of fellow-members who were wending their way toward the first tee. "Sorry, old man," one of them assured him, "but we already have three!"

∴

Woody Allen, who has made a fortune deprecating himself, insists that he's been a hopeless student all his life. "Even in kindergarten," he mourns, "I flunked milk."

∴

Rodney Dangerfield recalls that his first engagement as a stand-up comic was in a place so far out in the woods, his act was reviewed in *Field and Stream*. Opening night the boss said, "Kid, I want to talk to you in the basement." Rod asked a waiter, "Did the boss ever summon YOU to the basement?" "Yes," was the answer. "It was the night he made me a waiter." Rod said, "What were you before—a busboy?" He said, "No, his partner."

Dangerfield claims that the neighborhood in which he matured was so tough that a sign in the post office read, "One hundred dollars reward for information leading to the arrest of ANYBODY." Further proof? They raffled off a police radio car—with two cops still sitting in it!

∴

A brassy old burlesque comic burst into his booking agent's office to exult, "Have I got a new night club act for you! It involves me, my wife, and my two beautiful daughters."

"What do you do?" asked the agent.

"Wait 'til you hear this," bubbled the actor. "First, all four of us take off our clothes. Then we start throwing cream pies in each other's faces. Then, for a finale, we dash up and down between the tables smacking the pies on all the bald heads in the audience."

"That's some act," murmured the agent, shaking his head. "What are you going to call yourselves?"

The comic answered, "The Four Aristocrats."

7. *Pics*

In the depression days of the early thirties, the upper balconies of the big Broadway movie palaces (now all torn down) proved a haven for the unemployed. For a quarter, admission could be obtained for the early morning show, and a fellow could be protected from the cold wintry wind for hours, at the same time free to boo the vaudeville acts and fall asleep during the movie.

Jack E. Leonard was one of the big-time comics who broke in during these trying times. He opened one engagement at the Paramount by striding onstage and booming, "Good morning, opponents." He then added, "I've got my eyes on you boys in the second balcony. Yesterday some bum stole an aisle!"

∴

Comic Jackie Vernon recalls that in his youth he idolized Charlie Chaplin to a point where he wrote him a long, effusive letter almost every week. He never got an answer, but religiously kept up the one-sided correspondence for ten solid years. Finally, he grew up and stopped writing. This fall—many, many years later—he finally met Chaplin in person at the Connaught Hotel in London. Chaplin pricked up his ears when he heard the name Jackie Vernon. He scratched his head thoughtfully for a moment, then brightened and remarked, "Of course, Jackie Vernon! Tell me: why did you stop writing?"

∴

Undoubtedly the most famous dog in motion-picture history is Rin Tin Tin, but the actual fact of the matter is that the real Rin Tin Tin never appeared in a single film. On his very first day in the studio, he took a dislike to the owner of the company, Jack Warner, and bit the seat out of his pants. Mr. Warner got even by banning him from the lot—and it was the SON of Rin Tin Tin who went on to fame and fortune.

∴

There was a time in the good old days in Hollywood when the Four Marx Brothers signed to star in a picture called *A Night in Casablanca* for Warner Brothers, and the Warner legal department was rash enough to demand a final script before shelling out a fortune for production costs. Groucho found this demand restrictive and wrote Warners as follows: "Dear Brothers: Since I last discussed our picture with you, I regret to state that we have made a few minor changes in the plot. In the new version, I now play Bordello, the sweetheart of Humphrey Bogart. Harpo and Chico are itinerant rugpeddlers who are weary of laying rugs and enter a monastery just for a lark. This is a good joke on them for it develops there hasn't been a lark in the place for fifteen years. Shall I continue?"

The Brothers Warner decided he didn't have to. "Just make the picture your way," they beseeched.

∴

Frank Sullivan once overheard S. L. Rothafel, the man who conceived the idea of once all-popular movie palaces like the Roxy Theater in New York, threaten to evict an insolent usher from the premises. "You wouldn't put a dog out on a miserable night like this," jeered Sullivan. "Oh, wouldn't I?" countered Rothafel, and, seizing a dog, he put him out. That's Sullivan's story, anyhow.

∴

Wilson Mizner, a confirmed practical joker, once drove a beaten-up, dilapidated jalopy up to the canopy of a super-colossal Hollywood premiere, and left it right where it would block the stream of Rolls-Royces driving up behind. "Hey, you can't leave that piece of junk here," screamed a frenzied eighth-vice-president of the picture company. "My good man," said Mizner airily, "that's your tip!"

∴

A veteran ham was boasting of the performance he had given in his latest role. "I played the part of Sitting Bull," he told his lady love of the evening, "and was so convincing that six cows asked for my autograph!"

∴

In the lush days when Hollywood was Hollywood, the famed Cecil B. De Mille was wont to invite his bachelor friends for wild weekends at his retreat in the valley. Upon arrival, the guests were provided with pajamas in various solid colors. When they came down for dinner, there was a girl for each visitor—and he got the one dressed in the same color as his pajamas. Strong men fought hard for the privilege of being invited to these widely publicized (by word of mouth) little picnics.

One famous producer returned to Beverly Hills after a ten-year absence abroad, and immediately sought out Cecil De Mille to ask, "Are you still giving those wonderful weekend parties at your place in the desert—and, if so, can I come this Friday?" De Mille assumed the look of a martyr and answered piously, "Yes—and you can come this weekend, but I have to tell you that ever since I made *King of Kings* every guest has to bring his own girl."

∴

Harry Cohn, late Mr. Big of Columbia Pictures, respected only writers and directors who refused to be bullied by him and gave back as good as they got. Writer Jo Swerling won Cohn's respect, for instance, the day Cohn screamed at him, "Your blank blank wife just drove smack into my Rolls-Royce." Swerling answered calmly, "She must have thought you were in it."

Another subordinate, aware that Cohn did not like to be reminded of the fact that he once had been a trolley car conductor in the Bronx, always could cut his tirades short by simply shouting, "Clang, Clang, Clang."

Playwright Norman Krasna was a third who never let Cohn get the better of him. (You'll find these stories, and many more like them in Bob Thomas' book *King Cohn.*) One day Cohn demanded, "Where do you think I was last night?" Krasna guessed, "Night school." Krasna, striving mightily to induce Cohn to release him from an onerous contract, achieved victory when Cohn read about this provision in Krasna's newly drawn will: "I wish to be cremated when I die, and my ashes to be thrown in Harry Cohn's face."

Cohn himself coined the phrase that might be his epitaph: "I don't have ulcers; I GIVE them!"

.˙.

Occasionally a writer comes along—like John O'Hara or Jerome Weidman—who can sit down and bang out a first-rate story or column at will. Most writers, however, can think of more ways to delay getting down to work than even a temporary kitchen maid.

They tell of one Hollywood scripter who simply had to have a job completed for Sophia Loren by the following morning. His understanding wife disconnected the phone, inserted a fresh page in his typewriter, hustled both kids off to Disneyland, and left him in sole possession of the premises.

When they returned at the tag end of day, mummsie sneaked in to see how far popsie had gotten. He hadn't done too badly. As she walked into the study, he was just polishing the last piece of their eighty-piece sterling silver dinner set.

.˙.

When Technicolor was something brand-new in Hollywood, one celebrated producer, famous for his bursts of temper as well as his occasional misuse of the English language, offered "a great big musical in dazzling color." "Remember," he would caution his technicians, "in MY picture the vanilla ice cream must look like vanilla, the chocolate like chocolate, and the strawberry like strawberry." After hearing this admonition a hundred times, the crew made a special shot in color of a bowl of luscious chocolate ice cream and ran it for the producer. There was a moment of appreciative silence—and then the producer announced ecstatically, "Mmm, STRAWBERRY!"

.˙.

When Dore Schary made *Lust for Life*, the story of Van Gogh, for MGM, he invited the late William Goetz to a preview,

Goetz being probably the foremost authority on Van Gogh and his paintings in the country. After the screening, Schary anxiously inquired, "Do you think it's commercial?" "Of course it's commercial," Goetz assured him gravely. "Everyone who owns a Van Gogh will simply have to see it."

∴

Why do revivals of the old W. C. Fields pictures draw better than ever in movie houses, and pop up time and again on television? Penelope Gilliatt thinks it's because the whole world can identify with Fields' portrayal of the perpetual, but undaunted loser—"a brilliant enemy to privilege—the muttering straight man to Life, the counterblow to a punch in the stomach."

Miss Gilliatt happily reminds up of the picture in which Fields' grocery store was flooded with molasses by Baby Leroy. Fields let the little saboteur escape in one piece and simply hung on the door of his wrecked establishment a sign reading, "Closed on account of molasses."

Fields invariably brought a well-filled martini shaker to the studio with him. He explained blithely that it was filled with pineapple juice. One day a co-star emptied the shaker and actually refilled it with undiluted pineapple juice. Mr. Fields took one swallow, recoiled in horror, and bellowed, "What rascal has been putting pineapple juice into my pineapple juice?"

∴

W. C. Fields liked to tell about his difficult childhood in Philadelphia. "One of my jobs," he prevaricated, "was working on an ice wagon. I got paid thirty-five cents a week—plus all the ice I could eat." Fields said his pa whipped him so often that until he was twelve he thought he was a dog team.

∴

Hank Grant interviewed a rising young starlet who is not exactly a paragon of neatness and order. "I wouldn't say her apartment is a pigpen," says the ever considerate Hank, "but while I was with her the phone rang—and she couldn't find it."

∴

"I looked too thin in my last picture," grumbled a petulant film star to her cameraman. "Can't you do something to make me look round?" The cameraman did something and the star slapped him in the face.

∴

Years ago at the Goldwyn studio in Beverly Hills, the inimitable Sam Goldwyn celebrated his birthday in the very middle of his filming of the Gershwin epic *Porgy and Bess.* It was a happy and competent cast, and one of the happiest thereof was Sammy Davis, Jr., giving his all to the demanding role of Sporting Life. To show his appreciation of the opportunity afforded him, Sammy presented Mr. Goldwyn with a wondrous wrist watch which gave not only the time in seconds, but the date, the phases of the moon, low and high tides, and probably traffic conditions on Sunset Boulevard.

To further please Mr. Goldwyn, the cast prepared a special rendition of "I Got Plenty of Nothin'," with added features not meant for actual filming. Sammy Davis in particular gave his all for this feature of the day's entertainment, dancing his head off, and concluding with a slide clear across the studio, landing with arms outstretched smack in front of Goldwyn.

"Do you like it, boss?" panted Sammy. Mr. Goldwyn looked carefully at the watch just presented to him and made his only comment on the performance: "IT'S TOO LONG!"

∴

A disgruntled moviegoer insists that when Hitler sent General Von Choltitz his famous telegram, "Is Paris burning?" Von Choltitz replied, "Not yet—but wait 'til they see the picture!"

∴

Believe it or not, a brassy writer who specializes in science-fiction hoopla was rendered momentarily speechless in Hollywood last week. He had submitted a script concerning a gaggle of kooky Martians that the producer thought was great—with one reservation. "This speech by the head Martian," he quibbled. "You'll have to rewrite that completely." "Why?" demanded the writer. "Because," said the producer with conviction, "no Martian would talk like that!"

∴

A young movie actor had progressed in two short years from a twenty-five-dollar-a-day extra to a point where his agent could

—and did—demand for his services a million dollars in cash for a picture, plus a cut in the profits. And yet the actor sulked on an exploitation trip to New York, and told an interviewer that success and riches had not provided the happiness he had expected. "Money! Autograph pests! Beautiful women at my feet!" he sneered. "What good is all that to me when my poor old mother still has to live in a cold-water tenement?"

∴

There's a high-powered publicity man in the Hollywood sector who is generally acknowledged to be the most compulsive liar of our time. He tells lies seemingly for the sheer pleasure of so doing—not only when it's to his material advantage to do so. That's why the late Fred Allen got such a laugh when he reported to cronies one day, "I caught So-and-so in a truth this morning!"

Another time, Fred Allen and an executive of a major TV network were exchanging idle banter at the "21" Club when they suddenly decided to track down the champion whom we are describing and see who could catch him first in a whopper. They found their prey at a prominent table in Chasen's Restaurant in Beverly Hills. He was obviously delighted to receive a phone call from Fred and the executive and exclaimed, "You just managed to catch me here. George Jessel is with me and we're going back to his office at Twentieth to work out a big deal for one of my clients." "That's funny," answered Fred Allen. "George Jessel happens to be sitting right here with us at '21.'" Completely unfazed, the publicity man chortled, "That's great. Give him my regards!"

Case closed!

∴

One of the film colony's dizzier blondes hosted a big cocktail party recently, and hired an extra girl to help serve. "Now remember," cautioned the blonde. "There'll be nothing but big wheels and VIP's present, so be careful you don't spill anything." "Trust me, dearie," soothed the extra girl. "I won't open my mouth."

∴

A successful Hollywood screenwriter, famous for his conquests of a dozen reigning stars, begged off from a dinner invitation, explaining, "I'm working on something important." The hostess, unperturbed, answered warmly, "In that case, just bring your work with you, Arthur. We'd love to have her, too."

∴

A member of the staff of one of Beverly Hills' newer luxury hotels was showing visitors the beautiful new swimming pool. "But how," asked one lady, "do you keep out the riffraff?" "Madam," was the proud reply, "in Beverly Hills the riffraff have their own swimming pools!"

8. *TV and Radio*

In Michael David Harris' engaging book about TV star and columnist Ed Sullivan's career, *Always on Sunday*, there is told the story of the day when Ed and the great Jimmy Durante rode out to Halloran General Hospital to entertain the sorely wounded war veterans there.

Durante explained in advance that he had two very remunerative radio dates scheduled for later that very day, so that he would have time to do only one number. When he actually did that number, however, the audience was so ecstatic that he grabbed the microphone and did two more complete routines.

Sullivan cried, "You were just great, Jimmy. But now you'll never make those two radio dates of yours."

"Look at the front row of the audience," Durante told him. "You'll see why I forgot all about those dates."

Ed Sullivan poked his head through the curtain and spotted two soldiers in the center divan. They each had lost an arm and were applauding happily by clapping their two remaining hands together.

⁘

Sullivan, most successful and durable M.C. in the history of television, takes a great deal of kidding for his deadpan expression and deceptive sang-froid on the air. "In Africa," avers Henny Youngman, "the cannibals in particular adore Sullivan. They're convinced he's some new kind of frozen food."

Ed's wife, Sylvia, relates that her famous husband cannot taste most food and is continually faking his compliments to chefs the world over. When he doesn't finish a dish that particularly strikes his fancy, he sometimes takes what's left with him. Friends are occasionally startled to see him remove a chicken leg from his pocket at 2 A.M. and start nibbling.

∴

Milton Berle's greatest rooter is his mother, who has devoted herself almost exclusively to promoting his career since he was a precocious brat of nine. One day she called his room at the Waldorf from the lobby. When he answered, she demanded at the top of her lungs, "Is this my talented son who's such a sensation on Broadway, MILTON BERLE?"

∴

Famous comedian Phil Harris, happily married to movie star Alice Faye for many years, boasted on a recent TV show that they rarely squabble. He added, "I DO lose my temper once in a great while when Alice forgets something really fundamental—like applauding when I come down for breakfast."

∴

Early in his career, Fred Allen played eight straight weeks in the middle of winter in the icy stretches of western Canada and came back home almost frozen to death. "One day in Manitoba," he recalled, teeth chattering, "we played five shows —and the high of the day was sixteen degrees below zero." "How did they get the customers to clear out after each show?" he was asked. "Easy," Allen growled. "They just opened the back doors and let the wolves run through."

∴

Fred Allen's mock radio feud with Jack Benny added luster to many of their programs over the years. Allen had the advantage of authoring his own material; Benny had to depend on the wit and wisdom of a whole corps of highly paid writers. In fact, as Allen put it once, "Jack Benny couldn't ad-lib a belch after a Hungarian dinner!"

One evening Jack did surprise his audience—and himself—by a spontaneous crack. Accepting a plaque for a whole raft of charity performances he had given, he commented wryly, "I really don't deserve this plaque—but on the other hand, I have arthritis, and I don't deserve that either!"

∴

Red Skelton tells about the time his high-living agent came home very, very late for dinner and was confronted by a justifiably suspicious wife, who demanded, "Where have you been so long?" The agent replied loftily, "I've been visiting my poor old mother." "Oh yeah?" jeered the wife. "She happens to be sitting right inside that next room waiting for you." The agent rallied sufficiently to pipe defiantly, "Well, who are you going to believe: me or your eyes?"

∴

Garry Moore, emphasizing the passion with which TV fans identify with their favorites, recalls that he was resting for a moment on a park bench when a little girl about five years old spotted him and squealed ecstatically, "Garry! Garry!" Moore smiled and said, "Hi, honey." Whereupon the little girl burst into tears and sobbed, "You don't even remember my name!"

∴

When accosted by wild-eyed fans, Garry Moore has become so accustomed to waving genially and hurrying on that one evening, when a strange man materialized out of a fog, poked him in the ribs, and mumbled something unintelligible, Garry slapped him on the back, and said, "You betcha, buddy." Fifty feet down the block, he suddenly realized what the stranger had said. It was "Stick 'em up!" He turned, terrified, to see the would-be holdup man running just as fast as he could, with a gun in his hand, in the opposite direction.

∴

Gene Rayburn tells about a kid in L.A. who loved television commercials. After one long, long Sunday he came to his father with a novel request, "Pop," he said, "I want bad breath."

∴

A Manhattan sage who obviously has been watching TV too assiduously, summarizes modern civilization as follows: "Our subways aren't safe, our streets aren't safe, our parks aren't safe, but under our arms and our dentures we now have complete protection."

∴

A resourceful radio announcer arranged to do a local broadcast from the city dog pound, and as listeners heard a background chorus of mournful barking by the stray dogs, they were told that if they contributed just one dollar to the pound, they not only would save one animal's life but would be presented with the dog as well.

A week later the happy director of the dog pound called up the radio announcer to tell him, "What a hit that broadcast of yours made! The dollar bills have been pouring in so fast, I've had to hire three more dogcatchers to fill the orders!"

∴

There's an ambitious broadcaster whose job it is to disseminate news and play records on the all-night shift. While hoping for a daytime slot, he remains married to a lovely little blonde who works at public relations from dawn to midnight.

"Are you happy?" the broadcaster was asked. "Of course

we're happy," was his indignant reply. "WE NEVER SEE EACH OTHER!"

∴

When a TV game master asked a lady contestant to name her favorite author, she blandly replied, "My husband." Taken aback, the game master asked, "Your HUSBAND? What does he write?" The lady answered, "Checks."

∴

John Charles Daly, drooled over by bemused females all the way from Garden City, Kansas, to Federalsburg, Maryland, came home from his broadcasting chores one hot afternoon completely bushed. As he threw his coat wearily onto a chaise longue his young daughter, arithmetic book in hand, planted a wet kiss on his fevered brow and demanded, "Hey, Pop, how do you take one quarter from one fifth?" "Honeybunch," he told her solemnly, "watch me. I'm about to do it."

∴

Mother and father were in the kitchen washing dishes while their two spoiled kids ware sprawled out in the living room watching television. Suddenly the kids heard a crash of falling dishes.

They listened eagerly for a few moments, and then the young son declared, "It was Mom." "How do you know?" his sister demanded. "Because," he explained, "she isn't saying anything."

∴

Mrs. Mandell was used to seeing antique films on the late, late TV programs, but one popped up that set a new low. "That picture was so old," she told her husband, "that we saw it together way back when you used to take me out!"

∴

Joan Rivers doesn't think her parents appreciated her when she was a kid. "On Halloween," she recalls, "they used to send me out as is." Joan herself isn't too enthusiastic about the sex-mad movies of today. "I saw one so dirty last week," she replied, "that even the couples in the balcony were watching it."

∴

Dean Martin, the most relaxed, devil-may-care star in the history of television, has come up with a new song title that holds promise of great things: "It's June in January—'Cause I'm in Australia!" "I've licked worry," confides Dean, "because I now drink moderately. In fact, I'm never without a case or two of Moderately in my dressing room."

∴

Lucille Ball, watching Dean Martin do a full hour's show on TV without a single rehearsal, marveled, "That so-and-so makes cooked spaghetti look tense!"

∴

Lou Erickson notes that there's one sure-fire way of rating a television show. Zoom in on the kids. If they're real quiet, it's a show they shouldn't be watching.

∴

Comic Bill Cosby is now one of the highest-salaried stars in TV and filmdom, and maintains that in his new commodious home he has a dining room in which he eats breakfast and a breakfast room where he eats dinner. He explains, "I'm darned if I'm going to let any room tell me where to eat what in."

∴

As if you didn't have plenty of worries enough these days, Johnny Carson lists a lot more in his amusing book *Misery Is a Blind Date* (illustrated by the peerless Whitney Darrow, Jr.). A few Carson nominations: 1. Finding out your daughter's screen test has just been sold as an army training film. 2. Buying a sports car and finding that your bucket is bigger than the bucket seat. 3. Cooking an exotic, complicated French dish for five hours and then having your husband put catsup on it.

∴

One of the penalties of being a celebrity is the daily receipt of about forty letters requesting, if not DEMANDING, handouts for a prize assortment of grafters, freeloaders, and just plain lunatics. Jack Benny received this one recently: "If you don't send me a certified check for $50,000 by return mail, I can't buy four tractors I've got an option on. And if I don't get the tractors, I'll lose my whole farm. I never miss your show on TV, and you have a kind face, so I know you'll send me the $50,000. To prove to you I'm honest, I'll be glad to send you a photograph of the four tractors."

∴

Being a TV star, grumbles news expert Dave Brinkley, also has its drawbacks. In a single week, for instance, he was called upon to ride a horse in a parade, judge a high-school beauty contest, contribute a recipe to a cookbook, cut a ribbon at an all-night laundromat, serve on the sponsoring committee of six charities he never had heard of before, and "donate 27 neckties or other personal items to 27 different so-called celebrity auctions and bazaars."

Were he a publisher, too, Mr. Brinkley might also have received at his home address fourteen bulky collections of unbelievably awful poetry—not one of which included return postage.

∴

When a film star with one of the most famous sets of measurements in Hollywood turned up for a late evening talk show on TV, her costume was so abbreviated that noone was allowed into the studio without a prescription.

MUSIC HATH CHARMS

A keen sense of appreciation and familiarity with classical music sometimes stands a traveler in good stead. Top Amnesiac Oscar Levant was once bowling along a freeway at about eighty miles an hour when a traffic cop flagged him down. "But I was humming the last movement of Beethoven's Seventh Symphony," protested Levant. "You can't possibly hum the last movement of Beethoven's Seventh Symphony and observe the legal speed limit," objected the cop. Levant thereupon sang it perfectly in its furious tempo. The cop nodded in complete agreement—and let him go.

∴

A famous singer, now retired, was the proud possessor of a powerful bass voice. One night, he reported, he had a gratifying dream: "I was in a great heavenly choir: a thousand sopranos, a thousand tenors, a thousand altos—and me the only bass.

Suddenly the conductor stopped the singing short, turned to me, and said—quite respectfully, and a bit awed, in fact—'Not quite so loud in the bass, my boy!'"

∴

The late Arturo Toscanini once played host to violinist Yehudi Menuhin. The latter was in the middle of a sonata when the maestro's private phone began to ring. Toscanini gestured to Menuhin to continue playing, picked up a pair of scissors, calmly cut the phone wire in two, then leaned back happily to continue listening to the music.

∴

They tell about a famous maestro—unquenchable lady-killer on the side—who gets an average of two hundred requests a month by mail from adoring fans begging for a lock of his hair. He graciously grants every request, too. "At this rate," warned a Philadelphia music critic, "you'll be completely bald in another year." "Not I," corrected the maestro. "My sheepdog will."

∴

A shrewd violin teacher finally found the way to make his young pupil Irving practice. "Look at it this way, Irving," he suggested. "The more you fiddle, the stronger your pitching arm will get!"

∴

Peter de Vries was disconsolate when his township abandoned its old-fashioned picnic-and-fireworks celebration of July Fourth in favor of a Tanglewood-like music festival. "All we're going to hear now," he grumbled, "is Brahms bursting in air!"

∴

Turning upon her husband, a famous song writer, after their last guest had departed, his wife announced, "I simply cannot understand why you always plant yourself down on the piano stool every time we entertain. Everybody knows you can't play a note."

"I'm aware of that fact," said her husband complacently. "And while I'm sitting there, no other damn composer can play either."

∴

Harold Dum, music specialist in Missouri, reports these lulus excerpted from tests and essays submitted by embryo musical geniuses in recent months:

1. Handel was half German, half Italian, and half English. He was rather large.

2. Music sung by two people at the same time is called a duel.

3. The most famous fugue I know of was the one between the Hatfields and the McCoys.

4. A dirge is a piece of music played at sad occasions like funerals, weddings, and so forth.

5. Gregory, who wrote all those chants, lived from 640 to 604, but I can't remember whether it was AC or DC.

∴

Peter Lind Hayes has collected a few song titles that music lovers may not be able to recall: "When I Was a Blackjack Dealer and You Were 21"; "I've Grown Accustomed to Your Face—But I Can't Stand the Rest of You"; "I'm So Miserable without You, It's Just Like Having You Around"; "I Just Can't Forget What's-Her-Name"; and "Where Are My Glasses, or I Wonder Who's Kissing Her Now."

∴

When humorist Robert Benchley liked a tune, he believed in singing it. He drove his associates crazy one whole week by chanting over and over (and he was no Sinatra!) this lugubrious refrain:

"Abe, Abe, the office boy,
Sings all day to give folks joy.
But the only songs he sings real fine
Are 'The Robert E. Levy' and 'The Lonesome Klein.'"

∴

"Singing lessons are certainly helping my daughter's voice," boasted Mr. Goodson. "She used to be heard only two apartments away. Now I'm getting complaints from a building way down near the corner."

∴

Eye-arresting ad in a musicians' trade paper published in England: "Trombone player would like to sell 28 sports jackets with one arm longer than the other."

∴

A pompous, conceited opera tenor once hired a claque to stand at the rear of the theater and applaud madly every time he polished off an aria. Everything went splendidly until the singer got a bit careless about paying his claque their promised handouts. After a solid week of non-payment, the claque got its revenge. They applauded the tenor so ecstatically he had to give ten encores—and lost his voice for a month.

∴

Jimmy Dean is acquainted with a folk singer who's having trouble with his guitar. His audiences keep breaking it over his head.

∴

There's a girl singer, featured with a popular band, who's known as "Miss Cinderella of 1970." Regularly, at the stroke of midnight, she turns into a motel.

∴

A few interesting revelations made by David Ewen in his *American Popular Songs*. . . . "Take Me Out to the Ball Game," the song classic about America's favorite sport, was written by Albert von Tilzer, who didn't see a baseball game until twenty years after he wrote the lyrics; "My Blue Heaven," one of the most successful songs about marital bliss, was written by Walter Donaldson, a bachelor; the most celebrated songs about the Southland were the work of Stephen Foster, who never set foot below the Mason-Dixon Line; and Van Alstyne's "In the Shade of the Old Apple Tree" was inspired by the composer's visit to New York's Central Park, which has no apple trees.

∴

An old lady, unused to receiving telegrams, was put into a pleasurable tizzy when the Western Union operator called to say there was a wire for her. "Is it one of those singing telegrams?" asked the old lady. "No, ma'am," said the operator. "It's just a message to be read to you." "But I've always wanted a singing telegram," protested the old lady. "Now, you just sing that wire to me or I'll report you to the supervisor."

"Okay," said the operator, with a note of resignation in her voice. "You asked for it. Here goes: Da-Da De Dum Dum-Dum: [and to the tune of "Happy Birthday"] 'Your sister Rose is dead' . . ."

∴

Jack Benny, who has raised over five million dollars at benefits for musicians and musical scholarships, plays the violin faithfully but with frequent wanderings from the correct pitch. After one of his more venturesome solos, an anguished lady exclaimed, "My God, he's lost his ear!" Ever since, Benny likes to refer to himself as "the Van Gogh of the violin."

∴

After listening to a masterly rendition on the piano by Oscar Levant of George Gershwin's "Rhapsody in Blue," an ecstatic mother demanded of Oscar, "How can I make my boy a prodigy?" "Easy," replied Oscar. "Just lie about his age."

∴

Critic Kenneth Tynan once heard Levant do "Lady, Play Your Mandolin" on the piano. It was the only truly popular song Levant ever wrote. Tynan fractured him by remarking as he struck the final note, "That's right, Oscar. Play us a medley of your hit."

∴

In a book called *The Big Bands,* George T. Simon nominates as best of the lot the star-studded aggregation batoned by Tommy Dorsey. It included drummer Buddy Rich and trumpeter Bunny Berigan, and featured two young singers who didn't do badly when they struck out for themselves: Jo Stafford and Frank Sinatra. Dorsey was not above raiding competing combos for desirable talent. In fact, one rival, Joe Marsala, once wired him, "How about giving me a job in your band so I can play in mine?"

∴

An ingenious dress designer sought to lure the fairer sex with a line of fabrics made of spun glass. He even had a theme song for his wares: "I'll Be Seeing You in All the Old Familiar Places"—but the mean old ad managers of the town's newspapers wouldn't okay his copy.

∴

Did you ever stop to realize how dangerous leading a symphony orchestra may be? Take the case of the famous French conductor, Jean Baptiste Lully, for example. One night in Paris many years ago he was waving his baton majestically when he accidentally whacked himself on the head and was carried out of the hall unconscious! Danny Klaymen, demon statistician, has figured out, however, that the odds against a mishap of this kind are over ten thousand to one, so Leonard Bernstein and Stokowski can breathe easier.

∴

Famed motion-picture producer Billy Wilder tells of the day he tried to persuade Sam Goldwyn to let him do a picture on the life of the great Russian ballet star Nijinsky. Said star unfortunately had come to a disastrous end, spending the last years of his existence in an insane asylum—convinced he was a horse.

"Now listen to me, Billy," argued Goldwyn, "if you think I'm going to invest three million dollars in a picture about a man who thinks he's a horse, you're even crazier than he is."

"We can give the story a happy ending," pleaded Wilder. "We'll have him win the Kentucky Derby!"

NINE TO FIVE

1. *Business*

A man who had made a fortune in a relatively short time was showing his new home to less fortunate friends, and after savoring to the full their expressions of wonder and delight, he chuckled and said, "But this is nothing, my friends. You should see the place my son now has across the road. Three tennis courts, fourteen master bedrooms, his own movie projection room, and an indoor ice-skating rink."

"For heaven's sake," gasped one of the party. "Your son must be doing mighty well."

"I'll say he is," agreed the proud father. "On his last report card he had three A's and two B's!"

∴

A veteran plumber was trying to convince some callow apprentices that plumbing in the old days was a lot tougher than it is today. "You boys think you work too hard?" he jeered. "When I first started in this racket they let us lay two lengths of pipe, and then they turned on the water. WE HAD TO KEEP AHEAD OF IT!"

∴

Two partners who ran a prosperous garment business hired a new model—a darling, innocent young girl with the allure of Ali McGraw. "If someone doesn't look out for that kid," predicted one of the partners, "she's going to be taken advantage of. I think it's up to us to teach her what's wrong and what's right."

"Done and done," agreed the other partner cheerfully. "You teach her what's right."

∴

If you're puzzled by the intricacies of international currency and tariff problems today, you might take comfort from a comment made by the senior partner of the Rothschild banking consortium: "Only two men understand gold and balance of payments: a director of the Bank of France and a minor clerk in the Bank of England. Unfortunately," he concluded, "they disagree."

∴

"You've got to hand it to these scientists," marveled Rappaport. "I read about one this morning who predicted that by 1972 they'll be able to heat an entire apartment building with a single lump of coal." "By 1972?" sneered Himmelburger. "I've got a landlord who's trying to do it right now!"

∴

A lady called the builder of her brand-new house in Louisville, I am advised by John Hennessy, and complained that he had done his work so sloppily that the whole shebang vibrated violently every time a train went by a full block down the street.

The builder said, "Ridiculous," and went to see for himself. "Just wait till a train comes along," the lady told him. "It nearly shakes me out of bed. It will do the same to you." The builder scoffed, so she challenged, "See what happens if YOU lie on the bed." He had just stretched himself out when the husband came home, and demanded, "What are you doing in my wife's bed?"

The poor builder quavered, "Believe it or not, I'm waiting for a train!"

∴

Andrew Carnegie, one of the richest and most ruthless of the "robber barons" at the turn of the century, began giving away some of his fortune in his later years. 2,505 Carnegie libraries accounted for only a small part of his philanthropies. One day he demanded of his accountants, "How much have I given away so far?" The accountants knew down to the last dollar: $324,-657,399 to be exact. Carnegie blinked when he heard the total, and exclaimed, "Good heavens, where did I get all that money?"

∴

A top executive told a newly hired secretary to inform Allis-Chalmers in Milwaukee he had been called suddenly out of town for an emergency and would not be able to keep a scheduled appointment. Returned to his office, he found this carbon: "Alice Chalmers, Milwaukee. Dear Alice: I'm leaving for Houston, Texas, so our date is off." Horrified, he phoned the Allis-Chalmers people and begged them not to show the letter to anybody. "Not show it to anybody!" was the answer. "It's been on the bulletin board for three days!"

∴

Eighty-year-old Banker Michels still had an eye for a pretty girl and there was a hint of excitement in his demeanor as he ushered a stunning new client into his private sanctum. Just before he closed the door, however, he whispered to his secretary, "If you hear anybody scream, it will be I!"

∴

Mr. Kilbride has a ready explanation for hating women in business. "If you treat them like men," he grumbles, "they bawl all over the place, and if you treat them like women, sooner or later your wife is going to find out about it."

∴

A storekeeper fell behind in his payments to a supplier, and, furthermore, completely ignored three increasingly sharp letters demanding payment. Finally the supplier appeared in person, waving the sheaf of unpaid bills in the storekeeper's face. The storekeeper thereupon astounded him by paying up in full without a moment's hesitation. "Why didn't you send me a check and save both of us all this unpleasantness?" demanded the supplier.

"I didn't have the cash to begin with," admitted the storekeeper, "so I copied your letters and mailed them out to the people who owed me. The results were so gratifying I held up my payments to you till I could get your complete set."

.·.

Two dilapidated bums sat idly in the sun in Battery Park. "You know why I'm here?" demanded one moodily. "I'm a failure because I never took advice from anybody." "I'm as badly off as you are," his bench-mate reminded him. "I took advice from EVERYBODY!"

.·.

There's a famous men's wear establishment on Madison Avenue that's been selling the same model suit to five generations of affluent and conservative merchants. In fact, scoffers claim there isn't a single mirror in the store—nor is one needed. They prop up one customer facing another customer.

.·.

"Where on earth are you?" a grumpy boss demanded when his secretary was not to be found at her desk. "I'm hiding," she answered coyly, still invisible. "Well, wherever you are, come out," ordered the boss. "I have a little present for you."

"I'm hiding," repeated his secretary—"in the closet just to the left of the door."

∴

A merchant brought his son for the first time to the garment center to buy a fall line of dresses, and haggled over the price of each item for a full ten minutes. On the way home, the knowing lad inquired, "Why did you work so hard to beat him down, Papa? You know as well as I do that you'll probably be unable to pay the bill."

"My boy," the father assured him. "That man is not only the salt of the earth but one of my dearest friends, and I was determined that he should get stuck for just as little as possible!"

∴

On his way out to lunch, a boss left a long, penciled draft of a confidential report on the desk of his lovely young, just hired secretary with a memo attached reading, "Please prepare for submission." When he returned to his office, the memo was back on his desk. At the bottom thereof the new secretary had written (in lipstick), "WHEN?"

∴

Steve Brenner notes that one of those phony Broadway merchandise marts plastered with signs reading "Last Few Days: Everything Must Go," has now been going out of business for so long that last week three "temporary" employees received gold watches for completing twenty-five years of service.

∴

One of those fast-talking insurance salesmen called up a wealthy prospect and gave his spiel for ten minutes straight—probably the first time he ever had gotten that far uninterrupted.

Suddenly, however, there came from the other end of the phone a series of bloodcurdling shrieks and hisses—followed by a butler's apologetic voice. "Begging your pardon, sir," said the butler, "but every time I'm not looking, the chimpanzee answers the phone."

∴

Elma Otto, who unaccountably had her life insured by a company in China, forgot to pay her premium last time round, and claims she received this reminder from headquarters: "Esteemed Policy Holder: Kindly refrain from joining illustrious ancestors while insignificant premium check reposes in purse or desk drawer, since meantime honorable family, not company, is holding the burlap."

∴

The wily owner of a mammoth department store has opened a barber shop for the young fry on the third floor and advertises haircuts for the modest sum of twenty-five cents. A tired mother who bit for the bait explained later, "The haircut was cheap enough, but to get to the shop you have to walk Junior right through the toy section!"

∴

One of the first patrons of the barber shop referred to admitted later, over a double Jack Daniels on the rocks, "I couldn't stand my boy's long hair any longer, so I dragged him with me and ordered, 'Give him a crew cut.' The barber did just that, and so help me, I found I'd been bringing up somebody else's son!"

∴

"Marvin is so forgetful," complained a sales manager to his secretary. "It's a miracle that he remembers his name. I asked him to pick me up a pack of cigarettes on his way back from lunch, but I'm not even sure he'll remember to come back himself."

Just then Marvin dashed into the office and cried, "What a break, boss! At lunch, I met old man Hess, who hasn't bought a penny's worth from us in five years and before we parted I talked him into a two-hundred-thousand-dollar order!" "What did I tell you?" sighed the sales manager. "He forgot the cigarettes."

∴

"Beware of status symbols," warns a big steel executive in an article in *Nation's Business*. "Put an expensive carpet in your office and pretty soon you'll begin to think you're as good as the carpet."

∴

The not too ambitious son of a wealthy industrialist pleaded a virus infection one day, and didn't show up for work. His father decided to pay him a surprise visit at lunchtime, and collided with a very beautiful young lady sneaking out of the sickroom. The son took a deep breath at sight of his beloved parent and murmured, "The fever seems to have left me." "Right you are," agreed the father. "I'm taking it out to dinner this evening."

∴

A young builder had just gone into business for himself and a wealthy old friend of his father told him, "To get you started right, I'm going to let you build me this ranch house. Here are the plans. Now, don't skimp on anything. I want the very best materials used. Forget the cost. Just send me the bills."

The greedy young builder wasn't satisfied with this generous gesture and instead of employing top-grade labor and buying the finest materials, he shortchanged his benefactor in every possible way. Finally the last secondhand nail had been driven into the last flimsy wall, and the builder handed over the keys and bills totaling a round seventy thousand dollars to his father's old friend. That gentleman promptly wrote out a check and handed the keys back to the builder. "That house you just built, my boy," he said with a hearty laugh, "is my present to you. It's all yours. May you live in it in happiness for the rest of your life."

.:.

Mr. Ullman angrily crumpled up the notes he had extracted that morning from the employees' suggestion box and dropped them in the wastebasket. "I wish these confounded people would be more specific," he grumbled to his secretary. "What KIND of kite? Shove WHAT? And what has Macy's window got to do with all this?"

.:.

Business briefs:

—A billing clerk had a harrowing tale to tell the analyst to whom she had been recommended. It seems she woke up regularly in the middle of the night hearing invoices.

—New office boy, handing check back to the boss: "I couldn't get this cashed, sir. I couldn't find a single place where you're unknown."

—Chairman to his Board of Directors: "Let me put it this way, gentlemen. If all of us were in the Army, three of you would be shot."

—A man in Florida believes he's ready to get a patent on the first vending machine that will really give the customer satisfaction. It groans when you kick it.

—Ollie James reports a fellow who got eighty-seven shaves from a single razor blade. He's nine years old.

—At a cocktail party for visiting buyers in the garment district, a tray of canapés was passed around. "Hey, hey," chortled one buyer. "Dinner swatches!"

—The head of one giant combine upstate is a man who believes in being ready for all contingencies. Right next to a spanking new, enormous computer is an old abacus in a glass case. The sign beside it reads, "In case of emergency, break the glass."

∴

The only elevator in an old office building got stuck halfway between the tenth and eleventh floors. The superintendent called up through the grillwork to the solitary trapped passenger, "Don't panic! I've put in a call for the elevator repairman and we'll have you out in a jiffy." Back came a tense voice: "I AM the elevator repairman."

∴

Cartoonist Hagglund depicts a man in triplicate emerging from an inner office. His explanation: "I fell into the Xerox machine." Incidentally, a brokerage house customers' man insists that he barely missed becoming a millionaire the easy way. "I bought Xerox," he mourns, "at eleven—but like a fool I sold it when I was fourteen."

∴

Walter Renden has compiled these definitions for neophytes in the jungles of Wall Street:

STOCK SPLIT: What happens to your certificates when a letter opener is improperly used.

INTERIM REPORT: A glowing dissertation on company progress between annual reports.

ANNUAL REPORT: A glib explanation of why year-end results failed to live up to interim predictions.

RIGHTS: The hard-to-find customers' men who guessed properly. The ones who served you are generally called wrongs.

POINT: What every customer does to the skyrocketing stock his broker failed to recommend.

TENDER: How your posterior feels after a sound market shellacking.

∴

An energetic boss went on an efficiency kick and tacked up signs all over the office reading "DO IT NOW." Within four hours, the cashier absconded with the money in the safe, the secretary eloped with the boss's son, the office boy threw a bottle of ink into the electric fan, and the entire office staff went off to the ball game.

∴

Early one January, a boss slapped a young assistant on the back and boomed, "I'm giving you a ten-dollar raise, Osbert —and I'm sure you know why you're getting it." "Thanks, boss. I'm surprised and gratified. And by the way, here's that tape recording of our Christmas party."

∴

Golconda was a city in India where, legend has it, everyone who passed through got rich. That's why author John Brooks ironically names his book about Wall Street in the tempestuous 1920's and 1930's *Once in Golconda.* Financial geniuses in 1928 were selling apples on street corners in 1930. Mr. Brooks's book makes you wonder whether the whole tragic script couldn't be repeated today!

Once in Golconda opens with a description of the Wall Street explosion at noon on September 16, 1920, smack in front of the marble edifice of J. P. Morgan and Company, killing thirty and injuring hundreds more. The top brass of Morgan's were fortunately closeted in a windowless office facing away from the blast. A visiting French dignitary was with them. As the echo of the explosion died away and the shower of breaking glass subsided, the dignitary asked in wonder, "Does this happen often around here?"

∴

It's about eleven times as easy to start something as it is to stop something, observes Robert Townsend in his invaluable book for business executives, *Up the Organization.* For an example, Mr. Townsend cites the case of the British, who created a civil service job in 1803 calling for a man to stand

on the Cliffs of Dover with spyglass. He was instructed to ring a bell if he saw Napoleon coming. The job was abolished in 1945.

∴

A respected efficiency expert describes a business conference as a three-times-a-week meeting of all the important members of an organization so they can talk about the essential work they would be doing if the conference had been dispensed with. Someday the phone operator who reports automatically, "Mr. So-and-so can't talk to you now; he's at a meeting," is going to get what's coming to her!

∴

Saddest story of the week concerns the rich Texan who confided to a computer dating system, "I own five thousand shares of IBM, thirty-two producing oil wells, three square blocks in downtown Dallas, and, as a matter of fact, have $130,000 in cash in my pocket right now."

So the computer mugged him.

2. *Secretaries*

In Detroit, they tell of a great big automobile tycoon, his mind always on his business, who relaxed long enough to marry his long-time and trusted executive secretary. For the first night of their wedded life he whisked her off to his hunting lodge in Wisconsin. The next morning he woke up, spotted his pretty bride, and exclaimed in horror, "My dear Miss Plunkett, what on earth are YOU doing here?"

.:.

Two weeks before her baby was born, a secretary felt the time had come to turn in her letter of resignation. This is what she wrote her boss: "Dear Slave Driver: I feel I've gotten too big for this job."

.:.

Occupational hazards: An experienced stenographer landed a decidedly remunerative job with a water works company in Pittsburgh. On her third day there, the boss dictated a letter involving a lengthy word. She interrupted to ask, "Pardon me, sir: is that all one word or is there a hydrant in between?"

.:.

Calling to take his old buddy to lunch one business day, a publisher I know very well indeed discovered that said old buddy's new secretary had much of the appeal of Tuesday Weld and Julie Christie. "When did you find HER?" demanded the publisher, consumed with envy. "And can she type?" "Not very fast," admitted Old Buddy complacently, "but I might add that she can't run very fast either."

∴

ALIBI OF THE SEASON: Dropping into the office unexpectedly a trusting wife found her husband with his miniskirted blond secretary firmly established on his lap. Without hesitation, the resourceful husband explained, "You see how terrible business is, Minnie? I've had to start studying to be a ventriloquist!"

∴

Early last January an unfortunate secretary in Oxford, Ohio, had a lot of explaining to do. Her boss decided to give each of his fifty-six best customers and friends subscriptions to *Time* as Christmas gifts, turned the job over to his secretary, and went on his merry way. December 28 he received fifty-six copies of *Time* in the mail. That's when he realized she had filled out the orders in reverse. What his customers and friends received for Christmas was a bill covering a year's subscription for HIM!

∴

A curvaceous young private secretary asked her immediate superior if she could have a week off to visit Las Vegas with a friend. "I admire your honesty," chuckled the superior, "but I think you ought to get an okay from the president of the firm for a jaunt like this. You go right in and check with him." "Oh, there will be no trouble from THAT quarter," she assured him. "You see, he's the friend I'm going with!"

∴

In a jam-packed bus a young secretary was having difficulty fishing for a quarter in her purse to pay her fare. A stalwart gent standing next to her volunteered, "May I pay your fare for you?" "Oh, no," she stammered. "I couldn't let you do that. After all, you're a total stranger." "Not really," he told her. "You've unzippered me three times."

∴

Overheard during business hours:

11:30 A.M.: "The nerve of my boss! I come in only an hour and a half late this morning—and he'd already opened all his private mail!"

1:30 P.M. (on the phone): "The boss is out to lunch now but he won't be gone long. Nobody took him."

4:15 P.M.: "Mr. K., I've taken all the criticism of my work from you I can stand. How do you spell 'quit'?"

∴

On the windy expanse before New York's famous old Flatiron Building, a comely stenog one morning clutched her hat tightly with both hands while her skirt billowed upwards in the tricky currents. When a friendly cop pointed out that she was beginning to block traffic, she nodded, and explained cheerfully, "What these gentlemen are concentrating on, officer, is twenty-four years old; what I'm hanging onto in the wind is brand-new."

∴

The boss summoned his new secretary and told her angrily, "You always must answer the phone the moment you hear it ringing." "If you say so," she agreed reluctantly. "But it seems so silly. Nine times out of ten it's for you."

.·.

A secretary's prayer:

"Dear Lord, help me to satisfy my beloved but slightly loony and unreasonable boss. Help me to have the memory of an elephant, and to be able to do six things at one time—answer four telephones, keep the boss from throwing a lighted match in a full trash basket, and take a letter that 'must go out today' and which he'll forget to sign until tomorrow.

"Help me keep my patience when he has me search for a report in the files that he finds later in his coat pocket. And, Lord, permit me not to destroy records that he'll want three days later, even though he's ordered me to get rid of them. And teach me how to say, 'He's in an important conference,' when he's watching a ball game on TV.

"And above all, Dear Lord, when I finally retire, grant me enough strength left in my weary bones to give the big lug one big sock right in the kisser. . . ."

LAW AND ORDER

1. *The Establishment*

A sinner trying desperately to evade jury duty demanded to be excused from what promised to be a long-drawn-out case because he was "prejudiced." "I took one look at that fellow's miserable face, your honor, with his shifty eyes, and decided at once that he was guilty as hell." "Get over into that jury box immediately," snapped the judge. "That's the district attorney."

∴

Fellow barristers are sympathizing with the legal eagle whose alarm clock failed to ring one morning. In his resultant rush, he seized his son's leather brief case by mistake and rushed down to represent an important client in court. When he opened the brief case, he found himself with a code book, a false mustache, a plastic dagger, and autographed pictures of Charlie Brown and Snoopy.

∴

News item in a London daily: "Lord So-and-so left the bulk of his fortune to his lawyers. If everybody did this, a lot of time would be saved."

∴

A famous trial lawyer in Virginia had just won an acquittal for his cleint in a scandalous and highly publicized case involving rape and heaven knows what else. An indignant society matron (not above elbowing her way into the courtroom every day of the trial) collared him in the corridor and shrilled, "Is there no case so low, so despicable, so outrageous that you wouldn't take it?" "That remains to be seen," answered the lawyer in equally resonant tones. "What have you been up to, madam?"

∴

Favorite cartoon department: Brian Savage's depiction of members of the country's highest court filing solemnly to their chairs while a hep page boy proclaims, "Let's hear it for the Supremes!"

∴

A distinguished Texas attorney was buttonholed at the Petroleum Club by a recent graduate from law school, who babbled, "I've got my first big case coming up before Judge X next week. Do you think it would help if I sent him a couple of bottles of fine old brandy?" "On the contrary," the older man assured him. "Judge X is the soul of honor. Such an obvious ploy would prejudice him hopelessly against you."

Some days later, the young lawyer reported, "I won! And your advice was invaluable. The brandy sure helped." "But I told you NOT to send it," spluttered the older man. "I know," beamed the victor, "but I sent it anyhow—in the name of my opponent."

∴

An actual verbal exchange in a Brooklyn courtroom, as reported by Jerome Beatty, Jr.:

Q. What is your brother-in-law's name?

A. Borofkin.

Q. What's his first name?

A. I can't remember.

Q. He's been your brother-in-law for forty-five years and you can't remember his name?

A. No, I tell you I'm too excited. (Rising from the witness chair and pointing to Borofkin.) Nathan, for God's sake, tell them your first name!

∴

A pert little old lady was being examined for jury duty in a small-town courthouse. She was asked if she knew the defense lawyer. "I do," she snapped. "He's a crook." "And the plaintiff's lawyer?" "Yes, and he's a crook, too."

At this juncture, the judge beckoned both lawyers and told them in no uncertain terms, "If either of you birds ask her if she knows me, too, I'll fine you for contempt of court."

∴

Overheard in a Milwaukee night court:

Magistrate (to a woman accused of soliciting): "Why don't you shun this life of sin and go out with some nice man?"

Answer: "I do, but every time I meet a nice young man, he arrests me."

∴

A long-drawn-out murder trial finally drew to a close, and after the judge's charge, the jury retired to deliberate. "Before we all start talking at once," proposed the very businesslike foreman, "let's have one secret vote to see how we stand." He tore some sheets on the table into strips, passed them out to his fellow jurors, and continued, "As soon as we tabulate the result, we can begin to examine the evidence." "That won't be as easy as you think," observed an elderly member of the panel. "You just tore it up."

∴

The two cops who put a sudden stop to a spirited stickball game in a downtown side street the other day weren't just sadistic spoilsports. They had just made two interesting discoveries: one, their night sticks were missing; and, two, the kids were using said night sticks for baseball bats.

∴

A motorcycle cop flagged an elderly lady on an interstate highway and asked her how come she was speeding at a steady sixty-five in a thirty-five-mile zone. "I thought I was obeying the law," she protested. "I saw several signs saying sixty-six." "Madam," explained the cop wearily, "that is the route number of this highway." "Goodness," she reacted, "how am I supposed to know that? You should have seen me back there away on route one twenty-two!"

∴

An indignant judge fined a big lug a hundred and ten dollars for turning his wife into a punching bag. "The hundred-dollar fine is justified," admitted the lug, "but why the extra ten-dollar bite?" "That," said the judge, "is the amusement tax."

∴

A family had just moved into a rather exclusive subdivision, but the mother was deeply dismayed when the neighbors showed no interest whatever. No welcome wagon, no invitations, no nothing! She was relieved, therefore, when one afternoon her youngest son, a rapscallion if ever there was one, tore into the house to report, "Mom, the lady down the road asked me my name this morning." "Goody," enthused the mother. "What did she do then?" Replied the son, "She gave it to the policeman."

∴

A famous law professor, ultimately promoted to the Supreme Court bench, will long be remembered for his concluding remarks to his senior class just before the holidays. "Remember, gentlemen," he cautioned, "if she gives her consent but is under eighteen, it's rape. If she's over eighteen but does not give her consent, it's still rape. But if she's *over* eighteen and gives her consent—gentlemen, I wish you a Merry Christmas and a Happy New Year!"

∴

During a severe rainstorm, a distressed householder called the police and implored, "Come and rescue me quick! I'm standing in two feet of water." "Sorry," the police lieutenant told him, "but in this state, two feet of water do not constitute a flood emergency." "You don't understand," wailed the householder. "I'm calling from the third floor."

∴

A storekeeper, sunning himself in the doorway of his shop, watched a policeman, checking parking meters, stop at one car not too close to the curb, pull a dime out of his pocket, and carefully deposit it in the meter. "I saw you do that, officer," called out the storekeeper, "and I want to tell you I never knew a New York cop would be that considerate." "Considerate, my eye," grumbled the cop. "This happens to be my wife's car."

∴

A man who had never before been in a courtroom was subpoenaed as a witness in an accident case. Asked to tell what he had seen, he noted that his every word was being taken down by the court stenographer. He talked faster and faster, and the stenographer was having all he could do to get all the words down. Finally the witness stopped short—and complained to the stenographer, "Hey, stop writing so fast, will you? I can't keep up with you!"

2. *The Rebels*

A couple of dropouts were watching the overelaborate funeral of a notorious mobster. "But the hearse is empty. Where's the body?" inquired one of the dropouts. The other, infinitely more knowing, answered, "In the trunk, of course."

∴

A yegg high on the police "criminal wanted" list finally was tracked down and given a merciless grilling at headquarters. "Did you get anywhere?" asked the captain when it was over. "Nowhere, sir," regretted the inquisitor. "We browbeat him, and questioned him without a pause for a full hour. All the bum did was doze off mumbling, 'Yes, dear, you're perfectly right!'"

⁂

Lew Nichols tells of the bandit who had worked too long for a catalogue house. He telephoned a local bank and announced, "This is a stick-up. Mail me five thousand dollars."

⁂

In New York City there are several well-kept homes where young ladies from out of town can live within reasonable means. One night the sergeant in charge of the desk at the local police precinct received a frantic phone call from one of these Adamless Edens.

"There's a police officer wanted here," a voice gasped. "A burglar's trapped in one of the dormitories by some of the girls."

Noting down the address, the sergeant asked who was calling.

"It's me," was the anguished reply. "The burglar."

.:.

A retired banker heard someone prowling around the ground floor of his Florida beach house late one night, and caught him red-handed stashing loot into a burlap bag. "I'm not going to turn you over to the police," he assured the frightened culprit. "I just want you to come upstairs and meet my wife. She's been looking for you for the past twenty years."

.:.

A prisoner facing a ten-year sentence ran into a streak of extra bad luck shortly after he had been incarcerated in jail. First, he had to have his tonsils removed, then his teeth extracted, and finally had his right arm cut off in a nasty accident in the machine shop. To cap it all, the warden dropped into the infirmary to tell him, "You're not fooling me, Briggs. You're just trying to escape from here piece by piece!"

.:.

The owner of one of New York's oldest judo and karate schools is closing up shop next month. His excuse: "Our neighborhood is getting so full of muggers my instructors are afraid to come to work any more."

.:.

A desperado, fearless everywhere except in his own home, was finally collared by the cops and sent up the river for a twenty-year stretch. After twelve solid years of confinement, he effected his escape. The TV gave the details, and newspaper bulletins were rushed out to police everywhere.

The desperado finally wormed his way to his own apartment and rang the bell. His wife answered, glared at him, and demanded, "Where've you been, you good-for-nothing bum? You escaped four hours ago!"

∴

"Why," demanded an insurance agent of a lady claimant, "did you not report the robbery at once? Surely you suspected something when you came home and found every drawer opened, with the contents scattered all over the room." "Of course I suspected something," she nodded. "I suspected that my husband, as usual, had been looking for a clean shirt."

∴

A prison publication in New England announced a shake-up in the editorial staff, as follows: "The former editor of this magazine has reluctantly resigned. He was paroled. But we are fortunate to have back with us the previous editor, who has just become available for the next fifteen years."

∴

An actress who had received a magnificent diamond necklace as a gift from her admirer—one of those Greek shipping magnates—hit upon what she thought was a foolproof device for safeguarding it. She simply left it conspicuously open on her dressing table when she went out with a note nearby reading, "This is just an imitation, dear burglar. The original is stashed carefully away in my safe-deposit box."

One night, however, she returned to find the necklace gone. In its place was this penciled message: "Thanks, lady—the substitute is just what I wanted. I'm a substitute myself. The burglar who usually cases this hotel is away on vacation."

.·.

A salesman peddling unlisted Canadian oil stocks tried to high-pressure a girl who had just attained stardom into investing heavily in his portfolio. She insisted she'd have to think the matter over. Three days later she phoned him and said, "I've decided to buy twenty thousand dollars worth of your stock." "You're too late," he told her bitterly. "I'm already in jail."

.·.

Hy Gardner recalls a 1970 edition of Sir Walter Raleigh who gallantly offered his seat to a pretty girl in a subway train—only to get thrown into the jug for his pains. The new Sir Walter had failed to take three facts into consideration: one, it was three o'clock in the morning; two, the entire car was empty except for himself and the girl; and three, the girl turned out to be a policewoman.

.·.

Bill Kennedy reports an awkward moment in the life of a fine Los Angeles policeman. An expectant mother miscalculated the time it took to get to the hospital, and the husband frantically called for help from the taxicab. The good cop responded, delivered the baby, then knew enough to give the new-born babe a sound spank. The baby responded with the desired holler. Whereupon the father cried, "POLICE BRUTALITY!"

.·.

A murderer in Taipai was about to pay the penalty and grumbled to his guard that his last meal was not the traditional sumptuous one. "You're the only poor fish being hanged tomorrow morning," apologized the guard. "When there are two or more, we add egg rolls and barbecued ribs."

⁖

Ex-California Representative J. Arthur Younger tells about a stray who wandered into a federal office building and asked if it was headquarters for the war against poverty. "It is," said the lady at the entrance desk. "Good," nodded the stray. "I surrender."

PHYSICIAN, HEAL THYSELF!

1. *Doctors*

Dr. Bill Cahan recalls a day when he was an intern, and had vaccinated a kid from a very tough neighborhood. When he reached out to put a Band-Aid over the vaccination spot, the kid demurred: HE wanted it plastered on the OTHER arm. "But, son," said Dr. Cahan, "the Band-Aid's for the sore spot so the other boys won't hit you there." "Put it on the other arm, Doctor," the kid insisted. "You don't know those guys!"

∴

"Well, Doctor," asked the applicant for a life insurance policy, "how do I stand?" "Darned if I know," admitted the doctor. "It's a miracle!"

∴

A man about to undergo serious throat surgery received a call, designed to cheer him, from a friend who just had survived a similar operation. The message: "You haven't got a thing to worry about. . . . This is a recording."

∴

A mental patient complained so bitterly about severe stomach pains that the doctor finally decided to operate—and inside the poor fellow he found a bouquet of American Beauty roses. "Now, how in heck did those flowers get in there?" he exclaimed. "Darned if I know," said the patient. "Let's look at the card and see who they're from."

∴

A young lady who did very well for herself serving as first assistant in a children's nursery school was feeling distinctly under the weather and went to her doctor for a checkup. At its conclusion he shook her hand warmly and told her, "My dear, you are about to go into business for yourself."

∴

Two ladies were conversing on a hotel verandah. "Our doctor gave my poor uncle Sam ten pills to take, four hours apart," mourned one, "but after taking only four of them, he died." "Terrible, terrible," agreed the friend, "but just think what might have happened to him if he'd taken all ten of them!"

∴

"You're sicker than you think," a doctor warned an ailing candy manufacturer, "and I want you to go right to the hospital in an ambulance. I'll meet you there as soon as I get rid of another patient." The doctor made it to the hospital just in time to see the ambulance drive up—but instead of the sick man climbing out, it was his wife. "Didn't you realize this ambulance was for your husband?" asked the doctor. "I tried to tell her," broke in the husband, who had just come tottering on the scene, "but one word led to another, and, as usual, I came on the bus."

∴

Do you remember the story of the resourceful doctor who named his house Consultation so his nurse could tell his patients, "Dr. Schmaltz can't see you this afternoon. He's out on Consultation?" Well, it's now proposed that the good doctor acquire a dog named Physician, so that, when subjecting the pooch to an obedience test, he can command, "Physician, heel thyself!"

∴

To the most famous—and most expensive—doctor in the Hamptons came a woebegone soul who admitted at the outset he couldn't afford the fifty-dollar fee. In a good mood, the doctor reduced the tab to forty dollars. "But, doc," pleaded the man, "I have a wife and five kids to support." The fee was lowered to twenty-five. "For me that's half a month's rent," sighed the man—and it was in this wise that the fee went down to ten—and finally to five. "I'm the top specialist in my field," the doctor remonstrated, "and admittedly the highest-priced. Why ever did you come to me anyhow?" "Because," asserted the man vehemently, "when my health is involved, MONEY IS NO OBJECT."

∴

An incorrigible old reprobate of eighty-six consulted his doctor before taking unto himself a sultry bride of twenty-one. "Marry her if you must," said the doctor dubiously, "but restrain yourself. Overexertion could well prove fatal." The reprobate shrugged his shoulders and philosophized, "Well, if she dies, she dies."

∴

A sturdily constructed wife complained of increasing deafness. "It can't be helped," a doctor told the husband after thorough investigation. "Tell your wife her condition is simply an indication of advancing years." "Not on your life," cried the husband. "YOU tell her."

∴

A shipping tycoon, completing his annual physical checkup at a local hospital, was assured by the doctor in charge, "You're sound as a dollar, sir." The tycoon fainted.

∴

A Swiss handwriting expert declares that this business about doctors' handwriting being illegible is just one of those baseless myths. "They deliberately make it impossible for patients to read their prescriptions," elaborates this cynic, "so their friends at the pharmacies can charge two dollars for some pills or tonic that should cost a quarter. Take a look at the bills these same doctors send out on the first of the month. They're so darn legible a child of seven could read them readily."

∴

Doctor Jensen, convinced that he had lulled a six-year-old patient into a sense of false security, finally produced his hypodermic needle. The six-year-old backed away in sudden terror and whispered, "Doctor, I think I hear your mother calling you."

.·.

"Oh, oh," wailed a lady patient. "What I'd give for just one good night's sleep."

"Try taking a glass of warm milk and eating an apple just before you retire," suggested the doctor.

"But, Doctor," protested his patient. "Six months ago you told me not to eat a bite for three hours before going to bed."

"I know, my dear lady," bubbled the doctor, "but you have no idea what tremendous strides medical science has registered in that period."

.·.

On a pert little redhead's third day as a nurse at the hospital, the house doctor entered a patient's room and asked, "Have you kept a chart on this man's progress?" "No," she confessed with a faint blush, "but I can show you my diary."

.·.

Tom Parker tells about a colleague who tried to steal patients from the medico who shared his office with him and was promptly sued for alienation of infections.

.·.

"You'll just have to do something for my poor husband," a lady demanded of the family doctor. "I swear to you, he's convinced he's Aristotle." "You mean he goes around spouting philosophy?" wondered the doctor. "Not at all," she assured him. "I mean he goes around spending money like Onassis."

.·.

"I've had a way with the ladies ever since I was born," boasted a small-town Lothario. "I must tell you that five minutes after I arrived, the doctor didn't slap me—but the NURSE certainly did!"

∴

A Park Avenue physician, after examining a twitching, snarling, haggard businessman who had already amassed ten million dollars, but was avidly seeking twenty million more, advised, "I want you from this moment on to work and scheme only six hours a day instead of sixteen, and promise me that three days a week you'll drive out to the cemetery." "The cemetery," exploded the tycoon. "What for?" "Just look around," said the physician, "and meet some of the chaps you're going to have to compete with to be the richest fool there!"

2. *Dentists*

The town's most notorious deadbeat suddenly appeared in society dentist Pullman's torture chamber and paid a long-overdue bill in full. "That last letter you sent me," he confessed admiringly, "should get money out of a stone. How did you ever dream it up?"

"I didn't," admitted Doc Pullman, hastily pocketing the unexpected check. "I just selected the best parts from letters my son sends me from college."

∴

Buddy Hackett tells about an ingenious dentist who found a way to handle a particularly nervous lady patient. She panicked regularly the moment she seated herself in his chair, and clamped her mouth so tightly that he couldn't pry it open. So one afternoon he had his girl assistant sneak up behind her, and as soon as he was ready to drill, she got the signal to jab the lady in the rear with a hatpin. She opened her mouth to holler—and that was that.

His ministrations completed, the dentist consoled the patient,

"Now, that wasn't so bad after all, was it?" "Not quite," she admitted, still trembling, "but I certainly didn't expect to feel the pain so far down!"

∴

"Show me the father of our country's dentures," challenges Soupy Sales "and I'll show you the George Washington Bridge."

∴

"I want a tooth pulled," an imperious lady told a Cape Cod dentist, "and I don't want any anesthetic, because I'm in a hurry." Impressed with her bravery, the good doctor asked which tooth it was. "Donald," said the lady, turning to her husband, "show him your tooth."

∴

An unfortunate sufferer in a strange dentist's chair became convinced that the hole being drilled in his upper left bicuspid was inordinately large. When his wandering gaze fell upon the dentist's diploma, he understood why. The dentist was a graduate of Consolidated Edison.

∴

Dr. Hirschfeld, the famed periodontist, set to work on the gums of a lady patient with a mouth about as wide as the entrance to the Lincoln Tunnel. Furthermore, she opened it to its fullest extent as the brave master approached his task. He recoiled in horror and gasped, "Madam, not so wide, I pray you. I plan to stand outside."

3. *Psychiatrists*

"I really was worried about my son Timothy," confessed Mrs. Malone to her bridge cronies. "He had gotten into the habit of tucking all sorts of things into his pockets: twenty-dollar bills off my dressing table, other people's silver spoons, things like that. . . . Then my husband suggested that I take the boy to see that Dr. Thingamabob, who studied analysis with Freud in Vienna, and do you know, girls, my husband was absolutely right. That doctor solved my Timothy's problem after talking to him for just one hour. He told me, 'Mrs. Malone, your son is a thief.' "

∴

A psychiatrist called the police to announce excitedly that his couch had been stolen from his office. "Calm down," advised the policeman. "We'll get it back for you." "You'd better hurry," advised the psychiatrist. "There's a patient on it."

∴

A rabid football fan spent so many hours from August to January glued to his TV set, watching college games, exhibition games, pro games, and endless bowl games, that his wife began to question his sanity, and finally dragged him off to consult a psychiatrist. "It looks like a serious case to me," opined that worthy, "but I'm wondering how you managed to get the big lug in here."

"It wasn't easy," admitted the wife. "I had to red-dog him."

∴

A rising young matinee idol confessed to his analyst that relations with his wife were waxing more and more precarious. "It's that before-retiring ritual," he explained. "You know, the vanishing creams, wrinkle removers, hair curlers—all that sort of thing. But no matter how much she hollers—I'M NOT GOING TO GIVE THEM UP!"

∴

The usual worried husband invaded the office of the usual society psychoanalyst to plead, "You've got to help my wife, Doctor. She's convinced she's an elevator." "An elevator?" echoed the surprised analyst. "You'd better send her right up to see me." "I can't do that," demurred the husband. "She's an express elevator, and doesn't stop on your floor."

∴

"The money that I wasted on psychoanalysts," mourned Mrs. Mandelbaum, "before I discovered for myself the cause of all my anxieties and troubles!" "So what ailed you?" prompted Mrs. Schtuss. "I found out," declared Mrs. Mandelbaum triumphantly, "that I secretly believed I was a fox terrier." "Unbelievable," gasped Mrs. Schtuss. "But how do you know you're cured?" "How do I know?" echoed Mrs. M. "Just feel my nose!"

∴

Ralph Ellison tells about a despondent fellow who sought the advice of the city's most fashionable—and expensive—analyst. "You have acute melancholia," the analyst informed him. "The circus is in town this week. Go to it. It may give you some laughs." "Your advice is worthless," mourned the despondent one. "I'm the top clown there!"

∴

A woman strode into the office of a Park Avenue psychiatrist the other day with a live bird, marked black and orange, firmly tucked under her arm. "What's troubling you?" asked the psychiatrist. "It isn't I," explained the woman. "It's my husband here. He thinks he's a mynah bird."

∴

"I had the strangest dream last night," a patient confided to his analyst. "I dreamed that you were my mother!" "Your mother?" echoed the analyst, his interest instantly aroused. "I wonder what provoked a dream like that. Tell me the details." "Well," said the patient, "I dreamed that I woke up at my regular hour in the morning, and came to you for my regular breakfast of three hamburgers and an ice cream soda." "Ridiculous," interrupted the analyst. "What kind of a breakfast is that for a healthy young man?"

∴

An embarrassing moment ensued on upper Broadway the day the Queen of Greece came up to Barnard College to receive an honorary degree. One of the guests at the ceremony was a crusty old psychiatrist from Columbia University across the avenue.

"Come over and meet the Queen of Greece," smiled the dean of Barnard. The old psychiatrist shook hands graciously, then cackled to the dean—loud enough for Her Majesty to overhear, "She seems harmless enough. How long has she thought she's the Queen?"

4. Hospitals

The young nurses at Lenox Hill Hospital, N.Y., are more competent—and more pulchritudinous—than most. A newcomer to the staff, in fact, turned out to be a dead ringer for movie star Elizabeth Taylor.

An appreciative supervisor took her for her first tour of the establishment and paused at the entrance to the male convalescent ward.

"This ward is the most dangerous," he warned. "These patients are almost well."

∴

Most disgustingly cheerful nurse in medical annals must be the one who awakened a patient on intravenous feeding to chirp, "Wake up, Mr. Gubblebey! Time for your birthday cake injection!"

∴

When the floor nurse at Saint Mary's Hospital answered the phone, a voice asked, "Can you tell me how Mr. Donovan is getting along?" "He's doing splendidly," she answered enthusiastically. "I believe he'll be going home tomorrow. Who shall I say called?" The answer was, "This is Donovan. Those doctors won't tell me a darn thing."

∴

The editor of a big publishing house visited his ailing boss in the hospital, found him even grumpier than usual, and, bothered, took the very lovely young nurse aside after tiptoeing out of the room to ask, "Tell me the unvarnished truth, please. Is he making any progress?" "None at all," replied the nurse decisively. "He's not my type."

∴

A wealthy Grosse Pointe matron, used to having flunkies jump when she gave a command, was distinctly displeased by the service she received when a sudden illness forced her to spend a fortnight in a large Detroit hospital. While convalescing, she decided to dictate some letters to her private secretary. "I'll push the buttons meant to summon my nurse and my floor doctor," she proposed grimly. "That should assure us of at least a full hour of undisturbed privacy!"

∴

From his hospital bed of pain, George S. Kaufman offered as his own epitaph, "Over my dead body." It was Kaufman, too, who ticked off an overexpensive cat hospital as "a gyp joint where they charged four bucks a weak purr."

∴

At a hospital cashier's desk: "I can't pay my bill now. I slowed down like your doctors told me to, so I lost my job."

∴

Two expectant fathers were pacing nervously up and down in a hospital waiting room. "Darn it," grumbled one, "why did this have to happen on the first day of my vacation?" "YOU should complain," sneered the other. "This is our honeymoon!"

∴

Absent-minded Professor Headman sat in the hospital reception hall awaiting the arrival of his first baby in the delivery room upstairs. A smiling nurse finally popped her head in the door to exclaim, "Congratulations, Professor! It's a boy!" Professor

Headman looked up from his philosophical treatise to snap petulantly, "Well, what does he want?"

∴

There's a nurse at New York's Lenox Hill Hospital who's a past mistress at the art of suspense—not to mention sadism. An excited new father clutched at her in the reception hall one evening to quaver, "End my suspense, Nurse: is it a boy?" She studied him calmly, then answered, "Well, the one in the middle is."

∴

Already father of seven perky, superactive children, Mr. Abernathy followed the familiar path to the hospital to congratulate his wife on the successful delivery of offspring number eight. He tiptoed up to her bed and kissed her gently on the cheek. Half asleep, she smiled, and remonstrated gently, "Oh, Casper, starting in again, are you?"

DOWN ON THE FARM

1. *Farmers*

This clipping from what he claims is a leading New Hampshire newspaper has been turned up by an eager young Harvard graduate named Updike:

"Jared Hemp, one of the oldest residents of Pewter County, N.H., celebrated his 97th birthday at his home yesterday. When interviewed, Mr. Hemp was winding his watch. 'Yes, I still wind my own watch,' he said with a twinkle in his eye. 'I attribute my virile old age to my constant use of licorice losenges since I was a boy and to my never wearing a collar. This gave me adequate saliva and health-improving neck-play.' Mr. Hemp entered the business of making lasts at the age of 11 and has lasted ever since. He has 14 children, all of whom are in jail."

.·.

Reggie Putzvogel, chief of the Dusenberg Falls volunteer fire department, was asked what his brave lads did when they were summoned to extinguish a conflagration. "The first thing we do is to drench the premises with water, knock out the windows and chop up all the furniture and fixtures," explained Reggie. "What's the second thing you do?" inquired his interviewer. "The second thing we do," Reggie asserted proudly, "is to make absolutely sure we're at the right address."

.·.

A New York couple, lured by an ad, booked a room for a fortnight at a Vermont "hotel," but didn't like what they saw when they got there. "Why, you have more cows than you have guests here," expostulated the chagrined husband. "How do you explain that?" Snapped the Vermonter, "We prefer 'em."

.·.

We haven't heard too much lately about Charley Weaver—or his letters from his ma back home in Mount Idy. But he reported receipt of this new one from the good lady: "Birdie Rodd is pretty upset. Saturday night somebody broke into her house and stole her bathtub. She says whoever did it can keep the washrag, soap, and tub—but she would like to get back her Aunt Minnie."

.·.

There's a story about a new home owner who simply adored daffodils. So in late September, just after she had moved in, she and her husband spent a long, long weekend doing nothing but planting daffodil bulbs. They had just finished planting the last one and, completely exhausted, were heading for the bar when a neighbor stopped his car out front to call to them, "If you think this place is pretty now, just wait till you see it in the spring! It's one solid field of daffodils!"

∴

The mayor of a very, very small town in New England was a windbag of the first water and a particular irritant to Farmer John Daly, one of the more taciturn members of the community. After one of the mayor's longest excursions into the realm of empty phrases, Farmer Daly buttonholed him and rasped, "Well, sir, there's one thing President Richard Nixon and you have in common, my boy." Surprised and flattered, the mayor bubbled, "We HAVE? Thank you, John—but how do you mean that?" "Well," chuckled Farmer Daly, "you're both as high in politics as you'll ever get."

∴

From the giant redwoods sector of California comes the yarn of a truck farmer who decided to buy a power saw. A logging foreman sold him one that he guaranteed would cut down fifteen trees in a single day. A week later a very unhappy farmer came back to report that the power saw must be a faulty one: it averaged only three trees a day. The foreman grabbed the power saw and plugged it into the nearest outlet. The saw promptly went "BZZZZZZ."

"Hey," demanded the startled farmer, "what's that noise?"

∴

Jerry Morris tells of the hiker who was startled to come upon a farmer holding a pig up to a tree while he munched apples. When he picked up a second pig to repeat the process, the hiker inquired sarcastically, "Doesn't it strike you as a considerable waste of time to feed your pigs that way?" The

farmer threw him a contemptuous look, and countered, "What's time to a pig?"

∴

The prize bull of the year was on exhibition at the State Fair. Rumor had it that the owner had refused an offer of a million dollars from a would-be purchaser. Admission to see the animal was put at a dollar a head.

"I've brought my fifteen kids to see that bull," announced one youthful-looking farmer. "Do you think you could make a special rate for us all?"

"Fifteen kids," repeated the exhibitor with amazement. "You just wait here, mister. I'll bring the bull out to see YOU!"

∴

In front of a Wellfleet shop up Cape Cod way, two elderly ladies stopped for a bit of chitchat. "What's this I hear about somebody dropping dead in Truro yesterday?" asked one. "Yep. Happened right outside my sister Bess's home," replied the other. "Everybody was het up for a while, but it wasn't as bad as we thought. Just one of the summer visitors."

∴

The marriage between an elderly farmer and his robust young wife wasn't going too well, and the farmer sought out his doctor for advice. "Show her more affection," proposed the doctor. "A kiss and a hug several times a day will keep reminding her of your love."

"It won't work," said the farmer. "When I'm out plowing the fields it takes me too long to get back to the house."

"Okay," nodded the doctor. "She's younger than you are. So carry a shotgun with you and fire it when you feel romantic. She'll come out to you."

A few weeks later the doctor met the farmer at church and asked, "Did my plan work out?"

"For the first few days," sighed the farmer, "it was wonderful. But then the hunting season opened and I haven't seen her since."

∴

Bill Gove has this to say about the small town in Maine he recently visited: 1. When you plug in an electric shaver, the street lights grow dim. 2. They don't take the sidewalks in at night because they never put them out in the morning. 3. To show you how conservative the natives are, Bishop Sheen came into the dining room of the local hotel the other evening, and they made him put on a necktie!

∴

Farmer Ross had one of the finest apple orchards in the state, and come fall, regular as clockwork, the kids from the neighborhood would sneak in to purloin apples. Regularly, too, Farmer Ross would come charging angrily out of his house, waving a shotgun, and threatening the fleeing youths with everything he could think of.

After watching one of these vain pursuits a neighbor said to Farmer Ross, "Danged if I can understand you, Bill. You're normally a calm and generous man—and you've got ten times as many apples ripening in that orchard as you can possibly use. Why don't you just let the kids have some?"

"Heck," laughed Farmer Ross. "I WANT them to have the apples. But I was a boy once myself, and if I didn't holler and chase them—they'd never come back."

∴

After a farmer had bought sixty-eight axe handles—at the rate of two a week—at two dollars apiece, the hardware salesman couldn't resist asking him what on earth he was doing with them. The farmer explained he was selling them to his neighbor for a dollar each. "But that's ridiculous," expostulated the salesman. "Don't you realize you're losing a dollar on each sale?" "Sure I do," was the answer, "but it beats farming!"

∴

A Maine farmer returned home from the State Fair with a large, sparkling diamond ring. "Do you reckon," asked a friend, "that that diamond is genuine?" "If it ain't," answered the farmer, "I've sure been stung out of a dollar and a half."

2. *Hillbilly Country*

From those old Blue Ridge Mountains of Virginny comes the story of the lad whose paw was taking him to town for the very first time. At dusk, they came to the top of a hill, and looked down at the little county seat—and the lad got his first sight of electric lights—a couple of hundred of them, turned on. He turned to his paw with astonishment and declared, "Dawgone, Paw, it looks like the whole world's done gone possum hunting!"

∴

The parson of a tiny congregation in Arkansas rashly lit out one night with the entire church treasury, and the local constable set out to capture him. This he did, dragging the culprit back by the collar a week later. "Here's the varmint, folks," announced the constable grimly. "I'm sorry to say he's already squandered our money, but I drug him back so we can make him preach it out."

∴

Mrs. Ralph Palgrave reports that a famous Ozark character named Seth Abernathy was powerfully fond of an after-dinner cheroot. His wife smelled something burning one evening and hollered, "Land's sake, Seth, you've set your whiskers on fire!" "I know it," he answered angrily. "Cain't you see me prayin' for rain?"

∴

They tell at the University of West Virginia of a penniless old mountaineer whose crude one-room cabin burned to the ground one winter night. Folks in those parts felt so sorry for him that they began bringing him gifts to get him back on his feet. Soon the old boy was sitting relatively pretty—better off by far than he ever had been heretofore.

One morning he was seated in a rocker outside his brand-new cabin when a friend appeared bringing him a whole bag of oats. "Take them oats away," ordered the old man. "From now on I ain't taking nothing but money!"

∴

"I reckon," announced a West Virginian mountaineer with an anticipatory gleam in his eye, "that good neighbor Seth

McHatry's been running off a new batch of moonshine this week." "How do ye figger that?" asked his wife. "Because," chuckled the mountaineer, "his rabbits have been over abusin' my coon hounds again."

∴

A tourist in the Blue Ridge Mountains sector spotted a native sprawled out on the grass listening to a ball game on a transistor radio while his wife was lugging firewood into the house. "Isn't that pretty strenuous work for a woman?" hazarded the tourist. "Could be," allowed the native, "but we work in shifts." "You mean when she gets tired you take over?" "ME?" yapped the horrified native. "When she gets tired out here, I let her shift to working in the kitchen."

∴

A motorist, driving through the Ozarks, came upon a burly bearded mountaineer wrestling with a big bear—and getting the worst of it. Serenely watching from atop a boulder nearby was the mountaineer's wife, a rifle slung under her arm.

"Quick," cried the motorist. "Shoot the beast."

"Not yet," the wife replied complacently. "I'm a-waitin' to see whether the bear won't save me the trouble."

∴

A country doctor had occasion to phone the town's only drugstore in the middle of a hot midsummer afternoon. "Hello," drawled a lazy voice from the man who, after a considerable wait, answered the call. "Now, listen carefully," ordered the doctor. "I need these two prescriptions filled right away." He thereupon rattled off the names of several ingredients, some in five syllables. When he was finished, he demanded, "Have you got all that straight?" The lazy voice answered patiently, "Mister, when I said 'Hello,' I done exhausted my entire vocabulary."

∴

An Arkansas lady achieved an audience with then Governor Faubus just to tell him, "They sent my husband to jail for three years for stealing one measly ham. I'd like for you to grant him a pardon." "Has he been a decent husband to you?" asked the governor. "Decent?" jeered the lady. "He's a no-good bum who beats the children and wastes the few bucks he makes on liquor and poker." "In that case," smiled Faubus, "why do you want him out of jail?"

"Governor," said the lady earnestly, "I feel it's high time we had another ham."

THE GRAB BAG

1. *Signs Here!*

In the window of a Times Square bookshop: "If you don't see the book you want, it's in the police station."

Under an office clock: "It's earlier than you think!"

Outside a Beverly Hills church: "Approved for general audiences."

On the door of a pet shop: "For sale cheap, a talking parrot. Owner no longer can stand parrot's political opinions."

Sign at outskirts of Bismarck, North Dakota: "Watch out for small children—especially when they're driving."

On a Las Vegas divorce lawyer's door: "Satisfaction guaranteed—or your honey back."

In a reducing salon: "Fattery will get you nowhere."

In a pawn shop: "Hock it to me, baby."

At an Old Miss. student rally: "Help stop air pollution: muffle our Congressman!"

In a liquor store window: "Pay now, glow later."

On snow-covered mountain road: "Deluxe ski lodge one mile ahead. Eight doctors. No waiting."

On the gate of Montana nudist camp: "Clothed for the winter."

The new pedestrian lights in Las Vegas are marked, "Stop," "Go," and "Three to one you don't make it."

Outside a loan company branch: "We're here for the man who already has everything—but hasn't paid for it."

Outside an Italian opera house: "Tonight: *The Barber of Seville*. 2,000 chairs. No waiting."

On a roadside near Atlantic City: "Our hotel is so near the beach we have to station a lifeguard in every room!"

Sign in Oregon repair shop: "For sale: foreign sports car. Ask for Clyde, the guy with the cramped legs."

At the box office of an Ozark movie house: "Children under fifteen not admitted unless accompanied by their husbands."

In a Greenwich Village barbershop: "Only one haircut to a customer."

On the padlocked door of a bankrupt bookshop: "WORDS FAILED US."

In an art gallery: "We hung this picture because we couldn't find the artist."

In the window of a garage: "Mechanic wanted. Must look honest."

On a municipal golf course: "Please don't find golf balls until at least they've stopped rolling."

In a Division Street bar: "The opinions expressed by the bartender are those of his wife."

On an army camp menu: "Dreaded veal cutlet."

At a roadside antique shop: "If you don't know what you want, we've got it!"

In the workroom of a wig maker's shop: "NO TRESS-PASSING."

In the vestibule of a Tennessee funeral parlor: "For sale: hearse with 1968 body."

In window of a strike-bound bar and grille: "Closed for altercations."

On a self-service elevator: "Eighth floor button out of order. Please push five and three."

At a perfume exhibit: "Don't risk using this scent if you're only bluffing."

In a travel agency: "Spend your honeymoon in Iceland. The nights last up to 18 hours."

In the window of a liquor shop: "A soft drink turneth away company."

At a zipper display: "Grand opening sale."

In a clothing store: "How about a blue splurge suit?"

On the back of a private refuse disposer's truck: "Satisfaction guaranteed or double your garbage refunded."

Outside a maternity shop: "We provide the accessories after the fact."

In a Niagara Falls motel: "Honeymooners treated with studied neglect."

On the window of T. Ginsberg's Delicatessen: "Mr. Ginsberg himself eats here."

At a shop specializing in fireplace accessories: "Anything your little hearth desires."

On a peddler's cart in Division Street: "Don't be fooled by imitators. This is my only pushcart."

In a barbershop window: "During alterations customers will be shaved in the rear."

In an optometrist's window: "If you don't see what you want, you've come to the right place."

At a canoe rental shop at Lake Hopatcong: "No tipping allowed."

Near Woodlawn Cemetery: "Second-hand tombstone for sale. Extraordinary bargain for family named Schwarzendorfer."

A used-book dealer in Brooklyn has a sign in his seldom washed window proclaiming "My assets are over ten million dollars." He isn't kidding, either. His office is directly above a branch of the Chase Manhattan Bank.

On the back bumper of a wedding party limousine: "Letter writing caused this."

Over a cocker spaniel in a pet shop window: "Reduced: Obedience School Dropout."

At the entrance of a circus wild animals enclosure: "No trespassing. Survivors will be prosecuted."

Outside a cannibal snack bar: "Try our him on rye."

At a co-ed college in Long Island: "Save water! Shower with a friend."

On a boat being towed on a trailer: "Instant fun. Just add water."

On a highway in Indiana: "Don't just sit there. Nag your husband."

On a bus in Israel: "Passengers are requested not to stick their necks out of the country."

At a vegetable market: "Fresh corn: the stalk just brought it."

At snack and beer stand in Hyannis: "Frank'n Stein."

Outside a motel: "Courteous self parking."

In a New Hampshire ski shop: "Help stamp out summer."

Over new panty hose display: "For contented calves."

In a Maui discothèque: "Not responsible for dates left over ten minutes."

Outside the office of a brand-new doctor: "Small fevers gratefully received."

On a horrible Ozark back road: "Drive with extreme care. This road should be under construction."

In a swank hairdressing salon: "If you look like your passport photo, you've come here just in time."

In a department store toy section: "If you don't see what you want—cry for it."

In a business office: "This year's Christmas party has been canceled because of last year's Christmas party."

Add to the list of remarkable scrawls discovered on the walls of public institutions: 1."Ophelia! This way to the Nunnery!" 2. "Stop Stassen!" 3. "The Marquis de Sade really knows how to hurt a guy."

In an induction center: "We honor all draft cards."

On the window of a closed haberdashery: "We undersold everybody."

Outside a morgue: "Remains to be seen."

In a music shop: "Harp lessons. Learn now; play later."

On a wishing well: "Wish carefully. No refunds!"

At a gas station just outside the L.A. boundary line: "You have just left the city of Los Angeles. Resume natural breathing."

2. *Webster Revised*

ABALONE: An expression of disbelief.

ANATOMY: Something everybody's got—but it looks better on Raquel Welch.

ARCHAEOLOGIST: A man whose career lies in ruins.

ATHEIST: A man who has no invisible means of support.

BABY: Mama's little yelper.

BACHELOR: A smarty-pants who never Mrs. anybody.

BIGAMIST: Fog over Naples.

BODYGUARD: Deter gent.

BULLDOZER: One who sleeps through campaign speeches.

BUTTRESS: A female goat.

CASTOR OIL: Ugh nog.

CENSOR: A spoilsport who sticks his no's into other people's business.

COBRA: Underthing worn by Siamese twins.

CROQUETTE: Romantic lady frog.

DEBATE: What attracts de fish.

DIPLOMAT: A man trained to solve the difficulties created by other diplomats.

EPITAPH: A belated advertisement for a line of goods that has been permanently discontinued.

ESCALATOR: Stairway to the stores.

FIREPROOF: The boss's incompetent son.

FLOOD: A stream too big for its bridges.

GIRL-WATCHER: The ogley American.

GRANDPARENT: The only thing so simple that a child of two can operate it.

GRUESOME: A little taller than last year.

HANGOVER: The wrath of grapes.

HIGHLAND FLING: Kilt in action.

HULA: A shake in the grass.

JANITOR: A floor flusher.

KINDERGARTEN TEACHER: A gal who knows how to make the little things count.

LAWYER: A man who sees to it that you get what's coming to him.

LEISURE TIME: When your wife can't find you.

MATERNITY GOWN: A slip cover.

NEPOTISM: All the kin's men.

NUDIST COLONY: A retreat where men and women go to air their differences.

OPTIMIST: A man who says he's just going to watch the first fifteen minutes of the Late, Late Show.

PANIC: Kiss the poise good-by.

PARANOID: Couple interrupted by a cop in lovers' lane.

PATIENT: The raw material out of which a surgeon carves a career.

PILLAGE: About sixteen for most girls.

RECESSION: A time when we have to do without a lot of things our grandparents never heard of.

RED LETTER DAY: When Moscow citizens get their mail.

RICH UNCLE: The kin you love to touch.

SCREEN DOOR: Something the kids get a bang out of.

SEERSUCKER: A gullible fortuneteller.

SKEPTIC: A man who won't take know for an answer.

SORE THROAT: Hoarse and buggy.

SUCCESS: When your name appears in everything but the telephone directory.

SUMMER: When parents pack up their troubles and send them to camp.

TEETOTALER: An official golf scorer.

VICE VERSA: Poetry not fit for the kiddies to read.

WELL INFORMED: A person whose opinions are the same as yours.

3. *"Is a Puzzlement"*

Bright young lads and lasses in the Raffles Club set have revived a parlor game called "In the Name of." In case you're not familiar with it—and like puns as much as I do—here are a few choice samples:

1. A German plutocrat is showing his estate to an English friend, who praises the layout ecstatically. The German shrugs it all off in the name of what English author?

2. A southern lady bound for Quebec wakes up in her railroad lower to find the temperature of the car down to fifteen degrees. Ringing for the porter, she announces indignantly in the name of what famous composer?

3. A drama critic falls ill on the night of an important opening and sends his wife to cover it for him. Later he phones her verdict to his paper in the name of what Indian notable?

4. Mrs. Ullman thought the movers had taken everything out of her old flat, but suddenly discovered a valuable vase that had been left behind. She spoke to her Chinese houseboy, Allan, about it. In the name of what artist did he reply?

ANSWERS: 1. "Ach, it's Chesterfield." 2. "I'm Cole, Porter." 3. "Madam Pandit." 4. "Van Gogh, lady."

∴

There's at least one word in the English language, notes Roger Devlin, that contains the same vowel SIX times: Indivisibility. Mr. Devlin also lists six words containing only five letters, not one of which is *A, E, I, O,* or *U:* Crypt, Gypsy, Myrrh, Pygmy, Sylph, and Tryst.

∴

You can define each of the following by a single letter (and if you're right, you'll be the first to know it): 1. Blue and white bird. 2. Lowest note on the piano. 3. A large body of water. 4. A girl's nickname. 5. A vegetable. 6. An exclamation. 7. A beverage.

The answer is J-A-C-K-P-O-T.

∴

How carefully do you read a news item? Puzzle addicts are circulating this small test: Scan the following sentence and count the *F*'s therein: "Finished files are the result of years of scientific study combined with the experience of years."

If your count is four, you're supposedly above average, five you're a smart apple indeed, and if you caught all six, well, why are you wasting your ultra-valuable time taking tests like this?

∴

What words contain such unlikely combinations of letters as Tomo, Xyg, Dhp, Zop, Heon, Riju, Xop, and Omaha? Here, if you're too lazy or indifferent to dig them up yourselves, are the answers: auTOMObile, oXYGen, joDHPurs, schiZOPhrenia, luncHEON, maRIJUana, saXOPhone, and tOMAHAwk.

∴

The following arrangement of numbers has been made systematically: 8,5,4,9,1,7,6,3,2,0. Your job is to determine what the system is. (Answer: The numbers are arranged in alphabetical order: eight, five, four, nine, etc. Try it on those kids of yours who think they're so much smarter than their parents!)

∴

In a certain word of eight letters, KST is in the middle, in the beginning, and at the end, yet there is only one K, one S, and one T in the word. What is the word?

ANSWER: The word is INKSTAND. In the middle is KST. At the beginning is IN and AND is at the end.

∴

One little poem includes every letter in the alphabet but one. How long will it take you to spot the missing letter?

A jovial swain should not complain
Of any buxom fair,
Who mocks his pain and thinks it gain
To quiz his awkward air.

∴

A city slicker we know is winning money—and losing friends—by appearing at dinner parties and betting he can take a drink from a bottle without opening it or tampering with it in any way whatever. He then picks a bottle of wine out of his host's cellar—one with a hollow bottom, pours a shot of liquor into the cavity, drinks it—and collects the bet from a consistently outraged victim.

∴

Charles Rice, an admittedly shifty operator, suggests two other ways of separating a trusting friend from some of his hard-earned shekels:

1. Bet him that you can prove that there was one day in

American history when nary a soul either was born or died. Actually there were ELEVEN such days: September 3 to 13, 1752. It was the occasion of a great calendar reform, when by decree the day after September 2 would be designated September 14, thereby leaving a void of eleven days in our American heritage.

2. Bet the same gullible pushover that he can't pick out these correct colors:

A. A dime is what color (gray, silver, bronze)?

B. A penny is what color (gray, silver, bronze)?

C. A nickle is what color (gray, silver, green)?

What will destroy him is the color of a nickle. It's green. A nickle is a green woodpecker. It is not spelled like the coin, nickel. Now go out and get rich!

4. *It Could Be Verse!*
(*It's terse, at any rate.*)

She doesn't drink; she doesn't smoke;
She doesn't spend her dimes for coke.
She doesn't neck; she doesn't pet;
She doesn't even WALK as yet.

—Francis Duffy

Mary had a little lamb.
His hair was white as heck,
And everywhere that Mary went
This poor fish paid the check.

—Felix Travis

Someone hadn't much to do
The day they put "G" in gnat and gnu.

—Mary O'Neill

Nine times out of ten you'll find
No matter where you roam,
The big noise at the office
Is the little squeak at home.
—Joan Welsh

After studying great poetry for four years, a UCLA graduate produced the following classic of his own: "Rose's are red; Violet's are blue. They both wore miniskirts—and that's how I knew!"

It's often been found
When a girl looks around
With the all-seeing eye of a beagle,
That again and again
The likeliest men
Are illiterate, broke, or illegal!
—Ethel De Vitto

The bloke who plays golf
In the pouring down rain
And doesn't consider it screwy,
Is the very same pard
Who won't work in his yard
If the grass is the slightest bit dewy.
—Ralph Henderson

When she is the belle of the party,
Vivacious and bright as a flame,
And he is attentive and charming—
They quarreled before they came.
—S. Douglass

Though friends grow surly and kin berate her,
My wife thinks she's early if somebody's later.
—M. M. Parrish

When disagreement rears its head,
My spouse and I don't fight:
We talk it over calmly 'til
We find out why she's right.
—Dick Emmons

You can go barefoot in Syracuse
If you can't afford a new pyrachuse.
—Irene Keepin

Men seldom jump hurdles
For girls who wear girdles.
—Grady Johnson

We learn this after every war:
That life is not worth dying for.
—Yip Harburg

Thanksgiving Day dawns drear and murky
Invariably—IF you're a turkey.
—Don Quinn

Ladies love to drape their carcasses
In gowns bought at Neiman-Marcus's.
—Lon Tinkle

The room was hushed; the speaker mute:
He'd left his speech in his other suit.
—Richard Adler

Old King Cole was a merry old soul,
Oh, a merry old soul was he.
He called for his pipe and he called for his bowl—
And was promptly run in by the narcotics squad.
—Jonathan Gabel

I cannot imagine what impelled Sandy Alan, author of that world-shaking juvenile *The Plaid Peacock*, to send me this pointless rhyme:

> If we can remember so many old jokes
> With all of the details that mold them,
> Why can't we recall with comparable skill
> The number of times that we've told them?

And even a venerable gravestone carver in Vermont has gotten into the act:

> Here lies the body of Lemuel Bone;
> He met his death in a safety zone.

5. *The Word Game*

The late Wilfred Funk was one of America's most indefatigable word specialists. He even knew more six-syllable words than David Susskind. Funk had his own idea of the ten most beautiful words in the English language: dawn, hush, lullaby, chimes, golden, melody, murmuring, mist, tranquil, and luminous. He cited as our ten most overworked words: okay, terrific, lousy, definitely, racked, gal, certainly, darling, swell, and contact. Wilfred Funk even compiled a list of over 200 words every self-respecting dog was supposed to understand, including: down, heel, slippers, siccum, and "BAD DOG!"

∴

A confirmed girl-watcher was forced to conclude, "Though men are fond of reading, More necks are craned to gaze, Upon a well-turned ankle, Than at a well-turned phrase."

∴

Chided by his teacher for his painful inability to spell words properly, a now repentant student proudly quoted an announcement once made by Gilbert Chesterton: "Lord deliver me from a man who can spell a word in only one way!"

∴

FAMOUS LAST WORDS DEPARTMENT . . . I THOUGHT that last drink had a peculiar taste! . . . Well, if he won't douse his bright lights, I'm darned if I'll douse mine. . . . Darling, give me a hammer so I can hang this picture while I'm standing on this pile of books. . . . So this is your bride! I thought it was her grandmother. . . . That gun doesn't scare ME: you couldn't hit the side of a barn. . . . So your name is Francis Scott Key, eh? Well, young man, you've got a good enough tune there, but it'll never catch on!

∴

Dorothy Beers is a girl who obviously relishes both her ups and her downs. "Did you realize," she inquires, "that for 'shut up' you can substitute 'pipe down'? Or for 'upbraid,' 'dress down'? Or for 'catch up with,' 'track down'? Or for 'downcast,' 'upset'?" Now you do, anyhow!

∴

A father has no greater reward on earth than to have a young son whose big ambition is to follow precisely in his dad's footsteps. Agreed? Then you'll appreciate this little poem, quoted by Morris Mandel:

> His little arms crept 'round my neck,
> And then I heard him say
> Four simple words I shan't forget
> Four words that made me pray. . . .
> They turned a mirror on my soul
> On secrets no one knew;
> They startled me; I hear them yet:
> He said, "I'll be like you."

∴

Just how much wisdom, wonders Sam Marx, can a savant cram into four short words? He lists these conspicuous examples: 1. In God we trust. 2. Live and let live. 3. Still waters run deep. 4. Bad news travels fast. 5. Love laughs at locksmiths. 6. Nothing succeeds like success. 7. Charity begins at home. 8. Politics makes strange bedfellows. 9. Nothing ventured, nothing gained. 10. Let sleeping dogs lie.

∴

In *The Treasure of Our Tongue,* Lincoln Barnett tells about a job he had with a big foundation to synopsize a pile of lengthy treatises and reports so that the directors could understand their gist more quickly. After completing over thirty of his summaries he discovered that they were being rewritten and expanded by another hireling before the directors could get a look at them.

In many instances, the resultant "expansions" turned out to be longer than the original manuscripts!

∴

The demolition crew on an old warehouse found this part of a slogan on a half-wall still standing: "—— Cures Women." One workman asked sidewalk superintendent Bob Sylvester, "I wonder what that advertised." "I haven't the faintest idea," answered Sylvester, "but whatever it was, it didn't work!"

∴

A savant at Southwestern Bell Telephone Company opines that the six most important words in the language are: "I admit I made a mistake." The five most important: "You did a good job." The four most important: "What is your opinion?" The three most important: "If you please." The two most important: "Thank you." The one most important: "We." And the LEAST important word? "I"!

∴

The smart set has been spending evenings over a new parlor game: matching names in incongruous combinations. Here are a few that you'll have to go a long way to top: Andrew and Mahalia Jackson; Lyndon and Howard Johnson; Sally Rand and Talley Rand; Chiang Kai Check and Canceled Check; Oscar Wilde and Deuces Wild; Samuel Pepys and Little Bo Pepys, and—oh, no!—Carson McCullers and French McCrullers.

∴

New York's most incurable cocktail party hound has compiled a list of the words most in favor this year with the smart-aleck bended-elbow set. How many of them can YOU define correctly: dichotomy, viable, serendipity, syndrome, pejorative, ambient, prestigious, consensus, and, of course, ecology.

∴

Grady Nutt, colorful Baptist minister who doubles as a TV monologist and after-dinner speaker, has any number of pert expressions that linger in the memory. He rattled off a few for me: dogwood straining at the leash . . . . traffic lights ripening from green to red . . . . maple trees blushing in the fall preparing to undress in public . . . . kids swimming out loud . . . .

∴

An artist was engaged by the Pentagon boys to design a label for a newly instituted Cost Reduction Austerity Program. A postscript to the general's okay of the price demanded by the artist read, "Under no circumstances are the program's initials to be incorporated into the emblem's design."

∴

A youngster with thick glasses was upbraided by his mother for punctuating his conversation with a string of four-letter words. "But, Mother," he expostulated, "Norman Mailer and Tennessee Williams use those words all the time." "So what?" snapped the mother. "Don't play with them!"

∴

Although TV star John Charles Daly labels this story a dastardly and transparent fabrication, I am reliably informed that a class in a certain prep school he favors was given a word test—with these strange results:

88 per cent of the class defined "Finisher" as a native of Finland.

62 per cent thought "Dispersion" meant "this Persian."

49 per cent identified "Sonorous" as "Mexican ladies."

And 70 per cent defined "Ominous" as "An English motor vehicle."

∴

Just before he rose to make an after-dinner speech, a publisher I know was handed a note from his wife that read, "KISS! Phyllis." "How dear of your wife to remind you of her love," beamed the lady at the speaker's right. "Why do you seem so displeased?" "You don't know the code to which my wife and I sometimes resort," answered the speaker. "What this note means is 'Keep It Short, Stupid.'"

GOING PLACES

1. *Automobiles—and the People Who Should Know How to Drive Them*

When a giant automobile corporation asked the public for some novel color combinations for a new car they were putting on the market, Houston's George Fuerman came up with the following suggestions: Thanks vermillion, Freudian gilt, Unsafe topaz, Tookmylast copper, Gesund white, Yes cerise, Lohan green, and Shrinking violet. That will teach those admen in Detroit not to challenge the columnists again for a while!

∴

There's no accounting for the oddball hobbies of some of our leading citizens. An eminent journalist I know, for example, spends hours every week tracking down unusual automobile license plates. A few of his prize discoveries include a Connecticut gent who is a triple-threat man, with three cars tagged, respectively, MUMZ, POPZ, and KIDZ. A high-priced model wangled license number 36-24-36. A Newark undertaker with a grisly sense of humor nailed down a license plate reading U-2. A Mr. Silpe—not Jack Benny—has AGE 39. And one of my friend's happiest moments came when he found himself behind a tow truck hauling away the battered remains of a wrecked sedan with the license plate OOP.

∴

A couple looking for a bargain in the used-car market almost fell for a sporty-looking job that the dealer insisted had been driven only four or five times by the proverbial old lady. At the last minute, however, they discovered that the old lady hadn't driven to church—but in the county stock car races.

∴

"I see your daughter now drives her own car," observed Mr. Stanton's neighbor. "How long did it take her to learn?"

"About two cars and a half," replied Mr. Stanton sadly.

∴

Chicago Editor Spectorsky returned to his snazzy sports car to find a freshly crushed fender and this note affixed to his windshield wiper: "The people who saw me sideswipe your fender are now watching me write this note, and doubtless figure I'm telling you my name and address so you can contact me and send me the repair bill. Ho, ho! You should live so long."

∴

A Mr. Radison, whose wife had already won two gold cups for being the worst automobile driver in Westchester, called his insurance adjuster to report another of her periodic mishaps. "What happened THIS time?" asked the adjuster wearily. "As near as I can figure it," replied Mr. R., "she was backing out of our garage when she hit two trash cans, knocked over our TV antenna, and sauna bath, ruined my son Phil's bicycle—and THEN SHE LOST CONTROL OF THE CAR.

∴

"I was framed," cried Juan Saparillo, "when they let me out of a jail in Mexico. Thirty days is too much just for speeding." "Speeding," echoed his friend Pedro. "How could you speed? You never drove an automobile in your life!" "Who said anything about automobiles?" inquired Juan. "The miserable police arrested me for speeding on the governor."

∴

Another citizen, just back from a year-long business sojourn in Mexico, was proceeding past a busy intersection when a confused driver ignored a red light and crashed into him amidships. Ruefully inspecting the wreckage, the victim complained, "For a full year I've been driving this car in the middle of all those crazy drivers in Mexico and never got a scratch on it. Now, two days back home in California, you demolish my car for me. What on earth were you dreaming about, anyhow?"

The other driver looked at him blankly, shrugged his shoulders, and said, "NO COMPRENDO, SENOR!"

∴

A punctilious traffic court judge, having fined a speedster twenty-five dollars, suggested, "Better get a receipt from the clerk when you pay up." "What do you expect me to do with it?" snapped the disgruntled speedster. "Save it," counseled his honor. "When you get three of them, you get a bicycle!"

.·.

An adventurous chap, driving from Boston to Palm Beach via little-used back roads, vows this happened to him in South Carolina. A local sheriff sirened him to a stop and thundered, "You city fellers ain't going to drive through this community at murderous speeds. I clocked you at fifty-seven miles an hour. Don't give me no arguments neither. Just take this pad and pencil and write what I tell you!"

.·.

Possibly the laziest hitch-hiker extant was spotted sound asleep on the greensward bordering the Governor Dewey Throughway one afternoon. Propped up beside him was a big sign reading, "LAS VEGAS." A line in smaller type below said, "PLEASE BLOW HORN."

.·.

A whole book of Volkswagen jokes will strike many people as too much of a good thing, but Charlie Preston has gotten away with it handsomely. Here are a few highlights: 1. Woman frantically phoning her husband: "George! You know that big dog on Elm Street that chases cars? Well, he's caught our Volkswagen!" 2. Gas station attendant to VW driver in Boston: "Shall I fill it up?" Driver: "No, thanks, I'm only going as far as Los Angeles." 3. An eccentric Texas billionaire who preferred a VW to a Cadillac was asked if his little car was air-conditioned. "No," he drawled, "but I always keep a couple of cold ones in the refrigerator." 4. Another attendant to another VW driver: "What will it be, sir? Regular, high test, or sauerkraut juice?"

∴

A parking lot attendant in the theatrical district complains that he has a frequently recurring nightmare. He keeps dreaming he has grease all over his hands with not one customer's steering wheel to wipe it off on.

∴

A motorist in Maine stopped to ask an old lady tending her garden, "Can you tell me the way to Moosehead Lake?" "No, I can't," was the reply. The motorist murmured, "Thanks, anyhow," and drove on, but suddenly heard a shout behind him. An old fellow had joined the gardner, and the pair were beckoning him to back up. When he obeyed, the old lady announced, "This here is my husband. He don't know either."

∴

A mother, with six obstreperous brats in tow, boarded a packed bus at the height of the rush hour. The brats immediately began screaming and tripping over angry passengers. The exasperated driver finally suggested, "Next time, lady, why don't you leave half of your obnoxious kids at home?" The mother answered grimly, "I did."

∴

A lady driver in Vancouver has genuine cause to wail about her streak of bad luck a few days ago. First, a circus elephant wandered out of its enclosure and sat down for a rest on top of the lady's new sedan. (It was red, the elephant's owner explained later, and this particular elephant just loved to sit on red sedans.) Anyhow, the car, though considerably squashed, was still able to navigate, and the lady headed it toward the nearest garage.

On the way she ran into a traffic jam caused by a crash. The cops and the ambulance arrived on the scene just about the time she did and immediately assumed that she was part of the accident. "No, no," she assured them. "I had no part in this crash. The reason my car is squashed is that an elephant just sat on it."

So they wrestled her into the ambulance and into an emergency ward to examine her for shock and head injuries.

∴

Phil Silvers, bent on repaying an old friend for numberless favors, borrowed his automobile one morning and had it equipped with an intricate $1,500 stereophonic phonograph set. He then called for his friend, pointed to the set, and said happily, "From me to you, my old pal! How do you like it?" The pal swallowed hard, grabbed Phil Silvers' arm and confessed, "This is a rented car."

∴

Herb Caen tells of one Oaklandite whose chariot has a gadget that automatically extinguishes the headlights ten seconds after the ignition is switched off. One evening he parked in front of his residence and a lady passing by called after him, "Hey, mister, you left your lights on."

The Oaklandite timed everything neatly. Counting off the seconds, he filled his cheeks with air, and "blew" out the headlights from a distance of fifteen yards. So far as he knows, the lady is still standing there, trying to figure things out.

∴

A motorcycle cop finally caught up with a crazy lady driver who had blithely ignored three stop signs, gone through two red lights, and sideswiped a delivery truck. As he wrote out a ticket, she expostulated, "How dare you spend your time this way harassing a respectable citizen? Why don't you go after some of those drunken hooligans once in a while?" "Madam," he assured her gently, "I thought I had one."

∴

A gent who usually takes a bus to his place of business overslept one morning and decided to drive the family car. Opening the garage door he noted that the rear wall—the one his wife had shattered when she put the car into "reverse" instead of drive—had not been repaired.

He called his carpenter at once and stormed, "You've broken your promise to me. You swore you'd have that wall fixed by noon yesterday."

"Let me ask you one question," said the carpenter earnestly. "Did your wife take the car out again yesterday afternoon?"

∴

"Let's hear it," commanded Officer Flanagan to a scared-looking motorist. "How did you knock this pedestrian down?" "I didn't," maintained the motorist. "I just pulled up to this unmarked intersection, stopped to let him cross, and he fainted."

∴

A domineering wife, back-seat driver from Weehawken clear across the continent, even followed her poor husband to a slot-machine emporium in Las Vegas and watched grimly while he lost a bagful of quarters. Finally she could contain herself no longer. "Don't pull the handle so hard," she instructed him.

∴

Mrs. Jungfrau, reporting her third accident in a single month, told her husband, "This time it definitely was not my fault.

The drunk driving the other car came right down my side of the road and smacked into me." "How do you know he was drunk?" asked the husband wearily. "He must have been," maintained Mrs. Jungfrau. "He was driving a tree."

∴

The same unquenchable Mrs. Jungfrau insisted upon taking a nationally televised drivers' test one evening. "The very next day," mourned Mr. Jungfrau, "the commissioner of motor vehicles barged into our home and carted off our TV set."

∴

The next time you stand in the rain trying vainly to flag a taxicab, let your thoughts drift back to September 30, 1907. That's the day New Yorkers saw a taxicab in operation for the first time. Twenty-five of them chugged down Fifth Avenue in line and pulled up in front of the new Plaza Hotel, which was celebrating an opening of its own.

Nobody realized it at the time, but these taxis marked the

beginning of the end for the smelly old hansom cabs. The few still in operation make their last stand at the very spot where the taxi invasion began—opposite the Plaza Hotel!

∴

A New York taxi driver decided to turn in his cab for a new model. "But the car you've got looks as good as new," protested the honest dealer. "Nothing wrong with the car itself," admitted the taxi driver, "but the 'Off-Duty' sign is completely worn out."

∴

Taxi drivers come in for a lot of criticism these days, much of it amply justified, but once in a while you hear a story that renews your faith in them. During a sudden downpour, for instance, last month, a bank official succeeded in bagging an empty taxi, and had scarcely embarked on his ride uptown when he spotted a frail little old lady, her umbrella blown inside out, waiting forlornly for a bus. Impulsively, he ordered the cab halted and insisted upon taking the old lady to her door, though she lived a good two miles out of his way. When he finally reached his own home and took out his wallet, the taxi driver told him, "Please give me half of what the meter shows, mister. It would please me to go fifty-fifty on that old lady!"

2. *Aviation and Outer Space*

A plane was roaring through the air at 600 miles per hour when one motor conked, then a second, then a third, leaving only the fourth one functioning. That is the moment when the pilot stepped out of the cockpit, his parachute harnessed to his uniform, to reassure his passengers, "Not a thing to worry about, folks! I'm on my way down to seek help."

.:.

Has the story reached you yet about the pilot of the big jetliner who was sailing along on the automatic controls, but had forgotten to turn off the intercom? Relaxing in his seat, he remarked amiably to the copilot, "All I need now is a cup of hot coffee, some cookies, and a beautiful blonde." The passengers perked up, several registered astonishment, and a young stewardess rushed forward to tell the crew the intercom was on. As she opened the door to the forward section, a sweet little old lady pulled at her skirt and reminded her, "You forgot the cookies and coffee!"

.:.

An amateur pilot brought his plane down at a big airport in a series of jolting bounces and finally skidded to a stop at the very end of a long runway. He then radioed the control tower for the time of his landing, so he could enter it in his log book. Back from the tower came a sarcastic query: "Which one, sir?"

.:.

Informing the passengers of a West-bound jet that some turbulence was expected shortly, an on-the-job stewardess ordered seat belts to be buckled, then passed out sticks of chewing gum. A very proper lady from Boston announced, "I NEVER touch chewing gum," but the stewardess told her, "We're going up to 39,000 feet, and the gum definitely will keep your ears from popping at such a high altitude."

Just before the plane landed in San Francisco, the Boston lady summoned the stewardess in some embarrassment. "My two grandchildren are waiting to meet me," she said. "How do I get this confounded gum out of my ears?"

∴

Jimmy Durante arrived pale and shaking in New Orleans from a plane he had boarded in Los Angeles. "Rough flight?" queried the concerned agent who was awaiting him at the debarkation gate. "Rough!" echoed Jimmy. "Dis flight was so rough dat a hijacker who had ordered us to Havana got off at Dallas!"

∴

A nervous screenwriter had a particular aversion to flying, because of bombs on planes—even though his trusted actuary assured him that the chances of his being aboard a plane with a bomb carrier were something like a billion to one. "What," he persisted, "do you think are the odds against TWO bomb carriers on the same aircraft?" "At least three trillion to one," scoffed the actuary.

So now the writer travels gay as a lark and carefree on plane after plane—and every time he boards one he carries a bomb.

∴

It's Harry Hershfield's story about the astronaut who suddenly got worried in the midst of the first five-man orbit. "Do you realize," he asked his fellow space-explorers, "that there are over two thousand separate devices and instruments in this capsule—and that every darn one of them was supplied by the lowest bidder?"

∴

Two astronauts from whatever country you want to downgrade landed on the moon. One remained inside the capsule while the other traipsed about on the moon's surface for an hour.

When the wanderer tapped for readmittance to the capsule, the one inside queried, "Who's there?"

∴

A young astronaut who had not exactly won the full confidence of his mentors was sent on a trial orbit with a chimpanzee. Both of them were given sealed instructions and told not to open same until their space craft had circled the globe twice. And off into the stratosphere they were catapulted. At the proper time, the chimpanzee opened his envelope, then proceeded to push the various buttons and pull the levers indicated in his instructions. At this point, the not too bright astronaut opened HIS envelope. The directions therein read: "TAKE CARE OF THE CHIMP."

∴

Goody Ace likes to speculate what might have happened had one of our great astronauts remembered his childhood conviction that the moon was made of green cheese. Goody could see, in his mind's eye, the brave fellow stepping out of his capsule onto the moon's surface being greeted by a weirdy, and demanding boldly, "Take me to your Liederkranz!"

∴

Astronaut White made a lady author very happy at a Houston reception recently. "Ma'am," he told her admiringly, "I was reading your book while we were in orbit the other day—and I couldn't put it down."

3. *Railroads (Remember?)*

Back in 1866, notes Daniel Boorstin in his absorbing book *The Americans*, a superintendent of the Burlington Railroad was exploring sparsely settled terrain—what is now the center of the city of Ottumwa, Iowa. "This is barely a cornfield," he wrote, "so I cannot have it surveyed, but yesterday a man arranged to build a hotel here. This sure is a great country for hotels!" And even eight years earlier—in 1858—a man wrote to his wife from an almost vacant western site, "I predict there'll be a good hotel here by spring." He was a pretty good predictor. The site became Denver, Colorado.

∴

Attorney A. J. Priest recalls the long-past day when the Payette Valley Railroad, now part of the Union Pacific, was run independently on a shoestring by one Hyrum E. Dunn. Came the day when the Payette Valley's one and only locomotive broke down and was deadheaded into Salt Lake City for repairs—if possible. Dunn sent this telegram to the foreman of the Salt Lake yards: "Please return whistle on my broken-down engine. The Troy Steam Laundry from whom I borrowed it wants it back."

∴

A one-time president of the New York Central Railroad was taken to hear a sermon by the then Archbishop of Canterbury that dragged on for a full hour. "What do you think of our archbishop?" he was asked later. "He's excellent," nodded the railroad man, "but he has very poor terminal facilities."

∴

Commuters from Connecticut have become used to horrendous railroad service, but when a local limped into Grand Central an hour and a half late (on a scheduled forty-minute run) even one meek little shnook from Mount Vernon protested. The conductor reminded him, "We're always late when it's snowing." "I know that," persisted the shnook, "but this morning there isn't even a cloud in the sky." "We're not responsible for that," concluded the loyal conductor. "SNOW WAS PREDICTED!"

∴

The president of a large firm was taking an early train from New London to Manhattan, and found his way to the dining car for breakfast. Summoning the steward, he said, "I think I'll have a go at that eight-dollar special my salesmen always put on their expense sheets when they ride this train."

∴

Fred Birmingham has an ingenious friend who takes advantage of the free facilities provided at Grand Central Station to enhance his love life. He makes a date several days a week with his dream girl for noon under the Concourse clock. Then they spend a happy hour or two rapturously kissing each other in front of any gate announcing a departing train—moving on to the next departure when the gate closes—while boarding passengers smile tolerantly to see love still conquers all.

Two foreign gentlemen arrived in the Main Concourse another morning with a quantity of fresh fruit, vegetables—and lumber. Turned out that they had paid a couple of plausible strangers a goodly sum for the right to erect a fruit and refreshment stand in the middle of the action. Obviously, points out Birmingham, the boys who used to sell the Brooklyn Bridge now have moved uptown.

∴

Leo Rosten recalls a time when train executives still welcomed customers, and upper berths were actually in demand. A Mr. Fortescue was thus ensconced one night when a lady in the lower beneath him kept him awake for hours with her continual moan, "Oy, am I thirsty!" Finally, in desperation, Mr. Fortescue climbed down the ladder, padded the length of the car, filled two paper cups with water, and thrust them through the curtains to the grateful lady. Fortescue then climbed back to his upper, thinking, "That should keep the old girl quiet!" But just as he was slipping off to sweet slumber, she spoke up again. "Oy," she rejoiced loudly, "was I *THIRSTY!*"

∴

Sign at a railroad crossing near Sandusky: "The average time it takes a train to cross this intersection is twenty seconds—whether your car is on it or not."

∴

A little girl—1970 model—had been on dozens of jet planes in her time, but this was her first overnight journey in an upper berth of a Pullman car. Somewhat frightened, she called out at regular intervals to her mother below, "Mommy, are you there?"

After many hours of this a gentleman across the aisle piped up, "Yes, mommy is here. And I'm here, too. We're all trying to get a little sleep. So for heaven's sake, stop that confounded noise."

There was a moment of silence, and then a quavering little voice called out, "Mommy, was that God?"

4. Hotels

Boston is like no other city in America. Its hotels are different, too. When you're not allowed to go out of a certain door in most hostelries, you'll be warned by a pre-emptory sign reading, "No exit." In Boston's superb Ritz, however, the warning reads, "This is not an accredited egress door."

One early summer evening, an elderly guest asked a Ritz attendant, "Is the roof garden open for dancing yet?" "No, sir," was the respectful reply. "The roof is closed this evening."

What he neglected to add was that the roof garden had been closed for good twenty-five years ago.

.:.

A traveling salesman in the deep South hit one hotel where the rooms were infested with giant economy-size mosquitoes. Furthermore, he was told that no mosquito netting was available. "All you got to do is follow the example of the man who owns this hotel, Colonel Rip Clatterborn," the desk clerk told him. "And how," inquired the salesman sarcastically, "does your blasted Colonel Clatterborn manage to go to sleep without a net?"

"He doesn't," admitted the clerk. "But the colonel is what you might call a dedicated drinker. He goes to bed so well oiled he doesn't notice the mosquitoes for the first half of the night. And for the second half, the mosquitoes are so drunk they don't notice the colonel."

.:.

The late Bob Benchley was one of the most generous and open-hearted of men, but he did object to all the utterly dispensable flunkies who lined up for tips when he checked out of a fashionable hotel. Once, having already given handouts to a half-dozen servants he never had laid eyes on during his entire stay at a West Coast luxury den, he was confronted by a pompous doorman who specialized in never being on duty when he actually was needed. "Leaving us, eh, Mr. Benchley?" he boomed, holding out his palm. "I hope you're not going to forget ME."

Benchley shook the outstretched hand warmly. "I certainly am not," he promised with a tremor in his voice. "I'll write to you!"

∴

Claude, head masseur at a swank health resort, was unceremoniously fired last week. He rubbed a VIP customer the wrong way.

∴

A gentleman with a very military bearing drove his car into a parking lot of a hotel in Birmingham and looked about for the attendant. "Here I am, Major," called a lad from the rear of the lot, and ran up on the double. "I'm not a major," said the driver, descending from his car, "and I don't like to be called one." "Beg your pardon, Colonel, no offense intended," the boy assured him. "I'm not a colonel, either," said the driver. "In fact, I have no title at all. I don't like titles. Now, how much will it cost me to park here for three hours?"

"There'll be no charge at all, sir," grinned the attendant. "You're the first big shot that ever drove into this lot who was just nobody at all—and it's a pleasure to serve you."

∴

The closing of Washington's famous old hotel The Willard, set historians scuttling to record famous events that took place in the long history of the hotel.

Don Maclean dug up the part it played in the Civil War's first battle of Bull Run. Washington gentry had not yet taken the threat of the Confederacy seriously. On the day the Union Army sallied forth to do battle with the upstart rebels, fancy carriages loaded with gentlemen and ladies dressed to the nines set out from The Willard, bound for the Virginia hills to witness what they expected to be an easy northern victory.

Hours later, they straggled back to the Willard bar, and spent the evening imbibing and trying to rationalize the North's decisive defeat. That's the last time the Civil War was mistaken for a spectator sport!

∴

"Is this town's water pure?" demanded a cautious tourist of his innkeeper. "Sure is," nodded the innkeeper. "First we filter it, then we take the iron out of it, then we add numerous chemicals to it—and then we drink beer."

Later, the same tourist asked, "Any night life in this God-forsaken hole?" "Gotta admit there ain't," sighed the deflated innkeeper. "She left for Rockford last Tuesday."

∴

Subtle are the stratagems of a successful publicist! Years ago, when the Waldorf-Astoria was still located on Thirty-fourth Street, New York, a rumor gained circulation that it was going to be torn down, to be replaced by a brand-new hostelry up on Park Avenue. This was indeed the plan that was afoot, but it was still years from fruition. Meanwhile, as a result of the rumor, business began to fall off alarmingly at the old location. Fashionable folk didn't want to be seen in a hotel that seemed doomed to oblivion!

A prominent publicist was called in to set things aright—and this he did very quickly. He announced that Oscar, the famous head chef, had been signed to a precedent-shattering million-dollar contract: one hundred thousand dollars a year for the next ten years! Patronage at the Waldorf was soon bigger than ever, particularly in the lucrative food and beverage departments—and half the customers invaded the kitchen to get autographs from the great Oscar!

∴

A bellhop had just ushered a lady and gentleman into a posh suite in an exclusive hotel and been tipped generously. "Anything more I can do for you, sir?" "Not a thing," he was assured. "And how about your wife?" "Thanks for reminding me," said the gentleman warmly. "You might bring me a stamp and a picture postcard!"

5. *Restaurants*

Just 132 years ago, in 1838, a Mr. Delmonico threw open the doors of America's first deluxe and exclusive restaurant—at 494 Pearl Street in lower Manhattan. The establishment prospered from the start, and flourished in various locations—moving always northward with the social tide, until 1933, when, in its most sumptuous headquarters on Fifth Avenue and Forty-fourth Street, it succumbed to the ravages imposed by prohibition.

Delmonico's very first menu ran to eleven pages, offering a choice of twelve soups, twenty-eight beef entrées, forty-seven of poultry, forty-six varieties of fish, fifty-one vegetable and egg dishes, and forty-seven choices of dessert! And the prices! Beefsteak went for twenty-five cents a portion, delicious pie for a dime a slice, any one of the twelve soups was yours for a nickel, and so was a cup of coffee with real cream. Costliest item on the menu was roast canvasback duck—with twelve side dishes!—at $1.50 a throw, and no tipping was allowed! If there ever was such a word as inflation in those days, it's a sure bet that no patron of Delmonico's ever had heard it.

Among the Presidents who favored Delmonico's with their patronage was Abraham Lincoln. Once, when Host Delmonico gallantly refused to present Mr. Lincoln with a bill for a sumptuous banquet, the President fished into his trousers and presented the restaurateur with a long-used pocketknife as a token of appreciation.

∴

A restaurant owner, sampling a newly hired cook's first pot of soup, remarked, "You say you served overseas?" "I did," said the cook proudly. "I was officers' cook for two years and was wounded three times." "You're a lucky man," decided the owner. "It's a miracle they didn't kill you."

∴

Hermione Gingold supped at a popular chop house recently and told the waiter, "I've decided to have the Chef's Special." The waiter came back from the kitchen a few moments later to tell her, "I'm very sorry, madam—but the chef ate it."

∴

The air conditioner in a rather elegant restaurant was blowing right on the back of a scantily dressed young lady, so she quietly draped a napkin over her bare back. A boy at the next table watched the operation with great interest. "Get a load of that lady by the window," he told his father. "She's going to eat backwards!"

∴

Salvatore, just added to the staff of waiters at the Venezia Bar and Grille, disappeared for a full hour after reporting for his first day's work. His excuse to the boss: "I've been filling the salt shakers like you told me to." "It took you one hour to fill a few miserable salt shakers?" echoed the incredulous boss. "Yes, sir," replied the waiter. "It's not so easy for an inexperienced man to pour salt through all those little holes."

∴

A hungry stranger once wangled a table at Toots Shor's exclusive saloon on Fifty-second Street and ordered four cocktails, a bowl of soup, two thick slabs of roast beef, a baked potato, three bottles of beer, and two slices of apple pie à la mode. Toots tapped him lightly on the shoulder and asked, "What time are you being electrocuted?"

∴

A customer in a Second Avenue restaurant beckoned his waiter to complain, "This sauerkraut isn't sour enough to suit me." "That isn't sauerkraut," pointed out the waiter contemptuously. "That's noodles." "Oh," apologized the customer. "For noodles, it's plenty sour!"

∴

Another patron of the same establishment asked the cashier, "How's business?" "It could be worse," allowed the cashier. "I might own it."

∴

On his first trip abroad, an unsophisticated old rabbi, treated to the vacation by a loving congregation, was considerately steered in Paris to nothing but kosher restaurants, so that he would not inadvertently break the orthodox ritual. When the old man returned home he told his friends, "I don't know why they make such a fuss about that French cooking. We have exactly the same food at Mrs. Rosenberg's boardinghouse!"

∴

Two Wall Street speculators, badly bent by a steep decline in the averages, dined together in a very expensive restaurant.

When the check was presented, it turned out that each of them, confident that the other would pick up the tab, was strapped for cash.

"Let's split the check fifty-fifty," proposed one, straightening his shoulders. "You wash, and I'll dry."

.˙.

Max Asnas, late owner of Broadway's Stage Door Delicatessen, was a kindly man and many was the moocher he staked to a free meal. One night a particularly bedraggled derelict appeared upon the scene and was promised a handout as soon as a big crowd of paying customers had been served. This took longer than the derelict thought it should, so he angrily accosted Mr. Asnas and cried, "Hey, I've been waiting for that meal you promised me now for a full twenty minutes. How much longer will I be ignored?" Mr. Asnas answered, "What's the matter, you bum? Are you double-parked?"

.˙.

The biggest deadbeat in town, in debt to just about everybody he knew, proposed to take a new girl friend to the most expensive restaurant in town. "But aren't you afraid," he was asked, "that you'll run into a couple of outraged creditors there?" "Not a chance," sneered the deadbeat. "When I get through with them, they can't afford a place like that!"

6. *Table Talk*

Speaker at a businessmen's luncheon: "I will speak only fifteen minutes at most because of my throat. Your president threatens to cut it."

Exasperated mother to stubborn child: "Eat it, Chester, dear. Pretend it's mud."

At a lunch counter: "Did you say you wanted these eggs turned over?" "Yes—to the Museum of Natural History."

Small boy to his father: "How come a Coke will spoil my dinner and martinis give you an appetite?"

Fat lady at Schrafft's: "I watch very carefully what I eat—and then I eat it."

In a hotel dining room: Wife: "What are the snails like here?" Husband: "They're disguised as waiters."

At "21": Ambitious starlet: "I'm looking for a sugar daddy." Her aged escort: "Look no further, my dear. I've got diabetes."

At the bar atop the Fairmount: "I got this black eye fighting for a girl's honor. She wanted to keep it."

∴

Mike Romanoff, destined to become Hollywood's most elegant restaurant tycoon, spent many of his younger days posing with indifferent success as a Russian nobleman—but he even starved with distinction. One night Heywood Broun found him doubled up with pain and obviously suffering from some vile bootleg brew on the steps of a speakeasy, and rushed inside to fetch him a bottle of milk as an antidote. Shivering, Mike rallied sufficiently to read the label on the bottle, then flung it into the gutter. "A Romanoff," he informed Broun haughtily, "never drinks Grade B milk!"

∴

Chop suey, contrary to the belief of 95 per cent of U.S. citizens, is not a Chinese dish at all, but purely American. You can't get a decent dish of chop suey in the whole of Hong Kong—unless you patronize a restaurant catering exclusively to American tourists.

Chinese gourmets aver that chop suey—THEY call it "beggar's hash"—originated in the San Francisco region during the gold rush in the 1850's. A group of miners allegedly descended upon a Chinese restaurant there after hours clamoring for chow. The canny proprietor threw all the leavings in his kitchen into a big kettle, heated up the mess, and served same, ready to run for the hills. But the miners LOVED it. And THAT, chuckle the Chinese food experts, is the "chop suey" silly Americans demand!

∴

It was in an East Side chop suey emporium that a customer encountered a waiter who didn't look exactly Chinese to him. The proprietor explained, "You're right, sir. He's really from Flatbush. He kept chopping away at his real name till all he had left of Horowitz was Ho."

∴

An ambitious young man persuaded the daughter of the town's richest man to be his guest for dinner. He became increasingly nervous as she ordered the most expensive entrée and beverage on the menu, finally reminded her weakly, "Order anything you want, dear girl, but remember we have to get out of here at $10.50."

∴

One of those West Coast nighteries that feature topless waitresses has offered jobs to two very pretty midgets. They'll wait on customers who are under the tables.

∴

"I beg your pardon," said a diner, "but who are all those girls staring at me?" "I'm not supposed to tell you," confided the waitress, "but we get the bulk of our food from the cooking school next-door. If you don't eat every morsel on your plate, those poor girls have all flunked their final examination."

∴

A communiqué from the proprietor of a ritzy delicatessen on the waterfront at Long Beach, California, boasts that he serves "kosher dishes with schmaltz," but that on October 31 he provides no hot dogs with meat therein—only "hollow weenies." To compound this atrocity, he adds that of eighteen of his doctor patrons who switched some years ago to Camels, sixteen have gone back to women, and that his wife, weary of cooking blintzes, has invented a new girdle that makes fat ladies look like Barbara Walters. It still has one small bug, however, that she cannot eliminate. The wearer's face turns blue.

∴

A hayseed approached a vending machine, inserted a quarter, and pressed the button labeled "Coffee, double cream, and sugar." No cup appeared, but two nozzles began functioning, one pouring coffee, the other cream. After the proper amounts had gone down the drain, where the cup should have been, the machine stopped pouring.

"Now, that's real automation," nodded the hayseed admiringly. "This thing even DRINKS for you!"

∴

A teacher making a guided tour with a group of schoolchildren picked a restaurant for lunch that boasted a slot machine in the corner. The kiddies, of course, demanded to know what it was, which gave the teacher a golden opportunity to deliver a lecture on the evils of gambling. To prove that you seldom get something for nothing in this world, she inserted a dime in the machine, pulled the handle, and—you guessed it—hit the jackpot.

THE SPORTING LIFE

1. *Panorama*

Richard Morland, U. S. Government Chief of Injury Control (Even money you never knew we had one!) rates the five most dangerous sports indulged in generally by America in this order: 1. Hunting. 2. Scuba and skin diving. 3. Pleasure-boating. 4. Swimming. 5. Football. I would have thought that skiing and bobsledding would show more mortalities than pleasure-boating. Not so, avers Mr. Morland. Leslie Lieber adds, "Remember that statistics don't tell all." He recalls an Ivy League senior who fell off his chair during a hot chess tournament—and broke his leg!

∴

Here are a few sports oddities from the bulging archives of the "Believe It or Not" organization:

—Gary Pertit, of Sioux City, Iowa, starred in a school basketball game from which he emerged as high point scorer for both teams. He dumped a ball in the opposition basket by mistake, scoring two points for the wrong team, then rang up sixteen points to help his own team conquer, 34 to 3.

—A league football game in Pullman, Washington, played in below-zero weather, attracted exactly one paying spectator.

—A man named Blackstone, in Seattle, bowled 299½ in one game he'll never forget. One pin split in half and part of it remained standing.

—And Mrs. Rose Kinnie, of Watertown, actually found that diamond in the rough you've always heard about. She sliced a ball into the woods on the right of the third fairway and found it nestling next to a diamond stickpin, which she sold, when no other club member claimed it, for fifteen hundred dollars.

∴

The editor of the religious page of a big-city newspaper—plus his wife—attempted unsuccessfully to brazen their way into a crucial hockey game during the play-off season. After their rebuff, he complained bitterly, "That so-and-so at the gate wouldn't forgive us our press passes."

∴

Conned by a famous gate-crasher into allowing him in without a ticket, to another hockey game that had been a sellout for weeks, the guardian at one of the main gates explained mournfully, "That bird walked in backwards so smoothly I thought he was coming out!"

∴

A visitor to a girls' high school noted that in a junior class basketball game in the gym, all the girls on one team were white and all on the other team were black. "I thought this was a progressive school," commented the visitor, "with full integration. How come you play basketball along racial lines?" "Racial lines have nothing to do with it," explained the gym teacher. "You see, if we mixed the teams up, we wouldn't know who to throw the ball to."

∴

A Las Vegas showgirl, obviously headed for the heights, has forsworn golf in favor of bowling. "It's cheaper," she explains. "Last night, for instance, I bowled for three hours and didn't lose a single ball."

∴

A pair of retired businessmen in Miami, bored with unaccustomed lack of action, invested in a greyhound dog on a fifty-fifty basis. Unfortunately, the dog finished dead last in six straight races, and the partners decided to cut their losses and get rid of him. At the bank of a river upstate, one partner suggested, "Here's our chance. Let's throw the dog in." "That would be too cruel," decided his more tender-hearted associate. "I know! Let's run away from him!"

∴

A girl got a job wrestling octopi at a state fair last summer. She was darn good at it, too. She got her training, she says, going to a drive-in movie with a different fellow every evening during the spring.

∴

Wearied of chasing elusive jackpots in Las Vegas, a visitor decided to have a look at nearby Boulder Dam. In the building that houses the giant dynamos he spotted a lever and pulled it from sheer force of habit. Would you believe it? He hit for seven million gallons of water!

∴

Overheard by sports scribes:

Angry golfer: "How do you like that? I come out here for exercise—and, instead, I get a hole in one!"

Minnesota housewife: "I certainly enjoy hearing the honking of a wild goose—except when he's driving our car."

Clerk in sports goods emporium: "You say your wife returns everything, sir? We have the perfect birthday present for her: a boomerang."

By Hy Gardner: "You know what I call a scoundrel who steals a Japanese motorcycle? A Honda-taker!"

Caddy at Sandy Lane Course: "Sorry, Mr. Canfield. That wasn't your ball. That was your wrist watch."

At a family bowling alley. Novice wife to her would-be helpful spouse: "If I do anything wrong and you can show me how to do it better—keep your big mouth shut!"

Mervyn Leroy tearing up tickets at Santa Anita: "Last week I had the perfect system for winning on the races. Then the track opened."

One girl golfer to another: "The nearest I ever came to a hole in one was an eight."

Race track addict to baseball devotee: "One thing we've got over you on TV, anyhow. We don't have to watch a horse shaving."

∴

"There's really nothing difficult about learning to ski," a sports-loving groom assured his timid little bride. "First, you just learn how to put the skis on. Then you learn how to push off the crest of the hill on them. Then you learn how to get along on crutches for the next five weeks or so."

∴

To hear him tell it, a big blowhard at a winter festival in Vermont had almost made the 1968 U.S. Olympic ski team. "Why then," asked a young lady innocently, "do you sit all day at that picture window sopping up liquor and watching other people exercise? Why don't you get out there, and ride up on that ski lift that operates from morning until night?" The blowhard looked at her aghast. "If I did that," he grumbled, "how would I get down?"

∴

An avid sportsman not only suffered a broken leg on a ski excursion in the Laurentian Mountains, but discovered that the only way he could fly home, what with the bulky cast on his leg, was to buy two seats—one for himself, one for the leg. The ticket seller at the airline counter had one helpful suggestion, however. "Wait over until Monday," she counseled. "Then your leg can travel family plan."

2. *Want to Bet?*

Phil Levin recalls the worst day he ever experienced at a race track. As the sun slowly sank in the West, he went to the snack bar, ordered a corned beef sandwich, then switched at the last moment to ham on rye. "Wouldn't you know it?" he demands mournfully. "The corned beef came in first at eighteen to one."

∴

A horse race enthusiast, charged by his shopping-bound wife to take care of their seven squawking kids, bundled the lot of them into the family station wagon, and headed for the Aqueduct track. Just after the sixth race a friend met him and inquired casually, "How are you doing?" "Not so good," grumbled the enthusiast. "So far I've lost five races and three kids."

∴

When Oscar Levant was still a youthful piano prodigy, and not drinking more than thirty cups of black coffee a day, he once fell into the hands of some professional card sharks who clipped him several times running for just about everything he had made between sessions. As he was paying up the last of many $500 payments, Levant suddenly declared, "I don't want to make a scene, but I think you fellows have been cheating me." The leader of the group admitted frankly, "Oscar, we'd been planning it, but after seeing you play, we didn't have to."

∴

A group of pale-faced Broadway characters spent a recent weekend in Atlantic City and played poker in their suite for the entire forty-eight hours of their stay there. As the heaviest loser toted his valise down to the hotel lobby, he grumbled, "That's the last weekend I'll ever spend in the country!"

3. *Baseball*

In the dear old days when the Dodgers belonged to Brooklyn, Ebbets Field fans waxed ecstatic at the mere name of Dazzy Vance, as great a pitcher as ever strode to the mound. One day a couple of his Georgia cousins came to New York for their first visit to a big city and Dazzy invited them to see him pitch against the enemy—the Giants. "Watch me strike those bums out," he ordered. "Then you'll see why they just raised my pay to $25,000 a year!"

Unfortunately, this was not one of Dazzy Vance's better days. The first six batters to face him, in fact, lined out hits, and Dazzy was yanked without having retired a single man. His Georgia cousins were waiting for him at their hotel after the game. "Dazzy," they assured him, "you got the easiest way to make $25,000 we ever saw!"

∴

Joe Garagiola, who has cleaned up a tidy fortune on the lecture circuit retailing funny stories about the days when he was a big-league baseball star, recalls one afternoon when he was catching a game for the Cards against the Chicago Cubs. At the Chicago park, the walls enclosing the outfield are covered with ivy. In the third inning of this particular game there, the starting Cub pitcher had been manhandled so by the long-hitting Cardinals that Chicago's manager, Phil Cavarretta, strode to the mound to relieve him, explaining, "I hate to take you out on your birthday, Bob, but all my outfielders are getting poison ivy!"

∴

Joe remembers another game, where the starting pitcher objected strenuously to being taken out of the game. "Lemme face one more man," he begged the manager. "I know I can get that bum out." The flint-hearted manager reminded him, "You already proved that when he led off the inning."

∴

Nat Benchley figures that the Ancient Mariner must have been a rank bush leaguer. His fielding average was a lowly .333: "He stoppeth one of three."

∴

Frankie Frisch, Fordham's greatest contribution to big-league baseball, and Bill Klem, toughest and most deeply respected umpire in National League history, conducted a long-time feud that erupted at least four times every season. Once, when Klem called out a Cardinal runner on a close play at third, Frisch, coaching there, let out the expected shriek of protest, then clutched a hand over his heart, and collapsed on the ground. The players and the fans in the stands were panicked —but not old Bill Klem. He shoved his way through the crowd of players, glared down at the prostrate Frankie, and roared, "Frisch, you faking bum, dead or alive, you're out of the game!"

∴

Art Linkletter tells about the time the peerless Willie Mays was engaged to portray himself in a TV baseball epic. The director told him, "Willie, we know that acting is not exactly your line. Do you think you'll have trouble just being your natural self?" "Well, I'll tell you," replied Willie calmly. "Just you turn your cameras on, and if it ain't me, lemme know!"

∴

A heartbreaking tale concerns the trip into Mexico by a chronic tail-end baseball team during last season's spring training period. To the gratification of the team officials, a great crowd was waiting when the bus arrived in town. Everybody and his brother crowded around the surprised players, and enthusiastic cries and comments abounded. That night, however, not a hundred people showed up for the game. A disheartened official asked an English-speaking native why there had been so much excitement in the morning and so much apathy at game time.

"I guess you no comprehend," explained the native. "None of my fellow-townsmen ever saw a Greyhound bus before."

∴

In the now hard-to-recall days when the "amazing" New York Mets were chronic losers—the League's patsies—the player who probably symbolized the team's inadequacy best was a first baseman named Marv Throneberry. The fans loved his every bobble and strike-out in a pinch. Reporter Arthur Daley remembers best the day manager Casey Stengel was presented with a huge birthday cake. "Why," mourned Throneberry, "didn't somebody give me a cake on MY birthday?" "We woulda," the voluble Casey assured him, "but we wuz afraid you'd drop it."

∴

Another time Marv banged out a triple with the score tied in the ninth inning—then was called out for failing to touch first base. Manager Casey Stengel came roaring out of the dugout to protest. "Save your breath," advised the umpire. "He didn't touch second base either."

∴

There's a young outfielder with one of the expansion teams whose mind is really on the game. Asked in the interim of a doubleheader if the report was true that he had married his childhood sweetheart during the off-season, he nodded, "That's right, and now my wife's expecting a baby." "When is it due?" asked the interviewer. The ballplayer did a moment's mental calculation, then told him, "Well, right now she's in the top of the eighth."

∴

There's a ballplayer in the big leagues known to his teammates as "Flakey." One of his memorable exploits was to persuade the club's star pitcher to drive him twenty miles to a certain ice cream emporium because it was the only one that advertised twenty-nine different flavors. Then he ordered vanilla!

∴

Dizzy Dean, colorful star of the St. Louis Cardinals of yesteryear, was a tough man to impress. Just before he strode to the mound at the old Polo Grounds in New York one afternoon, Dizzy's manager pulled him aside and whispered, "You know who that dame is sitting with the baseball commissioner in that box behind first? That's the Queen of the Netherlands!"

"Oh, yeah," nodded Dizzy with a yawn. "Where was she last night when I needed her for a full house?"

4. *Football*

Placed atop my desk recently was a mighty funny cartoon of a big lug in football togs carrying a squirming coach off the field on his shoulders with the coach screaming, "Put me down, you idiot! We lost!"

∴

Maybe you're under the impression that El Paso is merely the name of a big city in Texas. Wrong, asserts Johnny Carson. According to Johnny, it's also the cognomen of a Mexican football player who can neither el rusho or el punto.

∴

"About as tense a moment as you can imagine on the football field," opines sports expert Bill Vaughan, "is when a coach realizes that his team, one point behind, has only one time out and three commercials remaining."

∴

At a hick college with a fourth-rate faculty but a first-rate football team, the varsity fullback was a formidable brute who had just about enough sense to sit down when he was tired. Nevertheless, a determined English prof picked on him one morning to name three characters in Malory's classic *Le Morte d'Arthur*. The fullback pondered deeply, and then came up with a hopeful, "Well, first of all, I guess there was old Mort himself."

∴

Many big football games have been played in abominable weather, but never have two teams faced worse conditions than those confronting Penn and Cornell one Thanksgiving Day for their traditional contest. Rain was coming down in buckets, and the field—not to mention the spectators—was soaked. The Cornell captain won the toss and, asked whether his team would kick off or receive, decided, "I guess we'll be better off kicking with the tide!"

∴

A 300-pound linesman on the awesome Los Angeles Rams football team explained at a dinner his system of defense: "I just jam in there and grab a lot of them. I peel them off—and the one that's got the ball, I keep him."

∴

An award-winning football coach devoted part of the off-season to teaching his six-year-old son the fine old art of goal kicking. One day he got down on his knees, placed the ball meticulously, then ordered, "Now, when I nod my head, KICK IT."

And that's how the coach lost his two front teeth.

∴

Football buffs are chortling over the story of the captain of a high-school team whose pep talk to his squad before a big game concluded with, "You know our beloved coach is fifty-eight years old today. Let's get out on that old gridiron and give him something to remember in other birthdays to come!" So they dashed on to the field—and got shellacked—fifty-eight to nothing!

.·.

The squad of a big pro football team was startled at practice one early fall afternoon when a turkey strutted to the field and demanded an opportunity to show his stuff. Sure enough, he was not only a superb passer, but ran repeatedly right through the team's strongest defense unit.

"You're terrific," beamed the coach. "We'll give you a hefty bonus if you'll sign up for the full season." "Forget the bonus," said the gobbler. "What I want to know is: does that full season extend past Thanksgiving Day?"

.·.

Pro football players not quite good enough to make the regular team are often carried for practice sessions or as possible replacements for injured regulars as a separate unit called the taxi squad. One 250-pound bruiser was heard complaining that he's been on the Jets' taxi squad so long he now wears an off-duty sign.

∴

A famous gridiron coach who eats, dreams, and is interested in nothing but football, ended a perfunctory round of golf one afternoon, then wandered absent-mindedly into the ladies' locker room instead of the men's. Nude and semi-nude females apprised him of his mistake by screaming bloody murder. Recovering at the bar, the coach mourned, "It was horrible. Those fool girls ran with their heads too low, they kicked their legs too far out behind, they brought their arms too far across their chests. . . ." "But were they dressed or undressed?" demanded the entranced bartender. The coach admitted, "I didn't notice."

∴

Buford Ray, former Green Bay Packer, told Bish Thompson of the Evansville *Press* the story of one of his 280-pound guards who was not exactly a mental phenomenon. One night the well-meaning bruiser came home nursing a black eye and a swollen lip. His explanation was, "I just ran into Mike Maloney, the tavern keeper, and made some crack about the Pope. So he took a couple of pokes at me."

"For Pete's sake," exploded Coach Ray, "didn't you realize that Mike Maloney is a Catholic?"

"Yeah, sure, coach," nodded his brilliant guard, "but I didn't know the Pope was!"

5. *Golf*

A golf nut had a beautiful creature on his right at dinner and gave her an endless monologue on his extraordinary achievements on various courses here and abroad. All she got in was an occasional "remarkable." Finally he became aware that her attention was wandering and apologized, "I'm afraid I've been monopolizing the conversation and talking about nothing but golf." "That's quite all right," she assured him, "but do tell me this: what's golf?"

∴

At the Lyford Cay Golf Club in Nassau, a player was seen waving off a frantic girl in a bridal gown. "No, no!" cried the golfer. "I told you distinctly, Myrtle: ONLY IF IT RAINS!"

∴

It was a raw, windy November day, but a foursome of rugged senior citizens had no intention of letting that hold up their regular twice-a-week match. Off the first tee they drove, making bets galore, hurling time-honored insults at each other—and then stopping after each shot for a nip at their ample pocket flask. By the eighteenth green the four of them were so fried they could scarcely stand. They were also all even. The whole match depended on whether or not one of the inebriated antiques could sink a long uphill putt. Just as he was about to make the putt, a great big brown-furred dog dashed out of the caddy house, burst straight between the old gentleman's legs, and disappeared into the bushes beyond the green. Completely ignoring the interruption, our intrepid hero smacked his putt straight into the cup.

"What a man," enthused his partner as they made their way uncertainly to the locker room. "He sinks a tough putt like that even though a big dog dashes between his legs."

The old man gasped, "Great heavens! YOU DON'T MEAN TO SAY THAT WAS A REAL DOG!"

∴

Frank Sinatra persuaded golf expert Arnold Palmer to play eighteen holes with him at Palm Springs one morning. The round completed, Sinatra asked anxiously, "What do you think of my game?" "Not bad," conceded Palmer, "but I still prefer golf."

∴

A couple of overweight lady duffers waddled out to the first tee of a Detroit golf course one very sultry morning. "I don't want to play too long," declared the lady who drove off first. "Let's quit as soon as either of us makes a hole in one!"

∴

Endless are the adventures that may befall an intrepid golfer as, regardless of weather or obstacles, he plods doggedly around the links. Take the case of Rex Bartlett, for example, as told by Fred Beck in his highly amusing 89 *Years in a Sand Trap.*

Mr. Bartlett was leading the field in an interclub tourney in California until he bounced an approach shot into a bowl of mustard on a hot dog stand. Or the plight of Carl Boies, a pro in Texas. Playing under the old rule that provided that no player may touch his ball until he has holed out, Boies drove his ball into a sea of icky mud. He played out manfully, splattering himself and the gallery with mud in the process, and, miraculously, landed smack on the green. He carefully stroked his ball toward the cup ten feet away when, alas, he discovered that the ball was stuck firmly to the blade of his putter!

∴

A Sunday golfer trying doggedly to blast his way out of a trap complained loudly, "The traps on this course are mighty annoying, aren't they?" "They certainly are," called out another player, trying to putt on a green nearby, "and I'll be deeply obliged if you'll close yours."

∴

"How I love that game of golf," enthused Mr. Maxwell. "I'd like to shoot thirty-six holes every single day!" "You sound like a shark," smiled the man next to him at the bar. "What's your handicap?" "My wife," mourned Mr. Maxwell. "She won't let me play."

∴

The first time Toots Shor ever played an eighteen-hole round of golf he made a 211 (with several conceded putts). On the eighteenth green he asked his companion, one Jackie Gleason, "What do you think I should give the caddy?" Gleason suggested, "Your clubs."

∴

A flying saucer's mechanism went out of joint, and it came careening into a deep sand trap on the Burning Tree Golf Course. "What do I do now?" the pilot shortwaved to headquarters in outer space. Back came the answer, "Use your number nine iron, you meathead!"

∴

Ed Kosun tells a story about a choleric golfer named Harry who could be depended upon to fly into a rage every time he played, but finally hit upon the device of playing without a ball. This made him very happy.

A clubmate decided he'd play without a ball, too, and the two of them had a match every Saturday—complete with everything but balls!

One day they made a $100 bet on a round and the club members gathered to watch this most unusual match. The two players were all even as they hit off the eighteenth tee. Both had good drives, and they sauntered down the fairway to where a good drive would have landed.

The first player took a club and swung. Immediately, Harry started to yell at him and in a moment there was a big fight. Club members rushed down from the eighteenth green to see what was wrong.

"It's my match! It's my match!" cried Harry. "HE HIT THE WRONG BALL!"

6. Prize Fighters

The Gowanus Marching and Chowder Club was sponsoring one of its classier fixed fights, with Spike Clancy, favored at odds of eight-to-one to flatten Chicken Shtoonk, handsomely bribed to let himself be knocked out in the sixth round. Shtoonk, secure in the knowledge that his victory was in the bag, unreeled a couple of genuine haymakers that rattled Spike Clancy's back teeth. "You miserable little double-crosser," muttered Spike in a clinch. "Wait till I get you outside!"

∴

Ex-pro prize fighter Phil Rafferty, now a valuable member of the staff at P. J. Clark's famous pub in New York, boasts, "When I was boxing I was probably the best fighter in the country." Then he adds ruefully, "But they murdered me in the city."

∴

The death of former heavyweight "champion" Primo Carnera concludes one of the weirdest and most disgraceful episodes in the history of professional boxing. Carnera, a giant, good-natured oaf with the courage of a lion, but a glass jaw and a complete inability to learn the fundamentals of self-defense, was rocketed to the championship via a series of fixed fights, then robbed of the profits by the dirty crooks who controlled his destinies.

The sad part of the story is that Carnera himself never realized he was being played for a patsy—even when occasional opponents were "knocked out" by roundhouse punches that had missed them by three feet. Budd Schulberg has told the whole story in a fine novel called *The Harder They Fall.*

One of the countless Carnera anecdotes concerns the day a manicurist asked him, "What do you think of Los Angeles?" "Pouf," deprecated Primo, "I knock him out in two rounds!"

∴

Touching sight at Madison Square Garden: a manager working frantically over his battered warrior in a corner of the ring, pleading, "Try to hang in there just one more round, Spike. What he's doing to you is beginning to sicken him!"

7. *Fishermen*

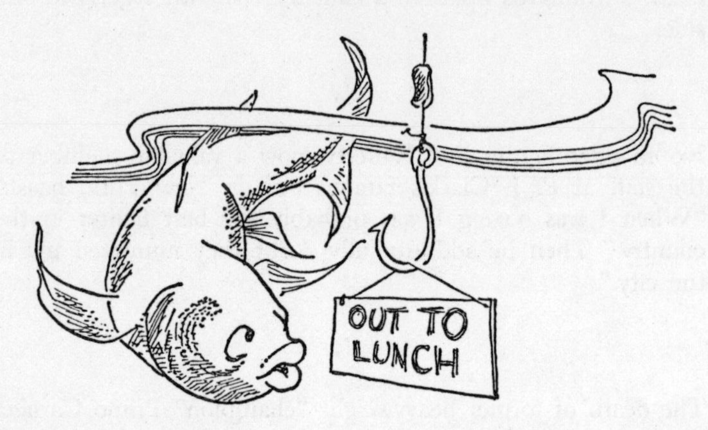

A little seven-year-old girl who had coaxed her daddy into letting her go fishing with him, grew understandably impatient when she failed to get as much as a nibble in over an hour of bobbing her line up and down in the placid waters of a nearby lake. She suddenly threw her rod into the bottom of the boat and announced, "I don't want to fish any more today, Daddy, I've got a worm that isn't even trying!"

∴

A tough old editor of a popular fishing magazine caught a member of the editorial staff relaxing at his desk, and barked, "What are you doing hanging around your office? Why aren't you out FISHING?"

∴

A personable young divinity student went fishing one day, accompanied by two extremely pretty young ladies. A fisherman downstream noticed that they hadn't had as much as a nibble in two hours, and commented, "You're not catching many, are you?" The divinity student explained haughtily, "I am, sir, a fisher of man." His tormentor nodded and remarked, "Well, son, you certainly have the right bait with you!"

∴

Two old retired cronies went fishing together one day at Rangeley Lake in Maine. For three hours neither moved a muscle. Then one got a bit restless. "Confound it, Joe," grumbled the other. "That's the second time you've shifted your feet in the past forty minutes. Did you come out here to fish or dance?"

∴

The recent arrival of a huge captive white whale, brought in a canvas tank to the Coney Island Aquarium from the Gulf of the St. Lawrence, caused unexpected trouble to a witless fishing enthusiast, who watched the huge creature thresh about for some moments, then said to his wife, "By the way, how's your mother?"

8. A-Hunting They Would Go

Aware of the fact that the woods would be full of a new crop of inexperienced hunters, an old-timer prepared for the opening of the deer hunting season by making himself a suit of awning cloth with glaring alternate stripes of black and white. Thus equipped, he sallied forth confidently on the first day and was promptly winged by a novice.

At the hospital, the doctors shouted at the quaking novice, "Anybody could see those stripes a mile away. How, from a distance of a hundred yards, could you possibly mistake this poor man for a deer?"

"I didn't," stammered the novice. "I mistook him for a zebra."

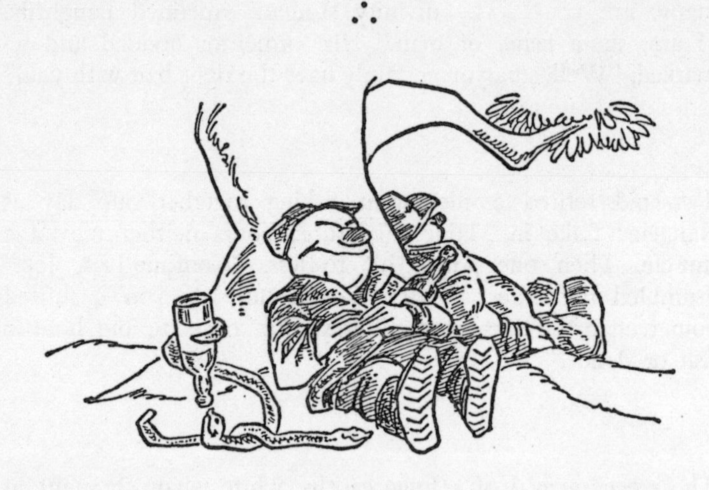

Jim Kelly tells of two business tycoons, off for a hunting trip, who cut their equipment down to barest essentials: four bottles of whiskey for snake bites—and two snakes.

There's one duck hunter in Georgia who won't take any kind of a drink in a hurry before he goes on another hunting expedition. Recently he found himself sharing a blind with a club member he couldn't quite place, though he nodded hello. The member happened to be famous ventriloquist Edgar Bergen.

A covey of wild ducks flew by. Both men aimed and fired. One duck fell, and both men claimed it was their shot that had brought it down.

"There's only one way to settle this," decided Bergen. He retrieved the dead duck, propped it up on his knee, and asked, "Who shot you, duck?"

The duck answered, "You did, Mr. Bergen." The other hunter fell out of the blind.

∴

During the quail season in Georgia, an Atlanta journalist spotted a farmer out hunting with his very old pointer. While he watched, the dog pointed twice, and twice the farmer peered into the brush, wheeled, and fired into the empty air. The journalist, intrigued, ran over for an explanation. "Shucks," said the farmer, "I know there ain't no birds in that grass—but my poor old dog's nose ain't what it used to be. But we two has had some mighty wonderful times together, and he's still doing the best he can. It would be mighty mean of me to call him a liar."

∴

An English huntsman was beating his way through the thick gorse and bracken when he came suddenly on a fair young maid taking a sun bath. "A thousand pardons and all that sort of thing," he stammered. "I'm looking for game." The maid smiled and said, "I'm game." So he shot her.

TRY AND STOP ME

1. 25 *More for Bennett Cerf's Riddle-De-Dee**

1. Q. What did Adam say when he heard that his wife had fallen out of the apple tree for the third time?
   A. "Evesdropping again, eh?"
2. Q. What's the past tense of Yankee Doodle?
   A. Yankee Diddle.
3. Q. What's a trampoline?
   A. A female tramp.
4. Q. What is covered with salt and has a twisted mind?
   A. A thinking pretzel.
5. Q. What is a panther?
   A. A man who makes panth.

* *Riddle-De-Dee*, published by Random House, Inc., 1962.

6. Q. Why is the cutest nurse at St. Luke's Hospital known as "Appendix"?
   A. Because only the doctors are allowed to take her out.
7. Q. What do they call a man who steals ham?
   A. A hamburglar.

8. Q. What's the best way to keep a husband from watching three football games on TV on Sunday?
   A. Shoot him Saturday night.
9. Q. How do you stop a herd of wild elephants from charging?
   A. Cancel their credit cards.
10. Q. What's yellow, smooth, and dangerous?
    A. Shark-infested custard.
11. Q. What has four legs and will sit in your lap?
    A. Two secretaries.
12. Q. What happens when you submerge a body in warm water?
    A. The telephone rings.
13. Q. Which pine has the longest and sharpest needles?
    A. The porcu.
14. Q. How do you tell girl pancakes from boy pancakes?
    A. By the way they're stacked.

15. Q. How can you get rid of repulsive fat?
A. Divorce him.
16. Q. What is the most austere hotel in the U.S.A.?
A. The Waldorf-Austeria.
17. Q. What do you get when you cross a movie house with a swimming pool?
A. A dive-in theater.
18. Q. What's the best way to clean an aardvark?
A. With an aardvarkuum-cleaner.
19. Q. Why isn't ten cents worth what it once was?
A. Because dimes have changed.
20. Q. What's the fastest thing on two wheels?
A. An Arab riding a bicycle through Moshe Dayan's rose garden.
21. Q. What kind of corsage did Lassie wear to the big ball of the year?
A. A collie flower.
22. Q. How was spaghetti invented?
A. Some Italian used his noodle.
23. Q. What did one IBM card say to another?
A. I'm holier than thou.
24. Q. How can a girl change into a river?
A. By marrying a hippie—thereby becoming Mrs. Hippie.
25. Q. What do you call a Shanghai maid who inherits ten million yen?
A. A Chinese fortunate cookie.

2. 25 *More for Bennett Cerf's Out on a Limerick**

1. An attractive, though silly girl, Ruth,
Had a horror of telling the truth.
To her dentist she lied
As his pliers he plied—
So he cheerfully pulled the wrong tooth.

* *Out on a Limerick*, published by Harper & Row, 1960.

2. A girl named Venuta Cellini
Came to school in a skimpy bikini.
Said her teacher, "Unless
You put on some more dress
I shall spank you betwixt and betwini."

3. It is never considered quite nice
To make passes at lady friends twice.
It is clumsy and crude
And exceedingly rude;
Besides, usually once will suffice.

4. In merchandise Macy's a symbol
For anything down to a thymbol.
But there isn't a doubt
That if they are out,
You'll be able to find it at Gymbol.

5. A critic refused, as reviewer,
To read the obscene and impiewer.
He soon quit the scene
For the books that were clene
Simply kept getting fiewer and fiewer.

6. In Rome dwelled a fair miss named Flettera
Whose necking grew better and bettera.
She'd hold hands in the park,
Kiss boys in the dark,
Etc., etc., etc.

7. When he met her, her name was Miss Fraser.
Now her husband most meekly obaser.
He did once refuse
To polish her shoes
But she soon changed his mind with a raser.

8. There was a young lady named Nance
Who attended a debutante dance.
She inspected the cellar
With an Ivy League fellar
And now all her sisters are aunts.

9. A seamstress named Lucy Levine
Caught her leg in a sewing machine.
Then observed with a cry
That she'd stitched on her thigh
Her telephone number in green.

10. An Englishman swears to his friends
As his wife's puffed-out figure extends
That he never complains
Of the pounds that she gains
But deplores all the pounds that she spends.

11. Said a cow in the pasture, "My dear,
Don't count on much romance 'round here.
I start with high hopes
But they come up with dopes—
And I end with the usual bum steer."

12. Quoth an erudite, envious ermine,
"There's one thing I cannot determine:
When a girl wears my coat,
She's a person of note;
When *I* wear it, I'm simply called vermin!"

13. "It is not in my nature to fiddle,
And thumbs I am lacking to twiddle,"
Said the hen as with pride
She laid sunny-side
Two fried eggs on a piping hot griddle.

14. A mouse who was mad about cheese
Developed a terrible sneeze.
His problem was this:
The holes in the Swiss
Admitted too much of a breeze.

15. A nuisance and pest is the rabbit.
When he spies your best lettuce he'll grab it.
He doesn't rate high
In brains, but oh my!
He surely knows how to cohabit!

16. There was a young lass from Connecticutt,
Who signaled a bus with her petticutt.
This her mother defined
As rare presence of mind
But a deplorable absence of etticutt.

17. There was a young poet named Peck
Whose verse earned him many a check.
Though he'd gathered them all
From an old washroom wall
In the Government House in Quebec.

18. Said a youth from Saskatchewan,
"You have something nobody can match you on;
I'm referring, my dear,
To a place at the rear,
That it gives me such pleasure to pat you on."

19. Mourned a swollen-faced man from Duluth
"I've got a bad tooth and itth loothe.
What I needth a martini
With, well, jutht a teeny
Or maybe not ANY, vermouth."

20. Said a farmer outside Albuquerque,
 "Tho Thanksgiving looms misty and murque
 All may still turn out well
 For I've managed to sell
 Some alfalfa, a cow, and a turque."

21. A mouse in her room woke Miss Dowd.
 She was frightened, it must be allowed.
 Soon a happy thought hit her;
 To scare off the critter,
 She sat up in bed and meowed.

22. There was a young girl from Missouri
 Who drove all her lawyers to fury.
 At her dumbness they'd frown
 But she sure went to town
 When crossing her knees for the jury.

23. Ten men in the town of Emporia
 All kissed a demure miss named Gloria.
 That was two weeks ago
 And so far as we know
 They're still in a state of euphoria.

24. The Mets playing baseball in Dallas
 Called the umpire names out of malice.
 While that worthy had fits,
 The team made six hits—
 And a girl in the bleachers named Alice.

25. There was a young damsel named Brooks
 Who was lavishly dowered with looks.
 But when parked in a car
 With her swain she would spar
 And insist on discussing good books.

(Her father was a publisher—and he had her on his hands until she was seventy.)

3. 25 More for Bennett Cerf's *A Treasury of Atrocious Puns**

1. Miguel Gonzalez, the Michael Caine of Juarez, was unlucky enough to suffer from insomnia. But then the resourceful fellow won the love of a Mexican beauty named Esta—and now, when he wants to sleep, he just looks at her picture. Miguel knew from childhood that when you see Esta, you sleep.

2. A post office exec in New Jersey has designated a special truck to expedite delivery of mail properly zip coded. The truck bears the sign "Zip Van," and, of course, it was only a question of time until a local wit added "Winkle" thereto.

3. A gaggle of prosperous optometrists is putting up a swanky new headquarters building in Los Angeles. Obviously, it will be a site for sore eyes.

4. A shameless pundit named Norbert Kearns cites the case of a barber named Cohen whose shop was located next to a bowling alley. Cohen became so determined to get his score over 150 that he began neglecting his barbershop. He had just made three successive strikes one afternoon, in fact, when the political boss of the county tracked him down and demanded an immediate shave. Cohen pushed him indignantly aside, however, declaring firmly, "A bowling Cohen lathers no boss!"

5. Jim Caldwell tells about a young lady who attended a famous Eastern college, but was bored by the proceedings. She vastly preferred to slip off either to New York or Boston and participate in the activities of the YMCA's there. One might say—in fact, Mr. Caldwell does—that this miss loved not Wellesley but two Y's.

6. There's a new dessert on the market whose ingredients are not being divulged by the bakery that's sponsoring it. Consumers are challenged to identify the ingredients for them-

* *A Treasury of Atrocious Puns*, published by Harper & Row, 1968.

selves. The new confection has been named "I am curious Jello."

7. An office secretary had a lovely face, but try as she would, could not develop a well-rounded figure. She stuffed herself with food from morning to night, but continued to look like a long string bean—especially when viewed from the rear. Heartless co-workers dubbed her "the bottomless pit."

8. Two professors of archaeology, avows Jan Harrison, were on a dig when they came upon a very odd rock formation. Furthermore, a strange, rhythmic sound seemed to be emanating from the rock, not unlike a heartbeat. "What do you suppose this can be?" one of the archaeologists wondered. Quoth his companion, "Doctor, living stone, I presume."

9. James Stewart and Josh Logan, we learn from James Powers, when they returned to Princeton for their twenty-fifth reunion, found themselves bedded down in Old Nassau, the hall in which they had roomed together so many years before. It was the first night of festivities and no formal activity had been planned. "How about a game of gin just to pass the time away," suggested Logan. "Okay," nodded Stewart. "Any old sport in a dorm."

10. When a recent Arabian potentate renounced his throne and vamoosed to Europe with twenty "dancing girls" and about forty million berries in Swiss currency, a wit at the Associated Press commented, "There's one king who could abdicate and eat it, too!"

11. The stingiest character in town ran up a six-dollar charge in a taxi ride the other day, and when he alighted from the cab paid the exact sum registered on the meter, then handed the outraged driver a half-smoked cigarette. "Here," he explained, "is your filter tip."

12. Fireman Epstein of Engine Company 29 is a proud man this day. He's just won an Extinguished Service Award.

13. A very, very dazzling girl whose knee was so far out of kilter that she made Joe Namath's underpinnings sound by comparison, visited a chiropractor in search of some relief.

Said chiropractor examined her with relish and rose to inquire, "What's a joint like this doing in a pretty girl like you?"

14. Richard Burton confided to Hank Grant that he once had a burning desire to smoke a hookah water pipe. Unfortunately, he couldn't find a hookah to sell him one.

15. A natural-born sucker bought a tract of land from a small-order real estate outfit, but discovered, when he visited the property, that nine tenths of it was bug-infested swampland. "There's not a thing you can do about it," advised his lawyer. "They've left you holding the bog."

16. A member of an old and exclusive club in New York was a hopeless egomaniac who never stopped boasting of his amazing accomplishments as, first, a college athlete, and later, a colonel in World War Two. "Every time that so-and-so opens his mouth," grumbled one exhausted fellow-member, "he puts his feats in it."

17. In Gloucester, an ingenious manufacturer of fishermen's supplies is advertising a new rod "guaranteed to get a pike's pique." In Sidi, Morocco, a smart apple has opened a saloon called "Sidi Limit." And in Great Neck, a doctor, summoned to treat a weekender who had swallowed an oyster containing an indigestible hard and gritty substance, removed the offending substance with the cheesy observation, "A gritty pearl is like a malady."

18. Anne Johnson, weekending at the Hamptons in Long Island, strolled over to inspect the brand-new Shinnecock Canal locks. Flying overhead was a covey of gulls. "What a natural for a delicatessen," enthused Anne. "Locks and bay gulls!"

19. Charles Kiser checks in with the story of a worker in a pants factory whose sole task was to place a small "X" in chalk on each completed garment. Along about 4:50 P.M. one day, he said to the man next to him with relief, "Thank goodness, I have only six more britches to cross."

20. Wayne and Schuster, two of TV's bright stars from Canada, confide that Jackie Onassis is taller than her bridegroom, and that he compensates for this by wearing built-up

shoes. "All of which proves," W. and S. dare to add, "that you should beware of Greeks wearing lifts."

21. Paul Stone, of Bowling Green, Kentucky, suggests that the first city of any size on the moon obviously should be named Mooneapolis—and that vacationers of the space age may soon be buying waterfront acreage on Saturn Island. Bowling's Stone gathers no Mars!

22. Ingenious garden tenders south of the border have found a new way to smuggle marijuana into the States. They stuff it into chickens—and then fly the poultry to a private airport in Texas. In that part of the country, at least, there now is pot in every chicken.

23. A renowned lady gardener in the New Haven area, her living room festooned with blue ribbons she had garnered, decided to plant some special fronds and anemones this spring. The fronds turned out in spectacular fashion, but the anemones, to put it mildly, were a distinct flop. The lady, unaccustomed to failure, was lamenting this minor setback, but a good friend hastened to bolster her sagging spirits. "Remember, Debbie," she counseled, "that with fronds like this, you don't need anemones."

24. A doctor in Toronto has come up with the theory that cheerful souls resist disease better than chronic grumblers. What he's trying to tell us, it seems, is that the surly bird catches the germ.

25. All afternoon a real estate agent had been showing a young couple empty houses. The ones they loathed always seemed to be available, but the ones that struck their fancy invariably had been snapped up by others. Finally they came to a house at the very edge of town and fell in love with it. "Please," they begged, "tell us that this one we can have."

"It's yours," beamed the agent. "It's last but not leased!"

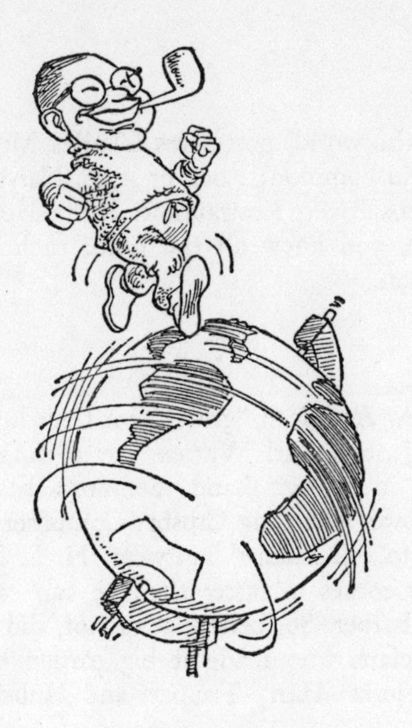

ROUNDABOUT

1. *Inside the U.S.A.*

The forefathers who named our towns and villages were not too imaginative. The U.S.A. today boasts twenty-one Milfords and Oxfords. There are seventeen Buffalos and sixteen Warrens, thirteen Parises, twelve Berlins, eleven Moscows, nine Dublins, and six Londons. There also are two Budas but no Pests.

Dreamers and lovers of the classics will be pleased to note that we have fifteen towns named Athens, sixteen Arcadias, and eight Paradises. Only one Utopia turns up, unfortunately —and that's in Texas.

∴

Now, what in the world, postulates Charles McHarry, do the following have in common: Rock of Ages, Naivilliwill, Whitefish Point, Brazos River, Keewaunow, Hesta Head, and Umpqua? Of course, you knew all the time: each one is a U.S. lighthouse station.

∴

Here's how a few American "greats" got their humble starts in life: Ex-Chief Justice Earl Warren was a union-card-holding clarinet tooter in a jazz band. Semi-pro baseball players: Dwight Eisenhower and Bing Crosby. Composer Dick Rodgers left Columbia to sell infants' knitwear. H. L. Hunt, now so rich the money comes in faster than he can count it, began his career as a barber. So, believe it or not, did Greta Garbo. And two politicians who made it big earned their first pay-checks as soda jerks: Harry Truman and Hubert Humphrey!

∴

If you're the kind of person who likes to celebrate holidays, take note of the fact that there's now a National Buzzard Day each March to celebrate the return of those lovable birds from their winter haunts in the Great Smokies. There's also an official International Whale Watching Week, a National Odor Control Month, and Honor-Your-Mother-in-Law Saturday, and a Sour Pickle Day. Keeps a chap happy!

∴

If you hear about a fellow whose head is buried in the sand, counsels Sidney Brody, don't jump to the conclusion that he's unaware of the dangers of the nuclear age. He may simply be spending the day on the beach with his children.

∴

A jaded professor of political science, bound for Tahiti to get away from it all, was pacing the deck with a new shipboard acquaintance. He announced confidently, "You live in the city governed by as mean, dirty, and corrupt a ring of thieves as there is in all the U.S.A." "How do you know where I live?" demanded the new acquaintance. The professor puffed placidly on his pipe and answered, "I don't."

∴

Polk and Company, publishers of innumerable city directories, would have you know that the first street in the country is Second Street! There are more Second Streets in the U.S. than those bearing any other name. Park Street is runner-up, Third Street is third, Fourth is fourth, Fifth is fifth, and Main is sixth. Poor old First Street straggles in seventh!

∴

Don't fret another minute about race relations, drug addicts, or pollution! A pompous old Park Avenue clubman has figured everything out to his own satisfaction. "What's wrong with the world today is very simple. You start treating people as equals, and the next thing you know the darn fools begin to believe it!"

∴

British stage star Robert Morley states in his lively autobiography that he's pleased that every time a foreigner arrives in the U.S.A., customs officials consult a long list of names of persons deemed *persona non grata* in this great land of ours. "I don't believe these people actually exist," confesses Morley, "but it does make one think, my goodness, I've been let into the United States!"

∴

Interesting coincidences reported by a New York newshawk: 1. An Alabama mayor proclaimed Crime Prevention Week. The next day his new automobile was stolen. 2. The U. of Washington, with an enrollment of 27,000, sponsored a symposium on "Student Apathy." Twenty students showed up. 3. A North Carolina city had to call off a "Disaster Exercise." The hall in which it was scheduled was flooded the morning of the show. 4. A Chicago bartender was relieved by a bandit of his gold watch and $150 in cash. The bandit tied him up with the cord from the burglar alarm system.

∴

A young Londoner, on his first visit to the States, asked a taxi driver to suggest a hotel and was driven to a house with a questionable reputation indeed. Two days later he was asked by an old friend and countryman what he thought of his first American hotel. "Well, I wouldn't say the decor is particularly striking," reported the Londoner, "but gad, what room service!"

∴

Deep in the Bronx, a bank failed—and its doors were shut to keep out a mob of outraged depositors. One of them mounted a soap box and began screaming, "The electric chair is too good for the crook who runs this bank! They should turn him over to the Red Guard in China! They should throw him into Niagara Falls for robbing poor workers of their savings!" A policeman stopped him and asked, "Did you have money in this bank, brother?" "Listen, officer," replied the orator, "if I had money in this bank, do you think I'd be taking it so lightly?"

∴

A stroller on the Coney Island boardwalk dropped into the lair of a Gypsy fortuneteller and got something of a surprise. "Say," he exclaimed. "Do you realize your crystal ball has two holes in it?" "Of course I do," nodded the Gypsy. "I put 'em there myself; on the side I give bowling lessons."

∴

The closing of the Nepperhan telephone exchange near Yonkers, New York, reports Beth Day, caused some temporary confusion. When one subscriber asked for Nepperhan 4508, only to be told "Nepperhan is now obsolete," she agreed amiably, "All right, give me Obsolete 4508."

∴

Alfred Bendiner tells about a visitor to Philadelphia who pointed to a building on South Broad Street and asked what it was. "That," said his guide proudly, "is our Union League Club." "What's the crepe doing on the door?" asked the visitor. "I guess one of the members died," answered the Philadelphian. "Hmmm," mused the visitor. "Cheers it up some, doesn't it?"

∴

A dashing young Argentinian met a beautiful young lady in Washington and persuaded her to spend four weekends with him at Virginia Beach, rewarding her with $250 on each occasion. As the fourth deliriously happy weekend was drawing to a close, the Washington girl said, "Incidentally, I have a brother living now in Buenos Aires. I don't suppose you ever ran into him?" "Indeed I have," responded the young Don Juan warmly. "In fact he commissioned me to look you up—and entrusted me with a thousand dollars to give you."

∴

Critic George Oppenheimer was taken to the prevue of a hackneyed motion picture with a Civil War setting. At its conclusion, the producer asked anxiously, "Do you think my picture will offend the South?" "It certainly will," answered Oppenheimer—"and the North, too!"

∴

Ben Wasson, harking back to the days when the first ladies of Virginia still left calling cards on their afternoon rounds, tells of one highly placed Richmond dowager who was breaking in a new footman. "Now, you bring along the cards I left on the table," she instructed him, "and leave one—or two, if I so instruct you—at each residence I visit." Late that afternoon they paused at the home of Richmond's undisputed society queen. "Here," said the dowager, "I want you to leave THREE cards." "Can't do it, mum," declared the footman. "Why not?" demanded the dowager. "'Cause we only has two left," explained the footman. "The ace of clubs and the seven of diamonds."

∴

In a sleepy South Carolina town, a luscious twenty-year-old bride was put on trial for shooting her miserly eighty-year-old husband. The jury knew to a man that she was guilty beyond all doubt, but they were darned if they were going to convict her. They filed back into the jury box to find out if her deceased husband had belonged to any club. "Yes," she sobbed demurely. "The Elks Club."

So they fined her five dollars for shooting an Elk out of season.

∴

A smug traffic cop nailed a tourist in a speed trap down South, and the magistrate slapped the customary ten-dollar fine on him. Then it developed that nobody in court could change the tourist's twenty-dollar bill. "Tell you what you do," proposed the resourceful magistrate finally. "Go back on that highway and SPEED IT OUT!"

∴

When Mr. Nussbaum cut his foot on a stone at Miami Beach, they rushed him to the hotel doctor—who, it developed, was a lady—and a darn good-looking one, too. "You're a DOCTOR?" jeered Mr. Nussbaum suspiciously. "Here's my diploma on the wall," she assured him. "Hmphh," snorted Mr. Nussbaum, unconvinced. "If you're a doctor, how come you haven't got a mustache?"

∴

Speaking of Mr. Nussbaum, when his wife was asked, "Have you been through menopause yet?" she answered, "With a husband as stingy as mine? He hasn't even taken me through the lobby of the Fontainebleau!"

∴

Mrs. Cameron was a bit uneasy as her touring group was led deeper and deeper into the Florida Everglades. "The very thought of alligators terrifies me," she confided to the guide. "How can you tell when one's nearby?"

"Nothing to it, lady," the guide assured her. "Say you and your husband wander off a few steps for a private conversation

and a smoke. All of a sudden you notice you're smoking and talking to yourself. Lady, you just located your first alligator."

∴

Lyndon Baines Johnson tells of a day when his brilliant political career was just dawning and he was seeking to win favor with his rural Texas audience by emphasizing the beauties of the state's landscapes. He started with the beautiful piney woods of East Texas, moved lovingly through the bluebonnets and out to the plains and down the hill country to the Gulf Coast and back to the piney woods, where he started all over again. When he got going on his third time around, an exasperated little cuss in the back of the hall hollered, "Say, Lyndon, the next time you pass through Lubbock, how about letting me off?"

∴

Stanley Marcus, bearded boss of the fabulous Neiman-Marcus store in Dallas, and his own best press agent, includes among his more improbable anecdotes one concerning a lady from a hole in the wall upstate who appeared at the store one day in a gingham gown and sunbonnet—barefooted. She bought a mink coat for $6,000 and paid cash for it on the spot. And while she was waiting for the coat to be wrapped—Stanley sold her a pair of shoes!

∴

A Texas lady, boasting about her new swimming pool, was interrupted by an unimpressed socialite from up North. "Virtually everybody I KNOW has a swimming pool," she declared. The Texas lady demanded, "With high and low tides like ours?"

∴

Three last typical Texas tidbits: 1. A cat in Dallas died and left an old lady four million dollars. 2. A Fort Worthy is so loaded with pelf that his son's piggy bank has four vice-presidents. 3. A Houstonite in Washington watched government minions at the Mint burning soiled currency and remarked ruefully, "Hot damn! Thought *we* were the only family that did that!"

∴

Robert Gottlieb has discovered why mountain climbers always are roped together. It's to keep the sensible ones from going home.

∴

A Wall Street kill-joy, never known to smile in the past ten years, had this to say about New Orleans' annual Mardi Gras: "You couldn't get me to attend if they were dancing in the streets!"

∴

A self-made tycoon in Cleveland freely admits that he owes the greater part of his success to his wife of forty years. "I keep a big picture of her on my desk," he explains, "and every time I look at it, I work overtime."

∴

A Jewish youth, equally adept at solving an intricate equation and throwing an accurate pass fifty-five yards downfield, elected to go to Notre Dame. Home for his first vacation, his rabbi, who had taken a dim view of the whole procedure, asked anxiously, "My boy, they aren't Catholicizing you there at South Bend, are they?" Indignantly, the youth replied, "I should say not, Father."

∴

Did you ever wonder how the ice cream sundae came into being? It was the result of a blue law, avers Sam Himmell. In the late nineties, a city ordinance in Evanston, Illinois, prohibited the sale of ice cream sodas on Sunday—another triumph for the bluenoses who were then cocks of the walk in those parts. One enterprising fountain operator found the way to outfox said bluenoses. He served ice cream with syrup instead of soda. The correction caught on, and soon was in demand all seven days of the week. Choosing the name "sundae" was easy!

∴

A beggar stood in front of St. Louis' most fashionable hotel holding out a hat in each hand. The doorman said, "I don't want to chase you, mister, but what's the idea of TWO hats?"

The beggar winked, and confided, "Business has been so good, I decided to open a branch office."

∴

The wife of a Tulsa zillionaire decided to give her spouse a 135-foot yacht for a birthday present. She instructed the salesman, "I want this to be a complete surprise. Be sure to wrap it so he can't guess what it is."

∴

There's a Pueblo Indian laboring in New Mexico who is far too obsequious to his white employers to suit his fellow tribesmen. They refer to him contemptuously as an Uncle Tomahawk.

∴

John Kohl, Allentown's leading literary light, tells about an ambitious young Indian, just released with honors from the U. S. Navy, who repaired to an Arizona reservation to help less fortunate members of his tribe. Anxious to freshen up for the dinner planned to welcome him, he paid his first visit to the head, only to find it shrouded in darkness. So he promptly had the head electrified at his own expense—the first time in history anybody wired a head for a reservation.

∴

The Rittenhouse clan—papa, mama, and four little Rittenhouses—elected to spend their vacation on a camping trip. Wearied by six nights at trailer camps, Mr. Rittenhouse returned from scouting the locale at their seventh stop to report sardonically, "Well, folks, there isn't a campground within a radius of twenty miles that isn't packed full. For this one night, I'm afraid we're going to have to sleep in some brand-new air-conditioned motel, with soft, downy beds, no bugs, color television, and breakfast served in our room—and just make the best of a bad bargain."

∴

An eastern visitor turned up at a big cattle ranch in Montana and asked the owner what he called the layout. "Our family had quite a fight over just that subject," admitted the ranch owner, "and we ended up by trying to please everybody. So this here ranch is named the Triple-X, Lucky Seven, Diamond T Bar, Lazy Mary Ranch." "That's quite a name," chuckled the visitor, "but where are all the cattle?" "Ain't none," sighed the owner. "Not one of them darn critters has survived the branding."

∴

Apropos of nothing, Joe E. Lewis suddenly announced in Las Vegas one evening, "I just met somebody who speaks perfect English." Frank Sinatra, seated next to Lewis, asked idly, "Who?" Explained Lewis, perfectly seriously, "A cat. It said, 'Meow.'"

∴

A tip-hungry bellboy knocked on the bedroom door of Jerry Lewis at 7 A.M. in a Nevada luxury inn and called out "Telegram, sir." "Dammit all," grumbled Lewis, "just shove it under the door." "I can't," replied the bellhop. "It's on a tray."

∴

Johnny Cash, visiting the headquarters of one of those weird cults that seem to thrive in the balmy air of Southern California, was startled to discover this notice posted on the clubroom bulletin board: "Due to the shortage of trained trumpeters, we have been compelled to postpone the end of the world."

∴

About the best way to treat the perpetrators of these irreverent, and sometimes infuriating buttons and rear-bumper stickers that are so much in vogue today, is, I think, to ignore them. Let the fad die out naturally—as indeed it will if it isn't kept alive by the very people most offended and sinned against thereby.

An example of my contention is one of the more widely circulated of these ridiculous slogans: "Mary Poppins Is a Junkie." Apparently the only man who took this nonsense seriously was some pompous legal eagle in or near the Walt Disney organization, who sought an injunction against the perpetrators. Obviously delighted, they promptly got out a NEW set of stickers reading, "Mary Poppins is NOT a junkie." That ended the litigation.

∴

Only in California, surmises Paul Nathan, could this happen: he ran into a crestfallen Pasadena father who just had been advised that his only son, a student at Caltech, had flunked golf.

∴

Two lissome surfboarders were sunning themselves on a virtually deserted California beach. "This spot is so secluded," noted one, "that I believe we could go nude into the water." "What's the point?" asked the other. "There's nobody to watch us."

∴

A very fat newcomer to San Francisco grumbled, "No other city ever bothered me—but these damnable hills are wearing me down." A native Chamber of Commerce booster cheered him with, "Ah, but you forget one wonderful thing about San Francisco, my friend. When you get weary you always can lean against it!"

∴

From the Oregon woods comes a story of a logging boss in those parts who slipped off of a wet log and would have drowned in the turbulent rapids had not an alert lumberjack spotted him and dragged him ashore. "Pretty lucky I was there to rescue you," panted the lumberjack. "Nonsense," snorted the boss (genuine villain!). "If you'd been paying strict attention to your job, you wouldn't have seen me fall in."

∴

An earnest little man told the clerk at a big travel bureau, "My wife and I are determined to find the real America." "Good for you," enthused the clerk. "But tell me, where did you lose it?"

∴

And here's a basket of five salty American oddballs rounded up by the ever vigilant Harry Ruby:

1. The woebegone character a policeman spotted sleeping on the marble steps of the Public Library. "Don't you have a home?" asked the copper sympathetically. "I do," admitted the character, "but my wife's there."

2. The realtor who told a home-seeking pair of honey-

mooners, "First, you tell me what you can afford. Then we'll have a good laugh, and go on from there."

3. The Swedish wife who walked out on her husband. She left his bed and smorgasbord.

4. The big executive who told his secretary, "Answer this letter for me, but be careful not to lose my temper."

5. The sweet young thing who told her roommate, "All I want is a decent man who will love and respect me. Is that too much to ask of a multimillionaire?"

2. *Outside the U.S.A.*

A. SOUTH OF THE BORDER

The wife of one of our Presidents—never mind which one—accompanied him on one of his Latin American good-will trips. Back at the White House, her daughter asked her, "What did you eat down there?" She answered, "Lots of beef, spicy side dishes, and 7,866 green peas." "Quit kidding me, Mom," protested the daughter. "How would you know exactly how many peas you ate?" "My dear girl," answered the President's wife, "how do you suppose I occupy my time while your father is speaking?"

∴

Former Secretary of the Interior Udall, an aide of his tells me, was standing outside a native crafts shop in San Juan when an American tourist tapped him, and apparently mistaking him for a native Puerto Rican because of his deep tan, asked him very carefully, "Pardon, señor. Can possible you tell me where comes el taxi?" Udall playfully answered, "Si, señora. You go across street, and ring, ring telephone. Taxi she come pronto."

The lady thanked him profusely, then boasted to her husband, "You see, Osbert? If you speak slowly enough they understand you perfectly."

∴

Rick Setlowe, in *Variety*, tells of the day Roone Arledge, high mogul of ABC's sports division, tried to get some TV color shots of the Acapulco cliff divers for whom the Mexican seaside resort is noted. It seems that these death-defying lads are also hep enough to have organized themselves into a union. The head thereof informed Arledge, "We know how many stations now air your 'Wide World of Sports.' You'll have to pay us a hundred thousand dollars for the shots you want." "Forget it," snorted Arledge. "Our whole show isn't budgeted for that much."

"Wait a minute," said the Mexican youth hastily, then ran over for a huddle with the other divers. When he hastened back, he announced, "We've just held a union meeting and decided we'll take ten dollars a dive."

∴

Down in a town in Ecuador, a restless manufacturer of foot powder he calls "Pulvapies" mailed out thousands of ballotlike throwaways urging recipients to "vote for Pulvapies." His copywriter did his work all too well. Came Election Day and Pulvapies received more votes than all the actual mayorality candidates combined.

∴

A salesman for a big Minneapolis outfit reports a trip aboard a train deep in the interior of an undeveloped South American republic. The station agent sold him a first-class ticket, but when the rickety wood-burning locomotive wheezed into sight it was pulling only one dilapidated coach.

"What's the good of having this first-class ticket?" demanded the salesman when the conductor came round. "Just wait and see," advised the conductor.

Sure, enough, fifty miles up the line, the train ground to a halt. The conductor shouted something in Spanish and all the other passengers climbed down to the ground, where they were handed an assortment of axes and buckets. "See?" explained the conductor. "First-class passengers don't work. Second-class carry water, and third class chop wood."

B. ENGLAND

Historic note for those who long for the good old days: In 1632 an author was hauled before England's Star Chamber on a charge of libel. The specific charge was that he had written disparagingly about a play at court in which the Queen had condescended to play a small role. Found guilty, he was fined 10,000 pounds, sentenced to life imprisonment, and had his ears cut off!

∴

Minor crisis in British history: when King George the Fourth (1762–1830) met his future bride, Princess Caroline of Brunswick, for the first time, he kissed her hand gallantly, then recoiled and whispered hoarsely to his attendant, "For God's sake, Henry, fetch me a glass of brandy!"

∴

Maybe you think women in England haven't made enough progress in the Battle of the Sexes in the past 160 years? Cast an eye on this legislation that was proposed in all seriousness in 1720: "All women of whatever age, rank, profession, or degree, whether virgin, maid, or widow, that shall impose upon, seduce, and betray into matrimony any of His Majesty's subjects by scents, paints, cosmetic washes, artificial teeth, false hair, iron stays, hooks, high-heeled shoes, or bolstered hips, shall incur the penalty of the law now in force against witchcraft and like misdemeanors, and that marriage, upon conviction, shall stand null and void."

∴

The Duchess of Windsor questions the authenticity of the remark so often attributed to Queen Victoria: "We are not amused." "Not only am I convinced she never said it," asserts the Duchess, "but I seriously doubt that she really was ever amused."

.·.

Britain's John Foster admits that his countrymen are on the phlegmatic side at times. He recalls a grisly moment in his schooldays when the headmaster came upon the pantry maid cruelly murdered, with her head all but severed from the torso and a bloody axe lying beside the body. The headmaster turned on the two horrified lads behind him and thundered, "What buffoon has done this?"

.·.

From a rural district of England comes the story of a driver of a small sedan braking hastily as the tweedy mistress of the largest estate thereabouts came hurtling around a sharp bend in the narrow road in her large Rolls. Before he could say a word, she shouted "PIG!" and drove on. "Fat old Cow," he cried after her in retaliation.

Then he drove round the bend himself—and crashed head-on into the biggest pig he ever had seen.

.·.

Claridge's in London continues to be the most elegant hotel in England, a reputation that it has jealously guarded for generations. To illuminate the management's ability to weather any crisis, the story is told of the time two reigning European monarchs, unbeknownst to each other, decided to visit London at the same time, and took it for granted that the hotel's fabulous royal suite would be reserved for them instanter. There was only one thing to do—and the Claridge management did it. They deliberately wrecked the entire royal suite, even pulling down the ceiling. The king's respective English ambassadors reported on the devastating flood that had done the damage, and the kings, neither of whom could claim one-upmanship, of course, were perfectly happy to be installed in identical lesser suites.

Two days after the kings had checked out, the royal suite was redecorated and ready once more to receive well-heeled and well-connected visitors.

∴

The British consul general in a Texas metropolis has a good sense of humor. Last summer, he had the following notice posted outside the entrance of his offices on July third: "Due to circumstances beyond our control, this Consulate will be closed all day tomorrow."

∴

A lady from Manchester was riding in a first-class compartment of a London-bound train with a baby in her arms. A gentleman (?) seated across from her peered incredulously at the baby and announced, "Madam, that is undoubtedly the most hideous infant I ever have seen in my life."

The outraged mother demanded forthwith that she be transferred to another compartment. "There you are, lady," soothed the conductor when the transfer had been completed, and then, to mollify her further, announced he was going to fetch her a cup of fine, hot tea. He was back in a few minutes with the tea in hand, and, "What's more, lady," he beamed, "I've brought a banana for your chimpanzee."

∴

An English guide was showing Kenilworth Castle to a gentleman from the Bronx. "For hundreds of years," he intoned, "not a stone of this edifice has been touched, not a single thing repaired." "Say," observed the Bronxite, "we must have the same landlord."

∴

A cockney mother in London regarded her sniveling ten-year-old daughter with considerable disgust and commented, "I've 'ad 'er vaccinated and I've 'ad 'er tonsils out, but nothing seems to please 'er."

∴

A Londoner, pinched for drunken driving, was submitted to a new testing machine which registered a staggering percentage of alcohol in his breath. "Your machine must be on the blink," insisted the Londoner. "My wife's a teetotaler. Try it on her." The police obliged and again the machine showed alcoholic content far above the allowable level.

"Now I KNOW your machine's out of order," cried the driver. "To prove it, let our little baby blow into the thing." The baby's breath was sampled, and sure enough, proved high on the alcoholic side. Sheepishly, the police tore up the complaint.

Driving triumphantly away, the Londoner told his wife, "That was one wonderful idea of yours to give the baby those two slugs of gin before we left the pub."

∴

An impatient American tourist was being driven through the English Lake Country when the road ahead was suddenly completely blocked by a very large contingent of quacking ducks. The driver of the tourist's car slowed down almost to a standstill. "Just don't sit there," grumbled the tourist. "Blow your horn, man!" The driver turned back to him and explained patiently, "Mister, those ducks are walking just as fast as they can!"

∴

The wise and experienced head of Wadham College in Oxford, Great Britain, knew just how to handle a gaggle of unruly students who suddenly forced into his hands a typical list of "non-negotiable" demands. Instead of losing his cool, the head sent them this note:

"Dear Gentlemen: We note your threat to take what you call 'direct action' unless your demands are immediately met. We feel that it is only sporting to let you know that our governing body includes three experts in chemical warfare, two ex-commandos skilled with dynamite and in torturing prisoners, four qualified marksmen in both small arms and rifles, two artillerymen, one holder of the Victoria Cross, four karate experts, and a chaplain. The governing body has authorized me to tell you that we look forward with confidence to what you call a 'confrontation' and I may say even with anticipation."

For the moment, at least, all is gloriously calm on the Wadham campus.

C. SCOTLAND

An Edinburgh excursion boat, jammed to the gunwales, obviously was about to sink, and frightened passengers were stampeding to the lifeboats. That's when the captain's voice was heard above the hubbub: "Remember, folks! Women, children, and those on the 'Go Now, Pay Later' plan first!"

∴

'Twas aboard the good ship *Mollie Burns* that the skipper and the engineer got into a bit of a row. The latter maintained that steering a ship was a lot easier than looking after the engines, whereas the captain asserted the engines were child's play compared with steering. They decided to settle the argument by changing places.

After ten minutes the captain was ready to concede defeat. "Mackenzie," he shouted, "I can't get these darn engines to start." "Don't bother," called back the engineer dispiritedly. "We're aground."

∴

A stubborn Scot from the picturesque isle of Skye boarded a train recently on the mainland, leading a large and nondescript animal which he insisted was an African mountain dog. The conductor protested vainly that it not only looked like a goat but smelled like a goat. Thereupon the "African mountain dog" proceeded to (1) butt the conductor in the stomach, (2) bleat, and (3) eat the mailbag. Furthermore, when the train reached its terminal, the animal butted the conductor a second time for good measure and then gave milk!

∴

An aged couple in Edinburgh were in their dining alcove listening to a church service on the radio. Suddenly the old man burst out laughing. "Sandy," cried his horrified wife. "Why this unseemly merriment on the Sabbath?" "Ho, ho," beamed Sandy. "The parson's just announced the collection, and here we are safe at home!"

∴

MacPherson had just attended his son's wedding at the little chapel in Gleneagles, and now he took the young bridegroom aside to slip him a rabbit's foot. "Always keep this in your pants pocket, lad," he counseled. "What for?" asked the son. "Because," said MacPherson solemnly, "every time your dam' wife sticks her hand in, she'll think it's a mouse."

∴

Three weeks after a good citizen of Glasgow had won the biggest football pool of the decade (over a hundred thousand pounds), his wife asked him, "Andrew, what should I do with all the begging letters?" Andrew, engrossed in his newspaper, answered calmly, "Just keep sending them oot!"

D. IRELAND

In the good old days in Dublin when the Irish were fighting for independence, one doughty son of Erin went to his confessor and told him he had just mowed down two British lieutenants. Hearing no response he announced in a louder voice that he also done away with a British captain. Still there was no comment from the priest, so the frustrated Irishman shouted, "Father, have ye fainted?"

"Fainted I haven't," the confessor finally replied. "I'm waiting for you to stop talking politics and commence confessing your sins."

∴

An Irish maid named Katie Flanagan was asked by the head of the house, Jerry Moriarity tells us, to put a nude statue on a pedestal in the front hall. "Faith, sir, and who is the indacent spalpeen?" demanded Katie. "He's a famous Greek god named Apollo," she was told. "He is, is he," concluded the unimpressed Katie. "And what's a murdering Greek with no clothes on his back doing with a fine old Irish name like O'Polly?"

.·.

A Dubliner named Flanagan was rash enough to attack Clarence Clancy while four other Clancy brothers were within firing range. Result: one Clancy was seen sitting on Flanagan's chest, another was punching him on the nose, a third was belaboring him with a barrel stave, and a fourth was whacking the soles of his feet with a baseball bat. When all the lads were hauled into court the judge looked at the fifth Clancy brother and asked sarcastically, "And what were you doing while all this fighting was going on?" "Me?" answered the fifth Clancy virtuously. "I was just circling around, your honor, looking for a vacancy."

E. EUROPE

It is the contention of Frank Sullivan—and who would be so bold as to dispute Frank Sullivan?—that when he was a callow youth in Saratoga, a reference he encountered in a textbook suggested that he look for amplification under Louis XIV. "I followed the suggestion religiously," avers Sullivan, "and there was Louis XIV asking indignantly, 'What are you looking under me for?' "

∴

A contemporary of the famous philosopher Voltaire was extolling the virtues of a protégé he was pushing for promotion in the government. "This man," declared the contemporary, "has a ready answer for everything." "Heavens," exclaimed Voltaire. "Is he as ignorant as all that?"

Another time, Voltaire was asked to join a symposium honoring a famous contemporary who just had passed away. Voltaire replied, "He was a sturdy patriot, a talented writer, a loyal friend, and a model father and husband—provided, of course, that he really is dead."

∴

Just arrived in Paris, a determined tourist from Reading, Pa., struggled in the Orly Airport snack bar to recall a smidgin of his high-school French. "*Nous voulons*," he stammered, "*deux consomme avec* bread and butter—that is, *beurre* and something or other. *Comprenez?*" "Sorry," shrugged the waiter, "but I hail from Boston, mister. I don't understand a word of French." "Well, dammit," exploded the tourist, "then get me some body who can."

∴

Leonard Gross tells of a tourist who approached the concierge of the posh Hotel George V in Paris and said, "I just saw ex-President de Gaulle praying at Notre Dame." The concierge asked, "To whom?"

.:.

From Paris comes the story of a young French boy and girl who were exchanging kisses in a parked car. The auto horn, stuck on a high note, was sending its piercing warning all over the neighborhood. The young couple obviously didn't notice, but the angry neighbors did—and summoned a gendarme. To his remonstrances, the boy only took out of his pocket a scrap of paper and wrote, "I love her very much." The girl, smiling happily, wrote beneath this, "We are going to be married." They were deaf mutes.

.:.

Just before the Manheimers flew off for a vacation in Italy and the Greek Islands, Mr. M. was asked, "Did your wife give the right age on her passport?" "She did," maintained Mr. M., "but it was someone else's."

.:.

Friends of the late Robert Sherwood remember the day he returned from an inspection of one of Italy's most famous monasteries. "It was splendid," he reported, "but it lacked the woman's touch."

.:.

A tourist back from his first visit to Italy was enthusing about the canals and gondolas of Venice, the Vatican and Coliseum in Rome, and the leaning Tower of Pisa. "But you haven't said a word yet about Florence," a friend pointed out. The tourist's face fell. "How did you hear about Florence?" he demanded. "She cost me four hundred dollars in American Express checks!"

∴

Have you ever stayed overnight at a strange hotel and gotten into the wrong room by mistake? A gentleman named Breiter won't forget the time this happened to him in Innsbruck, Austria. The key the desk clerk gave him opened the wrong door, all right. Mr. Breiter disrobed in the dark, climbed into bed, and found himself sharing it with a live, wriggling python! He made a wild dash for the door, fell down a flight of stairs, and broke his leg. The bona-fide occupant of the room, a lady of twenty-six, explained that the snake was her constant companion and bodyguard. "Every single girl should have one," she said—then magnanimously sent the injured Mr. Breiter a color photograph of her python.

∴

A few days after the Soviet troops invaded Czechoslovakia in 1968, a Prague patriot appeared at enemy headquarters to complain, "Two Swiss soldiers just stole my Russian wrist watch." The major in charge permitted himself a smile and suggested, "You mean two *Russian* soldiers stole your *Swiss* watch, don't you?"

The Prague patriot reminded him, "*You* said that. *I* didn't."

∴

If you saw three young ladies coming down the street with their hideous maxi-coats scraping the pavement, how could you tell which one was—(fill in here the nationality you respect least)? She would be the one whose slip showed . . . Nominate the same nation as the donor of a decoration to the first of its doctors to perform a hernia transplant.

∴

The junta ruling a country in Eastern Europe decided that one way to lure American tourists was to open a striptease establishment. One was duly established, and extensively advertised, but the tourists soon stopped coming.

Summoned to account for his failure, the manager wailed, "We can't put our finger on what's wrong. We serve fine food, the liquor is the best, and our service is excellent." "Then there's something wrong with your stripteasers," he was told. "Impossible," protested the manager. "Every one of them has been a model Party member since 1922!"

∴

There was a bit of a flap in one of Europe's few remaining kingdoms this summer. Seems the king was leaning over a washbasin one morning when an impulsive commoner sneaked up behind him and pinched his sit-spot. "How dare you, sir?" spluttered the outraged monarch, whereupon the commoner added insult to injury by stammering, "I didn't know it was you, Your Majesty. I thought it was the Queen!"

∴

A cartoon by Ruge worth pondering over depicts an armored Crusader carefully explaining to his companion, "The way it was put to me, it's like a row of dominoes toppling one by one. If we don't stop them in the Holy Land, all Southeastern Europe will fall, then Spain, then France, and first thing you know, they'll be on OUR OWN DOORSTEP!"

∴

In czarist Russia there once dwelled a rabbi with such a golden voice that everybody clamored to hear him. In his sleigh he made a triumphal tour. In every city he visited, pretty girls pelted him with roses and rich merchants plied him with compliments and gifts.

Outside one town the rabbi's faithful driver stopped the sleigh and suggested, "Rabbi, for once I'd like to be the one receiving all the honors and attention. Just for tonight, change clothes with me. You be the driver and I'll be the rabbi."

The preacher, a merry and generous soul, agreed, but added, "Remember, clothes do not make the man. If you're asked to explain some difficult passage of the Talmudic Laws, see that you don't make a fool of yourself."

The exchange was effected. When the two men arrived at their destination, the bogus rabbi was received with tumultuous enthusiasm, and obviously enjoyed every minute of it. Furthermore, since he had heard the rabbi's speech a hundred times, he delivered it faultlessly.

Then, however, came the dreaded question period. Sure enough, an aged scholar arose and propounded a tricky, delicate question. The real rabbi in the back of the hall groaned, "Now he'll make a fool of himself." But the driver was equal to the occasion.

"A fine scholar you are!" he scoffed. "Why, your problem is such a simple one that even the old dull-witted fellow who drives my sleigh must know the answer. DRIVER, COME UP HERE TO THE PLATFORM AND ANSWER THIS POOR FELLOW!"

∴

In the days when Khrushchev (and, somehow, we miss him) was Mr. Big in the Soviet Union, he often admitted that Stalin treated him occasionally like a court jester or clown and ordered him, "Dance the gopak." "And," Khrushchev would add, "I danced." Somebody in the crowd would always cry out, "Why did you let him make a fool of you?" And Khrushchev would demand sternly, "Who asked that question?" Inevitably, nobody answered, and after the appropriate pause, Mr. K. would conclude, "That, comrades, is why I danced."

∴

The scrubwomen cleaning up the General Assembly quarters at the UN retrieved an interesting document from the desk of a Soviet delegate who had delivered a bitter denunciation of the "Capitalistic Demons" that afternoon. It was a copy of his speech—and penciled on the margin beside one paragraph halfway through was this reminder to himself: "WEAK POINT. *SHOUT!*"

∴

Mickey Sharp is authority for the statement that a genuine novelty has been introduced in the voting process in the Soviet Union. Now, if a Russian citizen demands a secret ballot, he steps into a booth, pulls the curtain, and votes. When he opens the curtain, he's in a Siberian labor camp.

∴

A member of a troupe of touring artists from behind the Iron Curtain was asked by a reporter how he had received his theatrical training. "Well," he said complacently, "I served my apprenticeship in the national repertory theater, then I was promoted to small parts in the Moscow Art Theater, and finally I hit stardom in spontaneous ink-throwing and window-breaking demonstrations outside U.S. embassies and libraries."

∴

From abroad comes an invaluable book for trigger-tempered tourists: *The Insult Dictionary: How to Be Abusive in Five Languages*. Want to start a fight with a fresh French waiter? Just let him have a "*Vous avez meme additionné la date sur cette facteur.*" This means "You have added the date to this bill." Anxious to rebuff a larcenous Spanish innkeeper? Tell him, "*Cuando se organizan carreras de piojos?*" In English that's "How often do you run these bedbug races here?" German for "Kill the umpire" (very useful when ordering a glass of schnapps) is "*Knalt diesen Schiedsrichter ab!*" And when, like right here in the U.S.A., you simply cannot catch a waiter's eye in Rome, tell the maître d': "*Quanto mi addolara constatore che sono morti tutti i camerieri.*" That's Italian for "I'm mighty sorry to hear that all your waiters have died."

If this doesn't help make your next European trip a breeze, just blame the author of *The Insult Dictionary!*

F. ISRAEL

The most highly paid reporter on the Tel Aviv *Trumpet* was right on the spot when a bandit was gunned down near the King David Hotel. He grabbed a phone, and cried to the city editor of the *Trumpet,* "Stop the presses! Hold the back page!"

∴

Night club entertainer Pat Cooper is also a statistician of note. He has ascertained that the Jewish people eat more Chinese food than the Chinese and more Italian food than the Italians. Should the Jewish people decide to diet, warns Cooper, "they'd put two countries out of business."

∴

On the second morning of the Israelis' lightning advance across the Sinai Desert, according to George Fuerman, an Israeli lieutenant caught up with six fleeing Arab soldiers and beat the bejabbers out of them. The lieutenant then abandoned them with this parting shot: "It's a lucky thing for the six of you that it wasn't my husband who got you!"

∴

A private in the Israeli Army named Stein spent six months patrolling the captured Arab sector of Jerusalem. Others in his regiment, and numerous replacements, were winged by snipers, but Stein never received so much as a scratch. Decorated by no less a personage than General Dayan, Stein was asked how he had managed so successfully. Our hero explained modestly, "General, a niche in time saves Stein."

∴

Two out-of-towners were walking along the Hudson River docks in New York. One pointed to a new freighter in port and said, "See that trim-looking ship taking on cargo? It's Israeli." "That's funny," puzzled the other. "It doesn't look Jewish!"

∴

A story keenly relished in Tel Aviv these days concerns an Israeli bomber pilot who radioed his base commander, "I'm flying over a beautiful new steel mill built for the Egyptians by the Russians on the Upper Nile and I've got three bombs still on board. Shall I blow up the mill?" The commander answered, "Have you lost your mind? Leave that mill alone. Mismanaging it will cost those Egyptians a minimum of ten million dollars a year!"

G. AFRICA

The UN delegate from a tiny new state deep in the African jungle was without question the most magnificent physical specimen reporters at Kennedy Airport ever had seen. "How do you keep in such marvelous condition? Is it the diet you adhere to?" asked an admiring girl newshawk. "I just eat beans," shrugged the towering delegate. "Just beans!" echoed the girl. "That's amazing! You mean navy beans? Regular beans? Soy beans?" "No, no," corrected the delegate. "*Human* bein's!"

∴

Other cannibals in the news these days include the mother who chided her son, "How many times have I told you not to talk with someone in your mouth?" And the chief aboard his first jet plane disdaining the menu and snorting to the stewardess, "Pfui on this! Show me the passenger list."

∴

A Pan Am agent in the African safari belt had been reprimanded on numerous occasions for doing things without explicit orders from his superiors. So one day he sent this cable to headquarters: "Lion on runway eating pilot. Cable instructions."

∴

A TV producer, filming one of those series starring elephants, gorillas, and suchlike in darkest Africa, notified the home office that his budget of news was a mixture of very good and very bad. The bad news? A passel of bloodthirsty cannibals had broken into his quarters, sequestered all the film shot to date, and eaten it right on the premises. The good news? "We were two weeks ahead of schedule."

∴

A manufacturer had had a banner season, and decided his son's bar mitzvah party was going to be the talk of the town for years to come. "Have it in the middle of the African jungle," proposed his Broadway press agent. "It will be the first bar mitzvah in history where all the guests had to go on a safari to get there."

So the manufacturer flew three hundred guests by jet to Africa, then hired fifty porters, a hundred elephants, and two score beaters to lead them into the heart of Africa. Suddenly, on the third day, the whole winding procession ground to a halt, and stayed in one place for two hours before the manufacturer caught up with the head guide to ask, "What the blank blank is holding us up? If this keeps up, my son will be too old for the bar mitzvah ceremony."

"Sorry," apologized the head guide. "There seem to be two bar mitzvahs ahead of us."

∴

A famed English explorer was invited to Dartmouth to tell of his adventures in the African jungle. "Can you imagine," he demanded, "people so primitive that they love to eat the embryo of certain birds, and slices from the belly of certain animals? And grind up grass seed, make it into a paste, burn it over a fire, then smear it with a greasy mess they extract from the mammary fluid of certain other animals?"

When the students looked startled by such barbarism, the explorer added softly, "What I've been describing, of course, is a breakfast of bacon and eggs and buttered toast."

H. THE FAR EAST

Many years ago, Mahatma Gandhi was ambushed by newspaper reporters while on a mission to London. One question hurled at him was, "What do you think of Western civilization?" Gandhi smiled faintly and answered, "I think it would be a very good idea."

∴

Sign in a hotel room in Bangkok: "For the case that your electric light should fail, we beg to present you on bureau free postcard which please send us at once when you find your light out. We will then send you another postcard."

∴

Art Buchwald has counted over a hundred seemingly intelligent friends who spend thousands getting to Hong Kong principally to have a suit made to order for thirty dollars. Buchwald confesses he followed the same pattern. Deplaning at Hong Kong, a customs official asked him if he had anything to declare. "Yes," answered Buchwald. "I have one shoulder higher than the other."

∴

The representative of an American oil company, stationed in Tokyo, heard that an old college chum was contemplating a vacation trip to Japan. "When you get there," he urged, "be sure to give me a ring." "How will I find you?" asked the chum. "Simplest thing in the world," the oilman assured him. "Just look me up in the White Pages."

∴

Unfortunate souls who have to brave the New York subways day after day may find a bit of cheer in the report that the Japan National Railway has just hired 506 additional pushers and heavers to help squeeze passengers into its commuter trains. The procedure is now known (in Japanese, of course) as Operation Push Bottom and the total force is now up to 2,577. Furthermore, 754 of this number are postgraduates of courses on judo and karate.

∴

Hoping to close a big deal, a leading Japanese industrialist pulled out all the stops to give a visiting American tycoon a night to remember. An elaborate dinner with attendant geisha girls had gone off beautifully, and now, for the *pièce de résistance,* the three greatest Samurai swordsmen were summoned to do their thing.

Swordsman Number Three bowed low and drew his weapon, a fly was released from a box, the Samurai champ gave one slash with his sword—and the fly was cut cleanly in two. "Amazing," approved the American. "Wait," he was told.

Swordsman Number Two stepped forward and this time, when a fly was released, there were two lightning slashes of the sword—and the fly fell into FOUR parts on the floor. "Unbelievable," gasped the American. "How can Number One top that?"

And now the world champion, calm and confident, made his bow. The third fly was let out of the box, the champ flashed his sword through the air, and had it back in its scabbard in no time flat. The third fly, however, lived to buzz off into the air. "What a loss of face for the world champion," sympathized the American. "The fly wasn't killed!"

"He wasn't killed," agreed the host with a smile, "but, Honored Guest, HIS SEX LIFE IS OVER!"

∴

Caskie Stinnett has discovered a hotel in Kyoto, Japan, that leaves no stone unturned to make well-heeled foreign tourists feel at home. Its impressive wine card, for example, lists a variety of Bordeaux, Burgundy, Rhine, and Moselle, with their prices both in Japanese and English. Then, at the very bottom of the card, appears this last-minute tip: "Any other kind of world famous wine prepared to order."

∴

In Dennis Bloodworth's fascinating *The Chinese Looking Glass*, he emphasizes the futility of attempting to predict the Chinese reaction to any plan or happenstance. For example, he cites a day during a recent disturbance outside the British legation in Peking when the Chinese staff gravely requested permission from the chargé d'affaires to join the howling, threatening demonstration just beyond the gate. Permission granted (there was actually no alternative), the staff joined the rabble, yelled a while, hurled a few bricks at legation windows, then returned with dignity to their duties, which they proceeded to perform as punctiliously as before!

∴

When British journalist James Cameron toured Red China recently, a guide with an eye to future tourist trade led him to a corner of Shao-Shen Province to show him a house purported to be the one in which Chairman Mao was born. It sits in a picture-postcard setting in a valley guarded by an elegant mountain and a bubbling stream.

The skeptical Mr. Cameron slyly asked his guide, "Is it true that the government had to search the province for over two years to find such an ideal spot for the birthplace?" "Oh, no," was the serious reply. "It didn't take nearly as long as that!"

FINALE

What strikes me as an appropriate finale for *The Sound of Laughter* is the story of a cheerful truckdriver who pulled up at a roadside tavern in the middle of the night for a spot of refreshment. Halfway through his dinner, three wild-looking motorcyclists roared up—bearded, leather-jacketed, filthy—with swastikas adorning their chests and helmets.

For no reason at all they selected the truckdriver as a target. One poured pepper over his head, another stole his apple pie, the third deliberately upset his cup of coffee. The trucker never said one word—just arose, paid his check, and exited.

"That palooka sure ain't much of a fighter," sneered one of the invaders. The man behind the counter, peering out into the night, added, "He doesn't seem to be much of a driver either. He just ran his truck right over three motorcycles!"

Poetic justice indeed—and a last laugh in which I hope you'll join this resourceful truckdriver—and myself.

'Bye now!

INDEX BY CATEGORIES